1660

The Year of Restoration

1660

The Year of Restoration

PATRICK MORRAH

*Both my Nature, as I am an Englishman,
and my Reason, as I am a Man, have
bred in me a Loathing to that specious Name
of a Republick; That mock-appearance
of a Liberty, where all who have not part
in the Government, are Slaves; And
Slaves they are of a viler Note than such as
are Subjects to an absolute Dominion.*

JOHN DRYDEN

Beacon Press   Boston

To

DERMOT MORRAH

CONTENTS

ILLUSTRATIONS

Drawings in the text

PREFACE

THIS book is an attempt to chronicle the main events, and some of the minor ones, of a single year, that of the Restoration of King Charles II, and thereby to give some idea of the English scene during those memorable days when monarchy returned to Great Britain after the collapse of the republican régime.

I have endeavoured to present a straightforward account of events as they appeared at the time, avoiding the temptation to look forward or to interpret the past in the light of later developments. Nor have I attempted to burrow into economic causes as is the current fashion. There are enough economic historians arguing among themselves without a tyro adding to the confusion.

All dates are given according to the Old Style, and the year is taken as starting on January 1. Officially, of course, it still began on March 25, but by 1660 the new dating was being increasingly used for private purposes in England and had been officially introduced in Scotland, where the story starts.

The book is divided into two parts, with a slight difference of method. For the period leading up to the Restoration I have adopted a diurnal form, without attempting to cover every single day. For the latter part of the year, when things were moving less quickly and no single overriding theme can be discerned, this method is no longer suitable. I have therefore, without departing from chronological treatment, divided the narrative into longer periods, usually of a week but longer or shorter as is convenient.

A few words must be said on the spelling of surnames. There was still nothing like uniformity in this matter in 1660; names appear in a delightful variety of forms, and to

9

Preface

evolve a consistent system is impossible. My general principle has been to write a name roughly as one would expect it to be spelt today: Monk rather than Monck, Haslerig than Heselrige, Desborough than Disbrowe, Montagu than Mountague. I prefer Stewart to Stuart as having a sounder historical basis, though the latter was in more general use at the time of which I am writing.

As this book makes no pretension to being a contribution to scholarship, I have not thought it necessary to give my reasons for preferring one source to another in individual instances. A case in point is the very difficult question of the Duke of York's marriage. The few contemporary accounts that exist are hopelessly conflicting, none of them gives exact dates, and all are suspect for one reason or another. I have combined what seem to me to be the most probable elements in each, but I do not claim that my account is anything more than a reasonably likely reconstruction of what actually happened.

I make no claim to impartiality. My personal sympathies are obvious, and in my Prologue and Epilogue I have made no attempt to suppress them. The body of the book, however, I have tried to make as factual as I can, reducing my own comments to the minimum. This part is founded exclusively on contemporary sources, and only volumes containing these are listed in the bibliography and references. This, of course, does not mean that I am not indebted to modern historians for the general background and for the facts recorded in the Prologue and Epilogue. Those to whom I owe the greatest debt are Sir Arthur Bryant, Sir George Clark, Mr Godfrey Davies, Sir Keith Feiling and Mr David Ogg. My conclusions, I need hardly say, are my own.

In the preparation of this book I have received valuable help and advice. I should like to make particular mention of my brother, Mr Dermot Morrah, and the following who have assisted me in various ways: Mr A. W. Aspital, Mr Nicholas Bagnall, Mr Arthur Calder-Marshall, Mr Terence Mullaly, Mrs H. E. Parker, Mr David Piper, Mr Graham Reynolds, Mr T. E. Utley, Mr Kenneth Young, Mr H. D.

Preface

Ziman, and the staff of the British Museum Reading Room and the London Library. To all of these, and any others I may have inadvertently omitted, I record my deep gratitude.

PATRICK MORRAH

PROLOGUE

By the end of the year 1659 Great Britain's only experiment in republican government was dissolving in chaos. Since the eclipse of King Charles I's fortunes after his defeat at Naseby on June 14, 1645, the kingdoms of England, Scotland and Ireland had been subjected to the despotic rule which commonly results from the overthrow of hard-won traditions: administered first, at least nominally, by a Parliament responsible to nobody; next by a military clique; then by a single military dictator; finally by a mixture of the lot, with rival groups struggling and manœuvring for power and no man knowing who would come to the top next. During this period a King was murdered, the established form of church government proscribed, the House of Lords first abolished and then re-erected in a new form, and a succession of Houses of Commons, chosen according to electoral principles designed to ensure their subservience, sent packing as soon as they showed signs of kicking over the traces.

So long as Oliver Cromwell lived there was at least stability. Backed by an army which he had himself created, inspired by the driving force of puritan fanaticism, he imposed his will on every aspect of English life; if in Scotland and Ireland his personal dominance was less evident, his military machine, under the guidance of capable subordinates, successfully suppressed opposition. Parliaments he summoned from time to time when money was needed; the Army was always at hand to overawe them if necessary. He ruled with successive Councils of State, but always the power was military, even though the most extreme of his measures, the division of England into districts administered by major-generals, was not a success and soon had to be modified.

Prologue

Cromwell too, like many another dictator able to follow his own will without fear of opposition, pursued a vigorous and successful foreign policy, which enhanced his reputation abroad and stifled criticism at home. The bills incurred were met by assessments on the counties; if they became too large or too pressing, payment could always be deferred.

But Cromwell died on September 3, 1658, and England was at the mercy of a despotic system without a despot capable of working it.

Oliver had been empowered to name his successor as Lord Protector, and four days before his death he nominated his eldest surviving son Richard, who now, at the age of 31, succeeded him without opposition. Richard was not the 'Tumbledown Dick' of hostile legend. Kind-hearted, affable and easy-going, he was a far more attractive person than his father; he was good-looking and gracious, and he performed his ceremonial functions with ease and dignity. But he had no love for public life. In obedience to his father he had served in arms during his youth, and latterly had sat in Parliament and taken some part in administration. But this was never from inclination; he was by nature a country gentleman, and he was happiest when hawking, hunting and running unconcernedly into debt. He was unmilitary, unambitious and totally lacking in the qualities of ruthlessness and fanaticism without which he could hardly hope to retain power in the days in which he lived. It is safe to assume that he never wanted that power, and only took on the burden out of respect for his father's memory and in deference to his expressed wishes.

Two months after Oliver Cromwell's death Richard, feeling the need of money, decided to call a new Parliament. The last legally formed under the constitution of England was that known to history as the Long Parliament; it first met on November 3, 1640, and sat throughout the period of the Great Rebellion. Though that rebellion had developed from the long constitutional struggle between King and Parliament, the Commons during the civil war were in the main sympathetic to the idea of monarchical government.

Prologue

When the Army leaders proposed to set up a tribunal to sit in judgment on the King there was strong opposition in the Parliament, which in general was in favour of a treaty limiting the power of the monarchy. It was then, in December 1648, that 'Pride's Purge' took place. Colonel Thomas Pride, whether or not at Cromwell's order, surrounded the Parliament buildings with his troops and prevented some ninety members, deemed the most doubtful in their support of the Army, from entering. The remainder, varying in numbers from fifty to sixty and soon to be known derisively as 'the Rump', continued to sit as the Parliament of England until, having refused to dissolve themselves, they were ignominiously turned out of their seats by Cromwell on April 20, 1653.

Since then Oliver Cromwell had called other Parliaments; but in the eyes of its members the Long Parliament, which had received by statute the privilege of not being dissolved without its own consent, was still in being, though forcibly 'interrupted'. And the 'secluded members', as those ejected in 1648 came to be called, nurtured additional grievances; they had never consented to the murder of the King, and as time went on, and the nature of the republic became manifest, they tended to turn their eyes towards the dead King's son as the only saviour for whom the country could hope.

Richard followed his father in ignoring the claims of Rump and secluded members alike, and elections were held for a new Parliament, in which, however, members of the Rump were not precluded from sitting. Oliver Cromwell's nominated 'other chamber' was also revived. Parliament met on January 27, 1659, when the Commons turned out to be composed largely of moderates and Presbyterians, who could be relied on to support the Protector rather than the Army leaders who were already planning his overthrow. But there was also a vigorous minority of extreme republicans, men utterly opposed not only to a royal restoration but to any government by 'a single person'.

Their leader was Sir Arthur Haslerig. He had been one of Oliver's most capable soldiers and his staunch supporter in the Long Parliament; but when the Rump was turned out, and a few months later Cromwell assumed the title of Lord Protector, Haslerig went into opposition. He sat in subsequent Parliaments, but continued to assert the legitimacy of the Rump and refused all dignities from the hands of Cromwell. He was fiery and impetuous ('the Knight with the Hot Head', Thomas Flatman called him), and with the accession of the mild Richard he saw the chance of more effective opposition than he had been able to rally against Oliver.

A more volatile and a more sinister character was Sir Henry Vane the younger. His father had been the first King Charles's Secretary of State, but had gone into opposition after being largely instrumental in the condemnation of Strafford. The younger Vane, who had also been involved in the Strafford case, was influenced by puritanism early in life, and as he grew up adopted a strange, cloudy mysticism and a theory of allegorical interpretation which not even his most enthusiastic brethren could understand; Flatman pilloried him as 'the Knight of the Mysterious Allegories'. The abstract, apocalyptic nature of his religion was perhaps the basis of his political restlessness; he attached himself to no man, and followed where his inspiration led him. He too had quarrelled with Cromwell, and had been imprisoned during the Protectorate. He was a brilliant orator, and had at least been faithful to his republican principles; but no man trusted him, and all dissensions were laid at his door.

Two other leaders of the republican party were the regicides Thomas Scot and Edmund Ludlow. Both were uncompromising in their opposition to the rule of a single person, though Scot was never averse from compromise if it suited his book. Ludlow, on the other hand, was absent from the Parliament in its opening stages because nothing would induce him to take the oath of loyalty to Richard Cromwell. After a few weeks he unobtrusively took his seat without having sworn, and was allowed to remain. He was a solid, unimaginative man of limited intelligence; but he was upright and consistent, and his massive integrity was in refreshing contrast with the slippery self-seeking that characterised so many of his contemporaries.

Opposed to these rabidly republican parliamentarians were the leaders of the Army. They, ostensibly, appeared as Richard Cromwell's bulwark; they stood for the rule of 'a single person', and their influence came in the main from the prestige of their long association with the Protector's father. Two of the foremost of them were, indeed, connected by marriage with Oliver: Lieutenant-General Charles Fleetwood, his son-in-law, and Major-General John Desborough, his brother-in-law. Fleetwood had enjoyed his father-in-law's confidence as much as any man; he had been head of the Army, and it had been widely believed that he would be nominated Cromwell's successor. Now, after Oliver's death, he was the senior Army officer; but deprived of his patron he revealed his feet of clay. He was fundamentally timid and weak-willed, and had the unendearing habit of lapsing into tears when crossed. He soon degenerated into a figurehead, the tool of more forceful and more ambitious personalities.

One of these was Desborough, whose character was the reverse of Fleetwood's in almost every respect. He was a coarse and loud-tongued swashbuckler, all brawn and very little brain, vigorous and ambitious and out to get his way by force of arms if necessary. It was said that even Cromwell had been afraid of him, and that it was his violently expressed opposition that had made the Lord Protector refuse to declare himself King of England.

More formidable than either of these, though at the moment he was a member of the Parliament and not of the Army, was John Lambert. This restless, dynamic soldier had been the most brilliant of all Cromwell's subordinate commanders; his finger in every pie, he had played a leading part in all the main events of the Commonwealth. He was as responsible as any man for the establishment of the Protectorate in 1653; two years later he became major-general in charge of the northern counties, and he was at Cromwell's side in all decisions of moment. But like Fleetwood and Desborough he was opposed to the proposal to make Oliver King, and in his case the opposition amounted to a complete breach with his master. Cromwell deprived him of his commission, and Lambert retired into private life.

Now he had emerged as a member of Richard's Parliament, but despite his temporary civilian status he could never be other than a soldier and a leader of men. At forty he was younger than most of the leading men in public life; his place was with the military junto, and his energy and ambition were undimmed.

Ireland at this time was ruled by Henry Cromwell, Richard's younger brother, as Governor-General. He had more of his father in him than Richard; his government was harsh and strong, and he specialised in transporting Irish women and children by the shipload to Jamaica. Catholic Ireland was at heart royalist, as had been shown in the recent past and would be shown again; but Oliver Cromwell's brutal campaign of 1649, followed by the stern rule of his son, had subdued all overt opposition. Nevertheless, Henry's dominance was precarious; he could be sure of his position only so long as his brother remained in power in England.

Over the Scottish administration presided one of the most remarkable figures of the age. General George Monk, the Commander-in-Chief, was at this time fifty years of age. He was a Devonian of good family, and through the female line could trace his descent from King Edward IV. All his adult life he had been a soldier. In his early years he served as a volunteer in the Dutch service, and later commanded a regiment of foot under Charles I in Scotland. In the civil war he served with distinction in Ireland, then returned to England and was taken prisoner by the parliamentarians in 1644. He spent two years in the Tower of London, and after his release, when the royal cause was lost, he took service under the Parliament. Once having changed sides, he served his new masters with unswerving loyalty, winning Cromwell's confidence and being placed by him in charge of the Commonwealth forces in Scotland. From 1652 to 1654 he served at sea against the Dutch with Admiral Blake, and though without naval experience again proved himself competent and reliable. After the close of the Dutch war he returned to Scotland, and had been governing the country ever since with the maximum of efficiency and the minimum of ostentation.

Monk was of a type less common in the seventeenth century than in subsequent eras: a professional soldier first, last and all the time. He had learned his craft through and through from an early age, and he asked nothing better than to command troops when and where his superiors ordered him to. As a commander he was not spectacular; no dashing exploits stand to his credit. But his decisions were all carefully thought out, and his actions minutely planned. He was a rigid disciplinarian, and he never wasted the lives of his men.

He was never by inclination a politician. While generals all around him were undermining the Government and plotting their own advancement, Monk remained true to his creed of implicit military obedience. He obeyed his superior officers, and when he was himself in supreme command he gave the same obedience to the civil power. His change of allegiance in 1646, the only incident in his life concerning which a genuine charge of playing the turncoat could be laid, resulted from his view that it was his duty as a soldier to obey the Government in power. Only when it was uncertain where true power lay would he be forced to follow an independent line.

Monk was squat and thick-set, the personification of solidity. He was reserved and taciturn, and few if any of those about him were really in his confidence. His wife was not one of them, though for her part she bombarded him with advice. Contemporary writers have little good to say of Anne Clarges, who became Mrs George Monk. She was, we read, a woman of the lowest extraction, a sempstress, a common whore, devoid of breeding or education; after living with Monk for some years she had bullied him into marrying her, and thereafter made his life a burden to him by her virulent tongue and revolting manners.

It is doubtful if she deserved all these brickbats. Her birth may not have been exalted, but her brother Thomas Clarges, a physician, was looked upon as a gentleman; there is certainly no evidence that she was ever a prostitute, nor of any sexual scandal after her marriage. From the facts certainly known of her life, and the anecdotes of one or two more kindly writers (who incidentally knew her personally), she appears as a recognisable type: domineering, good-humouredly vulgar, indiscreet, garrulous, but at the same time kind-hearted, devoted to her husband and solicitous of his best interests: on the whole a rather endearing figure. Monk seems to have regarded her with kindly amusement. By 1659 she had become a confirmed royalist, and did not care who knew it. Her husband's chaplain Price paints a revealing picture: "Her custom was, when the general's and her own work and the day were ended, to come into the dining-room to him in her *treason gown*, (as I called it), and telling him that when she had that gown on, he would allow her to say anything. And, indeed, her tongue was her own then, and she would not spare it; insomuch that I, who still chose to give my attendance at those hours, (the general being alone), have often shut the dining-room doors, and charged the servants to stand without till they were called."

On the continent the exiled royal family watched events with renewed hope now that the arch-regicide was dead. Queen Henrietta Maria had lived for many years in Paris as the guest of King Louis XIV, dividing her time between her apartments in the Louvre and the convent which she had founded at Chaillot. Her religious devotion had increased with the years, but she was still politically active. In the civil war she had played a great and indeed heroic, if controversial, part; she was still under fifty, and was prepared again to rally to the royal cause should the call come. Unfortunately, however, her eldest son put less trust in her judgment and discretion than his father had done, and matters were not improved by the constant squabbles between her closest advisers, Lord Jermyn and Abbot Montagu, and the ministers of the exiled monarch. King Charles's personal affection for his mother never waned, but politically he held her at arm's length. And she felt slighted.

King Charles I and Queen Henrietta had had nine children. The eldest of all, a son, lived less than a day, as did one of the daughters, while another died before her third birthday. A third daughter, Princess Elizabeth, fell into the hands of the rebels and died in Carisbrooke Castle at the age of fourteen.

Five remained. Of these the eldest was Charles II, King of England, Scotland and Ireland since his father's death, but as yet without a throne (though he had been crowned in Scotland) and sometimes almost without means of subsistence. He had been through rough times since leaving his native country. In 1650 he had landed in Scotland and found some support there, though at the cost of degrading humiliation and of basely betraying his noblest supporter, the Marquess of Montrose: the most discreditable action of his life. He had then marched into England and fought gallantly for his rights at Worcester, but Cromwell's army was too strong for his and his forces were routed. There followed an extraordinary series of adventures during which, for six weeks, he made his way through England in disguise, dodging his enemies through his own resource and the selfless devotion of a quantity of humble people who succoured him at the risk of their lives. Eventually he escaped to France, and since then had been existing precariously at various places on the continent, living on the intermittent charity of France and Spain and endeavouring with only fitful success to raise forces for the re-invasion of England. Several attempts to inspire royalist risings failed, and the King's resources dwindled. King Louis was generous by nature, particularly to royalty in distress; but he had not yet taken power into his own hands, and France was ruled by the cold, calculating Cardinal Mazarin, in whose policy sentiment played no part and who preferred the powerful Cromwell as an ally to an indigent king without a throne. Philip IV of Spain was little more helpful, though he did assist King Charles to raise some troops.

Prologue

In the early months of 1659 the King was living with his meagre court at Brussels, in the Spanish Netherlands. At twenty-eight he was a tall, dark, good-looking young man, shrewd and humorous. His years of hardship had made him a cynic, devoid of illusions and sceptical on the motives of men. He was naturally kindly and the most approachable of men, but he had seen too much duplicity to have much faith left in the goodness of human nature. He was not scholarly, but his brain was of the keenest; nobody could outwit him. As yet he was content to leave his public affairs in the hands of others, but was always ready to intervene when he preferred his own judgment. He took his fun where he found it, and for some ten years he had been happily sprinkling the lands through which he passed with royal bastards.

Next in age, a year younger than the King, was the Princess Royal. Princess Mary took after her mother in her charm and beauty: the gayest and most vivacious of the children of Charles I. Her husband, William II, Prince of Orange and Stadtholder of the Netherlands, had died in 1650; his death was a tragedy for the royal cause, for he had been the staunchest supporter of his exiled brother-in-law. After his death Mary did all she could; she helped her brother with money and hospitality. But she was handicapped; her young son was as yet unrecognised as his father's successor and she was unpopular with the Dutch, who as stout republicans were always inclined towards Cromwellian sympathies. Mary felt little affinity to them, and annoyed them by preferring her English title of Princess Royal to that of Princess of Orange. Her court of Breda was a constant refuge to her brothers, but she had no authority and her help was limited by the hostility of the Netherlands in general.

James Duke of York, now twenty-five, was entirely different in character from his elder brother. In the civil war he had fallen into the hands of the parliamentarians and been imprisoned in St James's Palace, but at the age of fifteen had contrived his own escape, made his way across the Channel, and joined his sister Mary at The Hague.

Prologue

During the years of exile that followed he became a professional soldier, serving successively with great credit in the armies of France and Spain; the great Turenne formed a high opinion of his courage, his endurance and his assiduous study of his craft. Like his brother, the Duke was tall and handsome, fair where the King was dark. The years of struggle which had left the elder brother so gay and light-hearted had hardened the steely nature of the younger. He was slow-witted where King Charles was acute, rigid where the King was flexible; he was earnest and intensely conscientious. Above all he was of a passionate integrity; right and wrong were as clear to him as black and white, and he would follow what he believed to be right with a single-minded obstinacy that took no account of expediency. He was now with his brother at Brussels.

Henry Duke of Gloucester, seven years younger, completed a handsome trio of royal youth. He had already shown signs of equalling the eldest brother in charm and the second in steadfastness of character. He too had been a prisoner, and was with his sister Elizabeth when she died at Carisbrooke, but was subsequently released and joined his mother. When he was fourteen the Queen made a strenuous effort to convert him to the Catholic faith; King Charles, alarmed at the threat to his fortunes, intervened and Prince Henry himself defied his mother. When her plans miscarried the Queen behaved with petulant unkindness, and family recriminations followed which reflected no credit on anybody concerned. It was an unpleasant episode, for which only the strained conditions of exile could fully account. Thereafter the young Duke attached himself to his brothers and served gallantly with the Duke of York in the Spanish service.

The youngest of the family was Princess Henrietta, born at Exeter during the civil war and now fourteen years old. Since her infancy she had been continuously with her mother in Paris, and she alone of the brothers and sisters was brought up as a Catholic. Already she showed the grace and vivacity which were to make her such an ornament to the French court, and to endear her particularly to her eldest brother.

Prologue

The children of Charles I were a colourful family, all
endowed with varying degrees of grace and charm. There
were occasional rifts between them in the trying years of
exile, but they were united by a deep bond of affection
destined to weather all storms.

These were the immediate royal family. On the fringe
was another exile, that glittering personality Queen Elizabeth
of Bohemia, elder sister of Charles I. In youth she had had
the poets of England at her feet; Sir Henry Wotton, her
greatest admirer, had written exquisite lines in her honour.
When her husband was ousted from the Bohemian throne,
the chivalry of Europe burned to unsheath their swords in
her defence. Now she was in her sixties, but her dazzling
vivacity was undimmed. She spent her time mostly in
Holland with her niece the Princess of Orange, writing racy
letters to her friends and alternately quarrelling with and
fighting for the rights of her thirteen children, some of them
almost as vivid in character as herself. The most brilliant
was Prince Rupert of the Rhine, who had been Charles I's
Commander-in-Chief and the greatest soldier on the royalist
side.

Of King Charles's advisers at Brussels the most important
were Sir Edward Hyde, James Butler Marquess of Ormonde,
and Sir Edward Nicholas. Hyde was Lord Chancellor: an
eminent lawyer who had faithfully served the late King,
and was now the guide and controller of royal policy. He
was fat, pompous, erudite, fussy and pedantic; but shrewd
and far-sighted, with qualities of genuine statesmanship; and
he was the soul of loyalty. He fought steadfastly for a restoration; but it must be a real restoration. He would have no
truck with any suggestion that the King should be installed
by a compromise that would leave him the tool of unscrupulous parliamentarians.

The most illustrious of the King's servants was Ormonde.
He was the head of one of the greatest Anglo-Irish families,
and his lofty dignity, transcendent abilities and unswerving
loyalty commanded universal respect. In his youth he had
first opposed and then collaborated with Strafford in his

Irish administration; in the civil war he had fought to the last to hold Ireland for his King. Since then he had placed his whole life at the service of the new monarch, acting for him in every possible capacity, conducting endless correspondence with agents in England, and risking his life ('ready to try for a hanging', as he put it) by paying fleeting visits to England in disguise to further the royal cause. He was the guiding spirit of every move for restoration, and his powerful, buoyant personality was a tower of strength to his master.

Hyde was forty-nine years old and Ormonde forty-eight; Sir Edward Nicholas was sixty-five, and had been appointed Secretary of State by Charles I as long ago as 1641. He now held the same office under Charles II. He was loyal, honest, self-effacing and painstaking: an admirable office man who carried out the daily tasks of routine administration.

Such were the principal men and women at home and abroad on whom, in the main, the political future of Great Britain depended. Meanwhile the people at large were only intermittently affected by political developments. The rule of the major-generals had lain heavily on them, and the menace of harsh military government was always present in greater or less degree. But England was an agricultural country with a sparse and scattered population, communications were in many cases almost non-existent, and farmers in remote areas knew and cared nothing about what the men of Westminster might be doing, and seldom bothered their heads about the respective merits of monarchy and republicanism.

Religion, however, affected the lives of all men; and England at this time was in the grip of a religious tyranny harsher than any in her history. The parish system was the basis of English society, and church discipline could penetrate where political control was of the slightest. The Calvinist puritanism that now dominated England had penetrated into every corner of the land.

Puritanism took many forms, having as common factors an emphasis on the Old Testament rather than the New, renunciation of episcopacy, a dislike of church ceremonial, and hostility to all forms of levity and amusement. Officially the established religion of England, imported from Scotland, was Presbyterianism: a highly organised system of church government by elders. But early in the parliamentary régime the Presbyterian rule was challenged by Army leaders who called themselves 'Independents'. The Independents abjured the rule of elders; they believed in direct inspiration and extempore prayer. Each was in intimate personal contact with his Maker, over whom he tended to exert an ever-increasing domination. In Oliver Cromwell's speeches the Deity assumes the form of an influential but unquestioning supporter of Protectorial policy.

Presbyterians and Independents differed on questions of freedom and toleration. The Presbyterians were on the side of authority, and if they had had the power they would have set up an exclusive organisation such as prevailed in Scotland, with rigid suppression of all other forms of belief. The Independents adopted the watchword of toleration—toleration, that is, for all forms of puritanism, and liberty to persecute the two arch-enemies: prelacy and popery.

It was inevitable that the Independents should split into innumerable sects, some of which, the Levellers for instance, assumed a political rather than a religious significance. The most aggressive were the Fifth Monarchy Men, who believed in the imminent rule of Christ on earth and deemed it their duty to destroy all other governments in preparation for it. Individuals such as Vane, Dryden's 'numerous host of dreaming saints', developed their own mystical theories, unintelligible to all but themselves.

On the whole Presbyterianism tended to attract the men of property, believers in order and authority; Charles II had been accepted in Scotland, and royalist agents found much of their support among Presbyterians. Independents, anarchists in religion if disciplinarians in the Army, were mainly staunch in their opposition to a restoration.

Both were alike in their determination to extirpate all traces of the faith which had been England's for nearly a thousand years, and such ancient forms as had been retained

by the church which had succeeded it in power a century
ago. There were few crimes so heinous as 'prelacy'; bishops
had been deprived and in some cases imprisoned, though
the most distinguished of them, Juxon of London, had been
left in peace in Gloucestershire. While the established church
was not specifically denounced (the Presbyterian form
became officially the 'Church of England'), clergy who refused to renounce their allegiance to episcopacy were
ruthlessly ejected. The liturgy was proscribed, church
ornaments destroyed, and bare and barren rites substituted
for traditional ceremonial. On the surface puritan domination was complete, but Anglicanism survived underground
and men like Dr John Barwick, most selfless of royalist agents
in England, worked unceasingly for the only cause that
promised a return of the formerly established order.

The Catholics were far less numerous, but they too kept
their faith through these troublous times. Persecution was no
new thing for them. Since the reign of Elizabeth the Mass
·had been a criminal act, priests were liable to the death
penalty, and individual Catholics were subjected to crippling
fines which made it impossible for them to maintain any
status in society. The first two Stewart kings had tried to
mitigate the severity of the penal laws. King James had had
considerable intellectual sympathy with the Catholic view-
point, and the whole position might have been eased but for
the criminal folly of the Gunpowder Plot. King Charles,
with his Catholic wife, had made a real effort to introduce
some justice, particularly during the period when George
Con was in England as papal agent. The civil war had
brought a revival of persecution, and all the hopes of the
Catholics lay in a restoration of the monarchy. Many of
King Charles II's bravest and most faithful helpers after
Worcester had been Catholics. Neither they nor he had
forgotten.

Presbyterians and Independents were alike in detestation
of anything that savoured of frivolity. Sports and pastimes
were prohibited on Sunday (the only day on which a working
man had any leisure); numerous rigid fast-days were pro-

claimed on which it was illegal to do almost anything; even travel on the Lord's Day was denounced. Alehouses also were closed on Sundays, and their number was reduced; dancing was prohibited, extravagance in dress restricted, and heavy fines introduced for swearing. Constables were authorised to enter and search the houses of people suspected of breaking the sabbatarian laws. Christmas was abolished, and December 25 declared a fast day.

The puritans were obsessed with the sense of sin, and sexual sin, of course, loomed large in their minds. Thus the death penalty was introduced for adultery. This was a bit too much of a reversion to Old Testament standards, and the law became a dead letter owing to juries' refusal to convict.

Like all their kind throughout history, the puritans found there were limits to the extent to which human nature could be controlled. Rulers threatened dreadful penalties, and preachers launched thunderbolts from the pulpit, but brothels continued to flourish surreptitiously and as many illegitimate children were born as ever. Sometimes even staid elders lapsed from grace. Flatman in his hilarious satire, *Don Juan Lamberto*, has a story of Sir Archibald Johnston of Wariston, sternest of Scottish Presbyterians and a leading member of the Council of State. Johnston, he says, was alone in the council chamber when a lovely lady arrived with a petition for the redress of some grievances. Johnston agreed to her requests, on condition that she should pay a fee in kind; and he exacted the price there and then on the council table. Unfortunately they were interrupted by the arrival of other councillors, which was embarrassing for both of them. The tale may well have not even a basis of fact, but it probably reflects current scandal and the general view of the private life of such moralists as Johnston.

Nor were the regulations against sports and pastimes universally obeyed. It would take more than major-generals to stamp out the immemorial pursuits of the countryside: May games and morris dancing, archery, racing and cockfighting. Football flourished, and on village greens in the south cricket was being evolved. Cavaliers in hiding watched this curious rustic game, and took to betting on results; in happier times they would introduce it in higher society.

It was a rough, rumbustious age. The seventeenth-century Englishman was a tough character, and was never happier, it might appear, than in a fight. Duels were forbidden, but they took place from time to time. Lower down the social scale rival groups of apprentices fought with sticks and stones; butchers fought weavers and brewers draymen; lawyers were not above brawling in the streets, and the Thames watermen were a byword for rowdiness. Footpads flourished in the towns and highwaymen in the country.

Culturally, England was going through a bad time; neither literature nor the pictorial arts could thrive in a puritan atmosphere. Music fared slightly better, for provided it was not of a frivolous nature it was not frowned on by the puritans. English drama, the glory of the Jacobean age, had come to a full stop. The theatres were all shut; the fantastic William Prynne had denounced them in a whirlwind of invective, connecting the stage with every form of vice known to man, and the puritans had set their faces against all dramatic art.

There were plenty of fine poets living, but in the main they were silent. The taste of the day was for sermons of interminable length and for pamphlets of political propaganda. Yet at this time two of the greatest writers of the age were together in the employ of the republican administration. John Milton was Secretary for Foreign Tongues to the Government; and his assistant was Andrew Marvell.

But in the swiftly changing scene of 1659 those in the centre of the stage had little time or thought for anything but politics. Richard Cromwell's Parliament soon ran into heavy weather. The Army was in a restive state, and its pay was badly in arrears. The Commons, led by Haslerig, chose this moment to attack the Army and military rule, and in so doing they sealed their doom. The Army leaders prepared to resist and to assert their own authority; between the two forces the Protector found himself obliterated.

The act of parliamentary defiance that brought about the

crisis was the passing of a resolution that while Parliament
was sitting there should be no general councils or meetings
of officers without the consent of the Protector and both
Houses of Parliament. The senior officers defied the order
and continued to meet, and when Fleetwood was summoned to Whitehall by Richard he refused to go, and
ostentatiously called a general council of officers at St
James's. The Protector called a rival meeting, but when the
officers ignored him and rallied to Fleetwood it was obvious
that he was beaten. It was the end. Desborough took the
lead in demanding a dissolution of Parliament; Richard gave
in, and his only Parliament met for the last time on April 22.
The Protector remained in nominal authority for a few more
weeks, and then unobtrusively retired into private life, no
doubt with great relief.

The result was a power vacuum. The soldiers had got their
way, but they were not yet prepared for authority. They were
without effective leadership; Fleetwood was a broken reed,
and Desborough little more than a blusterer. They did not
know what to do with their victory and eventually decided
that there was nothing for it but to recall the Rump. So on
May 7 some eighty members of the old Long Parliament, led
by the timorous Speaker Lenthall who had so often been
unwillingly in the limelight, reassembled at Westminster. A
new Council of State was formed with Haslerig, Vane and
Ludlow as its principal members.

The Rump proceeded to adopt as equivocal an attitude
towards the Army as its predecessor had done. Fleetwood was
appointed Commander-in-Chief in place of the Protector,
and Lambert was restored to his commands; but the
Parliament tried to subordinate the Army to its own
authority by appointing seven commissioners to nominate
officers; the actual Army commissions were to be bestowed
by the Speaker in Parliament.

Everything was boiling up towards another crisis, similar
to the last. But its culmination was deferred by the discovery
of plans for a royalist rising. The King's followers had been
excited by recent events, though his wisest advisers counselled

prudence and patience. John Viscount Mordaunt, the principal royalist agent, was ardent for an attempt, and at length he was commissioned to co-ordinate risings in various parts of England. But Mordaunt, while brave and energetic, was an indiscreet leader. News of the plan leaked out, a few arrests were made, and the risings were called off. Only Sir George Booth, in Cheshire, failed to grasp the change of plan and appeared in arms on July 31. Lambert was sent north to meet him, defeated him without difficulty, and brought him captive to London. The King's cause had received a serious setback, and Lambert's prestige was enhanced.

He followed up his advantage by making new demands on the Parliament. In Fleetwood's name he called for real authority for the Commander-in-Chief, with himself as second-in-command. The Rump refused to be dictated to, and early in October counter-attacked. Fleetwood's appointment was annulled, and Lambert, Desborough and seven other officers were cashiered. The Army was henceforth to be governed by the seven commissioners—Fleetwood, Ludlow, Monk, Haslerig, Walton, Morley and Overton.

The Commons could hardly have expected that Lambert would sit down under such an affront. He was on the crest of the wave, and he acted promptly and ruthlessly. On October 13 his solders took up positions in Palace Yard and the members were once more excluded by force. The Army was again in undisputed control, and this time with Lambert for a leader.

The new rulers proceeded to set up a new constitution. The Council of State was transformed into a 'Committee of Safety' with a strongly military flavour; Lambert and Desborough were the leading members, while Fleetwood returned to his post of Commander-in-Chief. Lambert and his colleagues of course resumed their commissions, and Lambert appeared to be in control of the situation, with almost the power that Oliver Cromwell had wielded.

But in reality his position was precarious, and nobody knew it better than himself. The Army was ill-paid and ill-disciplined, and many of the junior officers were on the verge of mutiny. Another crisis could not be long delayed, and in this electric atmosphere all eyes began to turn northward.

Throughout the ups and downs of 1659 General Monk had made no move. He remained inscrutable. In August the King had approached him through Sir John Grenville, son of the incomparable Sir Bevil who had fallen at Lansdowne, and his own brother, the Rev. Nicholas Monk; but the General had promised nothing. Yet it was he who held the key to the situation. His army was small compared with Fleetwood's, but it was firmly under his control. Moreover, his prudent administration in Scotland had filled his treasury, and he had plenty of money to pay his troops.

Now he accepted his destiny. His creed was obedience; but he owed allegiance to lawfully constituted civil authority, not to a clique of generals who had seized power for themselves. He let it be known that he stood for the recall of the Rump, and that he was prepared to advance with his forces into England to bring it about. He made his plans with customary care and deliberation. First he purged his army of all potentially discontented elements, dismissing more than a hundred officers. Then he placed strong garrisons in the key fortresses of Edinburgh, Leith and Berwick. Finally he opened negotiations with Fairfax.

Thomas Lord Fairfax, of Nun Appleton in Yorkshire, was one of the greatest magnates in the North, and his territorial authority was enhanced by his immense personal prestige. He had been Commander-in-Chief of the parliamentary forces in the Great Rebellion, with Cromwell as his second-in-command. A man of honour and integrity, he had had no part in the killing of the King, and since 1649 he had veered increasingly towards support for a restoration. His views were not publicly expressed, but he saw eye to eye with Monk on the recall of the Rump as a preliminary to a free and full Parliament. Monk now got in touch with him, and the two agreed on joint action to be taken on January 1. Monk would cross the Tweed into England, and Fairfax would take up arms with his followers in Yorkshire.

Prologue

In the last two months of 1659 events moved rapidly. On November 3 Lambert marched north to meet Monk: ostensibly for negotiation, actually to oppose him should he advance into England. On November 24 nine members of the old Council of State sent Monk a letter of thanks and declared him Commander-in-Chief of all the forces in England and Scotland. Riots took place in the City of London, where vociferous demands were made for a free Parliament. On December 3 Colonel Herbert Morley, who had already defied Lambert at the expulsion of the Rump, marched to Portsmouth with Haslerig and induced the Governor and garrison to declare for Parliament. On December 13 the fleet in the Downs under Admiral John Lawson followed Portsmouth's example. The next day Dublin Castle was surprised, and the Irish army under Sir Charles Coote and Lord Broghill proclaimed its support for Monk.

The position of the Army leaders was hopeless; the country was sinking into anarchy. Lambert was in arms in the neighbourhood of Newcastle, but Fleetwood in London had no stomach for the fight. Declaring with characteristic delicacy of expression that God had spat in his face, he invited Lenthall and the Rump to take their places yet again at Westminster. They were down to forty now, but with unwearied optimism they took their seats on December 26.

This last move was unknown to Monk. On December 8 he had advanced his headquarters to Coldstream, on the Tweed. He now prepared for the next, decisive step.

PART I

---------------- ◊ ----------------

JANUARY

Sunday, January 1. So, on this first day of 1660, Monk gave
the order and his infantry crossed the border into England.
His plans had been carefully laid and all was ready; the
Parliament in London knew more about his immediate
intentions than he did of their return to authority. His army
was loyal and well trained: 2,000 horse and 5,000 foot, a
force of seasoned soldiers eager to take the road which after
ten years in Scotland would lead them towards their own
homes. Fairfax was already in arms, and Lambert, whose
presence in the field gave the pretext for the advance,
wavered irresolutely in Yorkshire as he found himself placed
between the two most eminent commanders of the day.

The risk Monk was taking was a very real one. He had no
official status as a commander in England; Lambert with
7,000 horse outnumbered him, and failure in the field would
transform his march for the defence of parliamentary
authority into an invasion of England at the head of a rebel
army. Nevertheless he was confident; Lambert's men, ill-
disciplined and with pay in arrears, had already begun to
melt away.

Lambert's position was in fact growing hourly more
desperate. When Fairfax rose it was with the support of only
about 100 gentlemen and their servants, but his name and
reputation soon won him recruits. And now came a hearten-
ing addition to his forces. Monk had sent Colonel Clobery,
one of his most trusted officers, to London to spy out the
land. Clobery had made contact with Colonel Redman,
former commander of the Irish Brigade now with Lambert,
and persuaded him to embark on a bold adventure. Redman
rode north and made himself known to his former troops;
disaffected as they already were, they acclaimed their old

commander and followed him over to the Fairfax camp. Fairfax found his force the stronger by 1,200 seasoned troopers.

Monk was not the only man who made history on this day. In London an obscure young clerk started a venture which, after more than 150 years, was to bring him fame far excelling the General's. Samuel Pepys, twenty-seven years of age and employed by George Downing of the Exchequer, decided to keep a diary. He wrote it in cipher, so that he could set down his inmost thoughts and his less creditable actions without the fear of anybody reading it but himself; he had, among other possessions, a jealous wife. His first day's jottings were not sensational; he wrote of his health, his home and his disappointed hopes of his wife's being with child; of the state of the kingdom and of his own attendance at church. More interesting revelations would emerge as he warmed to the task he had set himself.

Monday, January 2. Now Monk himself, with his cavalry, followed the infantry. It was a cold, clear, frosty day, and the descent down the bank of the Tweed on horseback was hard; the superstitious watched anxiously lest the General's horse should trip. But all was well, and the water was so clear that the colours of the pebbles on the bed could be plainly distinguished, even after many horses had churned up the stream. It was the Rev. John Price, one of Monk's two trusted chaplains, who noticed this. Musing on his ride, he went on to think of the mission on which the General had embarked, and how it would end. A sardonic thought struck him: if the 'men of Westminster', as Monk called the Parliament, had known 'what a loyal servant they were likely to have' in Monk, they would have done all in their power to prevent their champion's march. But this was conjecture; not a word had Monk said to suggest that his allegiance lay elsewhere than to the Parliament.

Meanwhile the men of Westminster were busy. Members of a new Council of State had been chosen by ballot and now the Council was officially established by the Parliament.

There were thirty-two members; most of the leading parliamentarians were included, Haslerig having gained the most votes, but there were ten outside members. They included, significantly enough, Monk and Fairfax; others were Sir Anthony Ashley Cooper and Vice-Admiral Lawson. Fleetwood, whose influence was waning to the point of extinction, was not a member. The Council was to hold authority till April 1.

Next came the matter, dear to the hearts of Haslerig and his friends, of safeguarding a republican form of government. An oath, it was resolved, should be taken by every member of the Council of State, to 'renounce the pretended title or titles of Charles Stuart, and the whole line of the late King James', and of any other single person pretending to the Crown or government of England, Scotland or Ireland or any one of them. The resolution was passed without much opposition, but when the ruling party went on to urge that the oath should be extended to all members of the Parliament, and that no man should sit who had not taken it, opposition was aroused. The more moderate members were dismayed. Where would this end? What further oaths would be proposed to fetter their consciences? The question was postponed for the moment, but it was decided that Haslerig should introduce a Bill next day.

Monk's army trudged on. The horse caught up with the foot, and the whole force halted for the night at Wooler, in Northumberland. The snow was still thick, and Price's colleague, Dr Thomas Gumble, watched 'the poor red-coats' wading knee-deep through snow, ice and water.

At Wooler the first fruits of success were seen. Gentlemen of the county, who a few days before had been fawning on Lambert, vied with each other in offers to raise troops for Monk's support: offers which the General acknowledged with sardonic smiles. More troops were of no interest to him now; they might have been useful when Lambert was still a danger. Lambert had shot his bolt, and both he and Monk knew it. When a messenger arrived from the Parliament ordering his forces to disperse to where they had been quartered on October 20, the great rebel submitted to the inevitable. He disbanded his army, and himself set out in the direction of London.

Late that night the same messenger brought a letter from the Parliament to Monk at Wooler. It was an unsatisfactory missive ('about six lines as cold as the night', says Gumble), giving notice of the Rump's resumed sitting. 'And because it wanted something to fill up, they put in thanks at the conclusion'. Of the General's march, of which he had proclaimed his intention, not a word was said. Monk was annoyed, and to those immediately about him he showed it. But he swallowed his disappointment. The hour was late, and Monk and his staff retired to bed for their first night on English soil.

Tuesday, January 3. Whatever his private feelings, Monk in public was out to display his loyalty to the Parliament, and his first act in the morning was to parade his troops and have the letter he had received read at the head of each regiment. The soldiers showed due enthusiasm, acclaiming their masters and shouting that they would march to London to see them re-established in their seats. There was, however, a suspicion that the stamping and shouting were more an attempt to get warm in the chilly morning air than a sign of spontaneous fervour in the cause of parliamentary government.

Monk, who had divided his force into two brigades, now set out for the next stop, Morpeth, but this was thirty miles ahead, a long stretch for troops in such conditions. A halfway halt was decided on. Whittingham, the village chosen, was quite unprepared for such an influx, but the army sorted itself out. There was something of a scramble for the best quarters, and Monk, reckoning that the clergy in such a place were most likely to do themselves well, imposed himself on the vicar. He had backed the wrong horse; the quarters were dismal and the vicar's hospitality not lavish. Gumble, a worldly cleric who liked his comfort, struck out on his own and did better; he managed to billet himself on a Catholic gentleman of the neighbourhood who regaled him with Christmas pie and strong beer. He was disconcerted when his host frankly confessed that he had hoped for Lambert's victory, but the food and drink compensated for political and religious vagaries. As he passed through the hall on his way to bed, he saw the private soldiers, exhausted after their march through the snow, lying uncomfortably on the hard boards.

In Parliament the Bill to impose the oath of abjuration on every member had a hard passage, but it was given its first reading by 24 votes to 15. Two other important resolutions were passed. One laid down that writs should be issued for electing members in place of those who had died, 'under such qualifications as should be agreed upon by the House'; no mention was made of the secluded members. The second provided for pay for the troops that had come from Portsmouth and Oxfordshire, but an ominous rider was added 'that it be referred to the Committee of Inspectors to see how the said fortnight's pay may be raised for them'. A satirical pamphlet entitled *The Acts and Monuments of the late Rump*, published anonymously a few months later, had its own version of this resolution: 'Ordered, that one month's pay be provided for the private soldiery, both horse and foot, and the rest of their arrears when they can get them'.

Wednesday, January 4. Definite news now reached the Parliament that Lambert was no longer in arms. So the only threat to the Commons was from Monk; he was their professed champion, but they looked on his progress uneasily. However, they were clearly helpless; only the Lord could succour them. The men of Westminster spent the day in prayer and fasting.

The same news was not entirely welcome to Monk. As long as Lambert was in the field his position as the upholder of law and order was unassailable. But with the enemy disbanded, what was the object of his march at the head of an army? Fairfax had already laid down his arms. Plainly it behoved the General to walk delicately.

At Morpeth he was met by the High Sheriff and gentry of Northumberland, who formally welcomed him to the county. A more important visitor was Mr William Man, Sword-Bearer of the City of London, who brought a message from the Lord Mayor and Common Council. London wanted a 'full Parliament'; in the House of Commons now sitting, the message pointed out, there was not one member to represent the greatest city in the world. This was the sort of message Monk liked to receive. Calls for a full and free Parliament could yet give him a popular cause to fight for. He returned the City a cordial if non-committal reply.

At the same time he decided to send his own messenger to the capital, and the man he chose was Gumble. This subtle, sententious clergyman had no apparent spiritual leanings; but he was highly intelligent, and he served his master with single-minded devotion. Till far into the night the General worked on his brief for his envoy, who was to make contact with both the Parliament and the City. Precise instructions were given in many instances, but Gumble was to use his judgment on the spot; his main object was not to negotiate, but to use his eyes and ears and bring back a full report of the state of affairs in London.

Monk understood fully the importance of the City in the events that were to come. So did the royalists across the Channel. Mordaunt was about to embark from Calais, and he was entrusted by Sir Edward Nicholas with authority to appoint commissioners for the City, who should prepare for the rising that might or might not eventuate. Detailed instructions, over the King's signature, were drawn up for the commissioners, whose names for the moment were left blank. They were to keep in close touch with commissioners for the neighbouring counties, who were also to be appointed. Mordaunt himself and Sir John Grenville were ordered to make it their particular care to let General Monk know 'the kindness and good opinion we have ever had of him'.

Thursday, January 5. A great reception awaited the General at Newcastle. To the good gentry of Northumberland it was now clear that Monk's was the winning side, and they thronged to town to welcome him, telling him to his face that 'he looked like a general'. Monk received the acclamations with his customary undeceived taciturnity. He had a great capacity for silence.

Some of the remnants of Lambert's army were now incorporated into Monk's. But the big business of the day was the sending off of Gumble. Armed with letters to the Parliament, the Council of State and the Commissioners of the Army, as well as to Fairfax in York, the reverend doctor sped on his way.

Meanwhile more and more was being heard of the demand for a free Parliament. The shadow of the secluded members loomed over the Commons, and behind it that of the King over the water. It was time to be decisive; a vote was taken to confirm the expulsion of the members in 1648 and 1649, and to issue writs for the election of new members in their place. The vote was unpopular in the City. That evening Pepys heard a report that 'unless there be a free Parliament chosen, . . . there are half the Common Council will not levy any money by order of this Parliament'.

Friday, January 6. Monk must be conciliated at all costs. That at least the sadly perplexed Parliament understood. So letters of thanks were ordered to be written to him acknowledging his faithful service and high deservings, and desiring him, at last but rather late in the day, to come up to London as quickly as he could. The *Acts of the Rump* summarised the motion rather differently: 'Resolved, that the parliament doth justify and approve of the actions of General Monk, because they dare do no otherwise.' Johnston of Wariston commented that the decision was 'good policye to weaken him and breake his army'. Johnston did not like Monk, and on this very day his wife came to him with the report that, at the General's instigation, the Commons had decided to deprive him of his Council office and give it to Dr Clarges, Monk's brother-in-law. Johnston meditated on the vanity of human ambition, but his wife only railed at him for playing his cards badly. His was a harassed life.

The atmosphere in London was one of restlessness and foreboding. Everybody felt that things could not drift on like this much longer, that a crisis must come, and with it probably violence and bloodshed. Francesco Giavarina, the Venetian Resident, described his impressions in a diplomatic dispatch. 'Everything is uncertain,' he wrote, 'in this inconstant country, which must amaze the world by the extraordinary things which are seen here daily.'

Saturday, January 7. Before embarking at Calais, Mordaunt wrote to the King. Letters from England had just arrived, and their contents were cheering. 'By the accounts I heare,' he told his master, ''tis the generall opinion if your Majestie could have landed 3000 men, that Kent itself would have raised an army might for numbers have reasonably disputed your right both with Monck and Lambert although united.' Mordaunt was of a sanguine temperament, though subject to moods of depression, and the royalist exiles were given to wishful thinking.

Mordaunt was equally optimistic about Dunkirk, which had been captured from Spain by Sir William Lockhart eighteen months before. Lockhart was still the Governor, but seemed to be losing his grip. He was so suspicious of his garrison, Mordaunt had heard from a good source, that he never went to bed till nine in the morning, and the soldiers had lately taken the occasion 'to complement him with snowballs, which he seems to take very unkindly'. A goodly bribe to Lockhart would soon bring Dunkirk over to the royal cause.

Sunday, January 8. Gumble had been riding by day and night through snow and slush and, what was worse, through the remnants of Lambert's disbanded army, to many of whom he was known, and who had no love for him. But he got through safely. At York he found that Fairfax had retired to his country house at Nun Appleton with an attack of gout, but he delivered his letter to Edward Bowles, a Presbyterian minister who was deeply in Fairfax's confidence.

Monday, January 9. The Parliament, which this day received Monk's letter from Wooler announcing that he had crossed the border, set itself to complete the subjugation of the military clique. The nine officers who had been cashiered in October were ordered to repair to their respective country houses furthest from London, and stay there during the Parliament's pleasure.

Sir Henry Vane was next on the list. Nobody had served the Commonwealth more ardently than he. But his was a restless and volatile soul; he had changed his allegiance more than once, and during the recent troubles had thrown in his lot with the Army. The Parliament now turned on him. He was summoned to answer charges; inflammatory speeches were made, and his defence failed to satisfy the House. He was declared expelled from the Commons and ordered to retire to his house at Raby, in County Durham, during the pleasure of the Parliament.

Johnston was convinced his turn was coming. He stayed gloomily at home, where his wife continued to bring him alarmist rumours. Monk was on his way, out for his blood; the Parliament was about to call for an account of money he had had in his charge, and he would be forced to refund it (Johnston had a guilty conscience about a certain £500); Fleetwood had been advised to retire to the country and counselled Johnston to do likewise. The good man began to think this was the best thing he could do.

In London Samuel Pepys had an interesting encounter with Henry Muddiman, the Parliament's newsletter writer and one of the most entertaining gossips of the day. He found Muddiman 'an arch rogue', but a good scholar and an amusing companion, and he spent most of the day listening to his talk. Eventually Muddiman took him to the coffee-house where James Harrington's Rota Club met. Harrington, author of *The Commonwealth of Oceana*, was a political idealist and philosopher strangely at sea in the welter of religious ecstasy and hard-headed time-serving that went for political thought in the days of the republic. He had founded the Rota Club in the previous November to discuss and improve his theories of the ideal state. Pepys paid 18d. to become a member.

Among the advertisements in the official newspaper, the *Publick Intelligencer*, was one for some pre-eminent toothpaste:

> Take notice, that most excellent *Dentifrices* to scour and cleanse the Teeth, making them white as Ivory; Preserves from the Toothach, fastens the Teeth, and sweetens the Breath, and preserves the Gums from Cankers and Imposthumes: Invented and made by R. Turner, Φιλομαδής; and is only had at *Thomas Rooks*, Stationer, at the holy Lamb at the East-end of *Pauls* Church, near the School.

Tuesday, January 10. A report emanated from Rome, and was published in the London press, that King Charles had become a Catholic and that the Pope (Alexander VII) was about to provide a large sum of money to bring about a restoration.

Wednesday, January 11. Monk arrived at York, and here he had his most important meeting. Fairfax had sufficiently recovered from his gout to come and greet him, and the two had a highly secret conference. Fairfax was now almost openly royalist, and few doubted the nature of the course he was urging on Monk. But the General gave no sign of having acquiesced. To all around him he was still the servant of the Parliament, and of the Parliament alone.

Gumble had made good time, and now reached London. By nightfall he had made contact with a number of Monk's supporters.

Thursday, January 12. Gumble presented himself in the morning at the House of Commons, produced his letter to Speaker Lenthall, and was immediately called in. Speaking from the brief Monk had given him, he told the Parliament what the General had done, how he had restored order in the North and what measures he had taken to ensure the public safety. He then produced the letter to Monk from the Common Council of London and Monk's reply to it.

The Commons took time to read the letter, and then Gumble was called in again. He was asked what more he had to say, and this time he spoke of the great services of the Scottish Army and asked that their views should be taken into account. Warming to his task, he took the opportunity of reading a homily to the Parliament, as coming from the officers in Scotland, on the wrongness of employing and trusting persons of seditious and unsettled principles in the Army, the militia or the fleets, or in any other places of authority. Gumble was enjoying himself; sedition and unsettled principles were so widespread among those employed and trusted by the Parliament that hardly a shot could fail to find a mark.

Next he lectured the legislators on church matters. The General, he told them, was anxious to see an able and learned ministry, and thought it a great scandal to the nation to see so many unworthy persons intruding among preachers of the Gospel. He further asked that some acknowledgment should be made to the Scottish nation for its services, and that Monk's senior officers, who had no commissions other than from himself, should be confirmed in their appointments. The final request was for an Act of Indemnity for all Monk's undertakings.

The Commons heard him patiently; then they meekly consented to Monk's demands. A resolution was passed 'that the Parliament doth justify and approve of what General Monk hath done, in taking up horses, and in his marching into England, and all other things by him acted and done, in order to the service of the Parliament and Commonwealth'; and the Solicitor-General was ordered to bring in a Bill incorporating the resolution. The officers' appointments were approved, and Gumble himself was voted £100 for his trouble.

Gumble's day was not yet over. That night he attended the Council of State, and sent in Monk's letter. But although he waited till midnight he was not called. Eventually he was directed to go to a private lodging and await the Councillors' convenience; there a deputation at last came to him, but 'rather to examine him, than to hear any proposals from him'. At this Gumble lost his temper. He was General Monk's representative, and he would stand no nonsense from these nonentities. He told them he had been riding day and night and was in no mood to answer their questions; when he was admitted to a full Council he would say what he had to say. The Councillors' one real worry was that Monk might be preparing for a restoration of the King; but Gumble refused to confirm or relieve their fears. At last he was permitted to retire to the bed a Scottish friend had found for him in King Street. Before he did so he sent off a private dispatch to Monk.

The General had settled in at York. His troops, dispersed over a large area of country, were resting after their hard march, and he was in no hurry to move on. He had a chance now to look about him and survey the prospects.

In London men were becoming bolder, and the name of the King began to be mentioned more openly. John Evelyn, of Sayes Court, Deptford, wrote to Colonel Morley, now Lieutenant of the Tower and a respected figure since the Portsmouth episode, imploring him outright to declare for a restoration of the Monarchy.

Friday, January 13. Speaker Lenthall found the atmosphere of strain a little too much for him. His was an unenviable position; no man was ever more anxious to avoid trouble, yet fate was continually thrusting him into the most perilous limelight. He simply could not face another crisis now; his health would not stand it, and he told the House 'that he was much indisposed in his health, and therefore prayed, that he might have liberty, for his health's sake, to retire himself for ten days'. The House was indulgent; it was ordered 'that in respect of Mr Speaker's indisposition of body, he have liberty to retire himself for ten days for the necessary recovery of his health: nevertheless, if his health do permit, that he do attend the service of the House sooner'.

Gumble addressed himself again to the Council of State, and was asked to go to see Fleetwood at Wallingford House. He haughtily refused. Fleetwood, he said, had been in hostility against the Army whose representative he was. So the matter rested.

In York deep discussions were in progress. Fairfax dined with Monk, and the two men were closeted together in the General's private chamber, discussing the shape of things to come. Price was deputed to act as host at the public table, where the frugal Monk had provided 'a half-crown ordinary for twenty men'. 'Large commons!' was the chaplain's terse comment.

Later, when Fairfax had departed, Bowles stayed on talking with Monk till far into the night. Price, entering the chamber for prayers, found them still at it, and was told by Monk to go out for a while, but not to go to bed. It was midnight before Bowles left, and Price was summoned to the presence.

Then, at last, out it came. 'What do you think?' said the General. 'Mr Bowles has pressed me very hard to stay here and declare for the King, assuring me that I shall have great assistance.'

Price was startled; he himself was a hardly concealed royalist, and indeed seems to have taken orders and joined Monk with the one object of furthering a restoration. But no such project had been mentioned before, however much it had been in men's minds. He asked his master if he had made any promise.

'No, truly, I have not,' replied Monk. A slight pause, and then: 'Or I have not yet.'

Price felt the delicacy of the situation. The General, it was clear, was perplexed in his own thoughts; he wanted advice. A story of the great Gustavus Adolphus of Sweden came into the chaplain's mind: how when that king invaded Germany in the Thirty Years War he said 'that if his shirt knew what he intended to do he would tear it from his back and burn it'. He told the story to Monk. His design, as he wrote later, was 'to entreat him to sleep between this and the walls of London; and, when he came within them (which I doubted not but he would do very shortly), then to open his eyes and consider what he had to do'.

Monk was glad of this advice. It accorded exactly with his own temperament, his own inclinations. So the General and his chaplain parted for the night.

Saturday, January 14. Monk returned Fairfax's visit, dining with him at his house at Nun Appleton. What passed between them nobody knew; but when Monk returned to York he was told that one of his subordinates had been heard to say that 'this Monk will at last bring in Charles Stewart'. He had him publicly flogged.

Johnston's nerves were cracking as his wife brought more doleful rumours. He went into hiding at the lodging of a pewterer.

Monday, January 16. Mordaunt, back in England, sent his appreciation of the situation to the King. The Parliament, he wrote, was rent by dissensions. Haslerig, supported by Henry Neville, wanted to restore Vane to his place, as a bulwark of the existing constitution; but Vane himself disowned him, and a rival clique was working for Haslerig's overthrow. Its leaders were Colonel Morley, John Weaver and above all Sir Anthony Ashley Cooper, a persuasive orator and a specialist in conspiracy. There was also dissension between the House and the Council of State; Parliament had ordered Monk to advance to London, the Council wanted him to stay in the North. Of Monk's army Mordaunt had heard it said that no force had been better disciplined since the Great Rebellion began; moreover, Monk had £50,000 in hand. The forces at Parliament's disposal were of little account, and could probably be bought over; the Navy was in poor condition.

Ormonde, who had an efficient intelligence network in England, echoed Mordaunt's words. Writing to Lord Jermyn, he spoke of discontent in the English Navy, where the pay of the sailors was as usual in arrears. A good part of the fleet could be brought over by the offer of money and assurance of safe harbourage. But where was the money to come from? Could Mazarin be persuaded to help?

By giving Monk precise orders to continue his march the Parliament had, as the members fully realised, delivered itself into his hands. It now proceeded to placate him. A grant of £1,000 a year to him and his heirs was voted, and a letter sent thanking him for his 'eminent and signal services'. But the Commons also took what precautions they could. It was decided that Thomas Scot, the newly appointed Secretary of State, and another member, Luke Robinson, should go to meet Monk with congratulations and expressions of good will. The private instructions given to them have not been preserved, but their nature was soon to become evident. The *Acts of the Rump* once more had its version of the grant: 'that there be a thousand pounds a year settled on General Monk and his heirs for ever, and that this act be repealed as soon as we can send him to the other world'.

This same day Monk received the order to advance. He knew it was not directed by goodwill; the longer he remained at York, in close touch with Fairfax, the greater was the danger that he might become too powerful for the Parliament's liking; and the men of Westminster would not dare, he knew, to order him back to Scotland. But the instruction suited him perfectly; he now had the official authority he wanted. He sent back two regiments to Scotland to keep the peace there, at the same time appointing a new governor for the Castle of Edinburgh; at York he left a garrison under Fairfax's nephew. Then he marched with four regiments of foot and three of horse: a total of 5,800 men. On the same day Gumble left London to join him.

Tuesday, January 17. A duel in high society was reminiscent of the more colourful days of monarchy. The Earl of Chesterfield, who had already fought two duels, fell out with a certain Mr Woolley about the price of a mare, and the two fought at Kensington, in the garden of Woolley's house.

Chesterfield wounded his man twice and was ready to stop; but Woolley refused to accept defeat. Another pass took place, and he was killed. Chesterfield bolted to the river at Chelsea, where he took a boat and fled overseas to the Low Countries. The inquest jury's verdict was 'chance-medley'.

Mordaunt was becoming more optimistic. He had raised £5,000 in London, and he wrote to his wife that he thought he could win over Portsmouth to the royal cause, provided King Charles would be ready to land at once in England, with or without forces, to exploit the success. He had also been in negotiation with the Catholics, whose loyalty was always assured; but they had backed the wrong horse in favouring Lambert, and were broken by their tribulations; little practical help could be expected from them.

At the same time Mordaunt was feeling the strain. He was worried lest his services should not be appreciated, and like many another man in hard and dangerous times he dreamed wistfully of future peace. His letter went on: 'After this blessed day which I no wise question but we shall suddenly see, you and I will retire, and serve God all our lives, and teach our children to serve God and be good subjects, for only those he will bless at last; I question not but they will be brave and it must be our care to make them good so far as education will lead to it. Indeed they are sweet children, the youngest has been ill of his health, but is past danger as I heare. These, Cosin, are wealth enough with content, which I hope we shall ever have.'

Wednesday, January 18. Monk and Gumble met at Mansfield. Gumble gave his master a full account of all that he had heard and seen in London; of the assurances of support and money which he had received in the City, and of the dissension that the oath to abjure the King, still not passed by the Commons, had caused in the House. There was 'great heat and passion' between the abjurers and the non-abjurers. But of even more interest was what he had to tell of the feelings of the people. The Rump, he said, was hated. The whole nation 'was absolutely determined to rush into blood, and all manner of hazzards, rather than to submit to their rule and government; and that principally for their great affection to the King's family, to which some of the Parliament were so peremptorily persuaded that he (Monk) was inclined, that no arguments could dispute them out of their fears'. Men in all walks of life were putting their one hope in Monk, the only man who could relieve them of their troubles.

This sanguine message must have delighted Monk. But still he gave no hint of his intentions. Everybody was longing for a sign; but none was forthcoming. 'Which way Monk leans,' wrote Mordaunt to one of his correspondents across the water, 'is not certainly known, but I feare he is nought as you will find by a letter I sent his Majestie.' Mordaunt's plans had been disrupted by Chesterfield's duel, for the Earl had been one of his most important fellow-workers. It was all very disturbing; no man had ever suffered more than Chesterfield to avoid fighting, but 'the insolence of Mr Woolley puld the sad judgment upon his head'.

Thursday, January 19. People were beginning to speak more openly of the King. Mordaunt implored His Majesty to come to England; should he but land, he wrote, a restoration was virtually certain. Only Monk (if he chose to do so) could prevent it.

The House of Commons turned its attention to Ireland. Ludlow had succeeded Henry Cromwell as Commander-in-Chief when Richard fell, but now new Commissioners, Sir Hardress Waller and Sir Charles Coote among them, were appointed for the country, while Ludlow, with his subordinates Jones, Corbet and Tomlinson, was ordered to attend the House to answer a charge of high treason. Ludlow, who was already in London, heard the news with indignation; he 'could not suppose them so abandoned of all shame, as to pursue such a design'. But he was a stout-hearted fighter and felt confident of defending himself against malice.

Monk arrived at Nottingham, where he was met by Clarges. Clarges was less sanguine than Gumble about the state of affairs in London; he told Monk that the troops in

London, under the nominal command of Fleetwood, were numerically superior to his own; their officers, moreover, with the exception of Morley and Fagg, were his declared enemies. Monk saw the danger, and took steps against it. A letter to the Parliament was drawn up, arguing persuasively that the regiments in the City had recently been in rebellion against the Parliament and could hardly be considered trustworthy. He was most unwilling that his own loyal troops should mix with them and perhaps imbibe subversive ideas. He therefore besought the men of Westminster, entirely for their own good, to remove Fleetwood's forces into the country before his own arrived; an exception might be made in favour of Morley's and Fagg's regiments, which had always done their duty. As for protecting the Parliament, his own troops would be quite sufficient. It was decided not to send this letter just yet; it would be more effective when Monk was himself closer to London and the Parliament would not dare to defy him.

Friday, January 20. Pepys had a convivial day. Having started by drinking with his friend Mr Woodfine at the Sun in Chancery Lane, he proceeded with other friends to the Swan in Fish Street, where they enjoyed 'a great and good dinner'. Then Mr Falconbridge persuaded him to go on to another place for a cup of ale. This was perhaps a rowdier spot, and Pepys would have liked to have shot at 'a scholar that lay over the house of office'. Later he went on to Westminster Hall to enjoy the company of Betty Lane, one of his more dubious acquaintances, who kept a shop there. Finally he took Mr Shepley home to his house for further drinks. Pepys had a strong constitution, and after Shepley had gone he settled down to his accounts.

The oath of abjuration was still causing dissension. Scot and Robinson set out to meet Monk, and it was believed that one of their objects was to induce him to take the oath as soon as he came to London.

Saturday, January 21. Monk, installed at Nottingham, settled down to letter-writing. He wrote to Lenthall, who had reluctantly returned to his post; to Chief Justice St John, and to John Weaver of the Council of State. To all he commended the services of his followers, and in particular of Gumble and of Colonel Redman of the Irish Brigade. He emphasised once again his devotion to the cause of the Parliament, and mentioned (no doubt with his tongue well in his cheek) that Fairfax had 'assured mee in a privat conference that hee would joyne with mee to the opposeing of Charles Stuart's family'.

The Commons turned to high constitutional matters. A committee was instructed to bring in a declaration on the following Monday 'that the Parliament intends forthwith to proceed to the Settlement of the Government; and will uphold a learned and pious Ministry in the nation, and their maintenance by Tythes and the known laws of the land: that they will proceed to fill up the house as soon as may be; and to settle the Commonwealth without a King, Single Person or House of Peers, and will promote the trade of the nation: that they will reserve due liberty to tender consciences; and encourage and settle the Universities: that they will not meddle with the executive power of the Law, but only in case of mal-administration and appeals; and that proceedings shall be according to the laws: and also, that they will ease the Burdens of the nation as much as is consistent with the pressing necessities of the Common-wealth'.

The King's finances were in a bad way. A memorandum of this day showed that the account of his laundress, Dorothy Chiffinch, was four and a half years in arrears.

Sunday, January 22. Monk marched to Leicester. On the way he was met by Scot and Robinson, whom he received with exaggerated humility, insisting that all around him should show greater respect to them than to himself. Henceforth these two, a Rosencrantz and Guildenstern echoing each other's sentiments with obsequious fidelity, would watch his every movement and intrude themselves into his most private affairs.

1660: The Year of Restoration

In London Evelyn, dining with his friend Colonel Morley, again approached him on the subject of a royal restoration. Morley was suspicious, saying he did not believe Monk intended to do the King any service. Evelyn then suggested that Morley should take the initiative without waiting for Monk, and have all the honour himself. The Colonel was still doubtful, and Evelyn left him to turn the matter over in his mind.

Monday, January 23. When Monk advanced to Harborough the nature of the Scot–Robinson mission was made clear to him. The commissioners insisted on staying at the same inn as the General, so that they would be on hand to help in replying to addresses. They constituted themselves his eyes and ears, and above all his mouthpiece.

This was brought home to all when Alderman Fowke, Alderman Vincent and Mr Bromfield, representing the City of London, met Monk at Harborough. At the same time Sir John Norris, with many of the chief gentry of Northamptonshire, welcomed him into the county. Bromfield spoke freely. After describing the calamities of the country, he proposed the readmission of the secluded members, 'that the Parliament might be made full and free'. This was too much for Scot, who elbowed Monk aside and took the words out of his mouth. He told the Londoners that, now that the Parliament had subjected the military power to a due subordination to the civil, it was perfectly free; that a judgment had been given on the question of the secluded members, and that it did not become anybody to insist on their readmission.

Scot's outburst brought a mild remonstrance from Fowke, who pointed out that it was unreasonable for the citizens of London to be governed by a Parliament in which they were not represented. Thereafter the argument became heated; through it all Monk alone remained silent, tacitly acquiescent in Scot's and Robinson's assertions. The episode was humiliating for him; but he was adept at preserving his own counsel, and according to Price he managed to convey by his looks some hint of his real feelings.

Part I: January

Yet Scot and Robinson had no reason to feel comfortable. The demand for a 'full and free Parliament' was reaching a crescendo: addresses from Norfolk, Devonshire, Northamptonshire and Buckinghamshire reached Monk at Harborough. And at this stage few people doubted that the return of the secluded members would mean the return of the King. Monk must have had his private chuckles. In the meantime he satisfied Scot and Robinson by writing ostentatiously to the men of his own county, Devon, telling them that the readmission of the secluded members would be opposed to the interest of the Commonwealth.

Parliament sat the whole day debating the constitutional declaration. But at last it was passed, and was ordered to be printed. Johnston of Wariston, still in hiding, was moved to melancholy at being absent from Parliament on this momentous day: 'As I am wryting this I heard the trumpet going by for their meeting in the House agayn. . . . When I looked throu the glasse and saw the boyes and maidens and everybody going to and fro, I thought they had by Gods providence mor liberty nor I.'

Tuesday, January 24. At Northampton more addresses awaited Monk. After the scene at Harborough the gentry were at first nervous of presenting them, till Dr Barrow and others of Monk's staff persuaded them. But again Monk was permitted to make no reply. Scot and Robinson 'eased him of that care'.

Monk omitted no occasion of showing the commissioners the most exaggerated deference, the irony of which appears to have been quite lost on them. Every time their coach passed a regiment the troops halted and expressed formal obedience to the Parliament's representatives. On one of these occasions the coach lurched on the uneven road, and Scot and Robinson banged their heads together. Scot's head was cut, and an army surgeon had to be sent for. Gumble saw the incident, and wondered if it was an omen of disaster. Could it foretell the severance of Scot's head from his shoulders at some future date?

Wednesday, January 25. A gibbet was set up in the middle of Cheapside. On it was hung a picture of John Hewson, one of the most unpopular of the republican soldiers. Six weeks before, Hewson had suppressed a riot in the City, killing two or three apprentices in doing so and wounding twenty others. The apprentices were out for his blood.

Thursday, January 26. The expense of the armed forces was a heavy drain on the republican government, and Parliament now passed an Act for a levy of £100,000 a month on the country for six months. Commissioners were appointed for every county in England, Scotland and Ireland, and elaborate machinery was set up for collecting the money.

The House spent most of the day discussing the assessment, but found time to deal with one or two minor matters. Monk's letter commending Gumble had arrived. The House recommended the good doctor for a fellowship of Eton College.

Samuel Pepys gave a dinner party at his house in Axe Yard. His guests were his father, his uncle with his two sons and Mr Pierce and all their wives, and his brother Tom; for this company his wife had provided a dish of marrow bones, a leg of mutton, a loin of veal, a dish of fowl, three pullets, two dozen larks, a great tart, a neat's tongue, a dish of anchovies and a dish of prawns and cheese. A fine dinner, and it was all a great success except for one thing: young Will Joyce drank too much and stayed too long.

Friday, January 27. Monk arrived at Dunstable. There was not far to go now, and the General called a conference of his senior officers, for once succeeding in dodging Scot and Robinson; the following Friday, February 3, was fixed for the entry into London. It was time, too, to send off the letter drafted at Nottingham. The finishing touches were put to it, and Colonel Lydcott, a kinsman of Lenthall, was deputed to carry it to the Speaker.

Mrs Monk, who had sailed by sea from Scotland, arrived in London and was lodged in Whitehall.

Part I: January

Saturday, January 28. The next halt was at St Albans. Here Monk sent Lydcott off with the letter. Clarges also left for Westminster; he was a member of Parliament, and might be able to help sway the voting when the question of moving Fleetwood's regiments was raised.

The conduct of Scot and Robinson was becoming intolerable. They were not content with clinging to Monk to the extent of sharing his quarters; he now discovered that, when they left him for their own adjoining apartments, they were in the habit of boring a hole in the wall through which they could spy on him. Even now he made no protest to them; he was determined to give them no ground for complaint. But he expressed his resentment to his staff in no uncertain terms.

King Charles was kicking his heels in Brussels. His hour was not yet come; despite his courage and resource at Worcester and after, he as yet had little personal influence on his destiny. Affairs of state were in the hands of Hyde, Ormonde and Nicholas; it was for them to decide whether or when he should stake his fortune in England. He beguiled the time by writing to his adored young sister Henrietta— 'Minette' as he called her—who was at Chaillot with her mother. 'I begin this letter in French,' he wrote, 'by assuring you that I do not mind you scolding me. I give in joyfully since you quarrel so charmingly with me, but I will never give up the friendship that I have for you. And you give me so many marks of yours that we shall never have any other quarrel but as to which of us shall love the other most, but in this I will never yield to you.'

Monday, January 30. On the eleventh anniversary of the martyrdom of King Charles I, Monk's fateful letter, on which might depend the future government of England, was delivered to the Parliament. A violent debate followed, lasting from 8 a.m. to 12 noon; Haslerig argued that the Council of State had decided that only four of the regiments in London should move out and four of Monk's be admitted. But Monk's letter prevailed; the House

57

decided that all Fleetwood's troops, except Morley's and Fagg's regiments, should be dispersed into the country. Quarters were to be prepared for Monk's soldiers, and money was provided to pay them.

It was a momentous vote. Monk's control of London was assured, and with it his mastery of the three kingdoms. Lydcott sped back to St Albans with the joyful news.

Ludlow appeared in the House to answer the charges against him. He was received 'very civilly', to the amusement of some of his fellow-members. It was not usual, they said, for men accused of high treason to be so well received in that place.

Tuesday, January 31. A woman was hanged at Tyburn for the murder of her bastard child. She had put it in a pot, covered it over, and taken it to the bakehouse to be baked. As the oven heated it cried, and the baker discovered it. The baby died after two hours; meanwhile the mother was traced.

A sudden calm seemed to have descended on London. The die was cast; Monk was master, and it remained only to wait and see what he would do. While the soldiers began to march out of London to make room for Monk's men, Parliament filled in time passing yet another resolution approving the General's actions. It was superfluous, but there was nothing else to do.

FEBRUARY

Wednesday, February 1. The general calm was disturbed by the soldiery. There were murmurings among those ordered to leave their London quarters, and some of them declared that they would not go without their arrears of pay. Colonel Fitch, in command in St James's Fields, went to the Parliament to see what money could be procured, but the men of Westminster were blind to the danger of mutiny. They were more intent on ordering the arrest of Sir Henry Vane; he was to be taken to his house at Bellew, and then to Raby.

Among those who had met Monk at St Albans was the Rev. Hugh Peters. This Independent cleric, hated for his reputed part in bringing Charles I to trial, had a style of his own in the pulpit. February 1 was a fast-day, and Peters was invited to preach before the General. He chose the text, 'He led them forth by the right way, that they might go to the city where they dwelt', and with his finger on the pulpit cushion he measured the right way from the Red Sea to Canaan. It was not forty days' march, but God had led Israel for forty years through the wilderness, on His own right way, 'crinkledom cum crankledom'. Peters applied the story of the wanderings of Israel to the current history of England; the English were not yet come to the City of Habitation, but were still being led in the right way. Price, listening with disapproval, thought Peters was preaching his own funeral sermon.

Thursday, February 2. The mutiny that had threatened the day before now burst into a blaze. The infantry quartered around Whitehall attacked their officers, killed a captain, took away the colours, broke the drums, and seized Somerset House. There they defied all attempts to eject them, mounting seven guns by the street door and threatening to blow up the Rump. Others paraded the streets in arms; Pepys, observing the scene from a safe distance, heard them 'bawling and calling for a free Parliament and money'.

The Council of State were now seriously alarmed, and hastened to promise the troops an immediate grant of a month's pay (about a third of what was owing to them). At this the mutineers wavered, and peace seemed about to be restored. But a new menace appeared; at nine in the evening the London apprentices, always ready for a brawl, joined in. About seven hundred of them assembled at the Old Exchange, armed with swords, halberds and any other weapons they could collect, and marched up to the stocks in the Poultry, calling on all apprentices to take up arms and fight for their liberties and a free Parliament. From there they marched down Cheapside, but were met by a party of cavalry who had remained loyal to the authorities. This was too much for the mob of apprentices, who quickly dispersed, about forty of them being taken prisoner and lodged in Lambeth House. This was virtually the end of the mutiny, and there was no more trouble from the soldiers, though the Somerset House garrison, surrounded by cavalry, did not yet surrender.

But panic had reigned in the Council of State. A messenger had been sent off post-haste to Monk, imploring him to march on London immediately. The General, meanwhile, had arrived at Barnet, his last stop before his planned entry into the capital on the following day. Here he contrived to take lodgings by himself, quartering Scot and Robinson in another part of the town. But he was not to be quite free of them. The messenger from Westminster reached Barnet at midnight, and it was to Scot that he went. That worthy, roused out of his sleep, did not stop to dress, but rushed through the town to Monk in nightgown, nightcap and slippers. Thus he presented himself before the General and demanded that he should then and there beat his drums and march. But Monk was not the man to be chivvied into instant action. He saw no reason to alter his plans. 'I will undertake for this night's disturbance,' he assured the miserable Scot, 'and be early enough in the morning to prevent any mischief.' Then, advising the Secretary of State to 'put his fears under his pillow', he retired to bed unperturbed.

Friday, February 3. Monk's appreciation of the situation was justified. The night passed quietly; in the morning the soldiers received their promised month's pay (it was said that the Parliament had to pawn its public plate to provide it) and marched in orderly fashion out of London. Only the Somerset House mutineers remained. The capital settled down to await its master.

So the great march came to its triumphant end. Monk led

BURNING OF RUMPS, FEBRUARY 11, 1660

From a print in a 1710 edition of Samuel Butler's *Hudibras*.
The original of the picture is believed to have been contemporary.

his troops to Highgate, where they halted to form up for the final stage: the horse in front with Monk at the head of them, accompanied by the inevitable Scot and Robinson. Bells were rung as the army, 5,000 strong, marched into London down Gray's Inn Road, but in general there was not much enthusiasm. Curiosity and anxiety were the keynotes of the citizens' reaction; nobody yet knew what Monk would do. But his soldiers came in for their share of admiration. Tough, ragged and weather-beaten after marching for three hundred miles through continuous snow, they looked what they were: a seasoned force of disciplined troops, capable of making short work, if necessary, of the rabble that had mutinied the day before. 'The foot,' wrote an eye-witness, 'had the best arms and were the likeliest men that ever I saw.'

Monk rode on down the Strand, and as soon as they saw him the men in Somerset House surrendered. A little further on he was greeted by Speaker Lenthall, who had come from the House of Commons to meet him. At Whitehall the General took up residence in the Prince's Lodgings, where his wife and family were already ensconced.

He spent the rest of the day receiving visitors. Among others came Ludlow with Vice-Admiral Lawson, and the old republican questioned him earnestly on his intentions. Monk assured him that he stood for the Commonwealth, but Ludlow was still suspicious. Lawson was more easily convinced; since the Levite and the Priest had passed by and would not help, he told his companion, he hoped they had found a Samaritan that would do it.

In other parts of the country there were restlessness and fear. Disturbances took place in Bristol that closely resembled those of February 2 in London, the apprentices again being prominent; and from Kent and Dorset came news of more cries for a free Parliament.

Saturday, February 4. Some of the soldiers who had been marched away from London were still in a mutinous mood. Five companies of Sir Brice Cockram's regiment were being sent to reinforce the garrison at Dunkirk. At Gravesend they disarmed their officers and besieged the commanding officer, Colonel Lilleston, in his quarters, threatening to kill him. Somehow he escaped and took refuge on shipboard; whereupon the troops marched out of the town.

This time Monk took immediate and vigorous action. Some troops of horse were ordered to Gravesend; the companies were disarmed and disbanded, and the ringleaders brought back to London under arrest.

On the same day Monk took his place in the Council of State, where he was invited to take the oath abjuring the Stewart family. This was embarrassing; Monk had disclaimed any intention of restoring the King, but an oath was another matter. However, he was equal to the occasion. He pointed out that others who had been nominated with him to the Council had not sworn, and suggested that there should be a conference between the abjurers and the non-abjurers to discuss the matter; until then he would defer taking the oath. The Council were not pleased, but they were in no position to dictate to Monk.

Sunday, February 5. The mercurial Mordaunt had again lost faith in Monk. He wrote to the King that the General had pulled off his mask and was clearly republican, and there was no prospect of support from him. But Mordaunt was still hopeful of a restoration.

A story reached Monk's ears of a plot against him. It came from a certain Mr Sturdy, a Catholic living in Russell Street, with whom a son of Secretary Scot had been lodging. Sturdy reported that young Scot had told him in great secrecy 'that not only Monk's power for commanding the Army should be taken from him, in a few days, but that he should be sent to the Tower, and questioned for his life; and that it was not doubted but that such things would be proved against him as would take off his head from his broad shoulders'.

It was all rather nebulous, and Monk may well have given little credence to the report. But it was as well to take precautions. He unobtrusively took possession of the Tower.

Monday, February 6. This was the day of Monk's eagerly (and apprehensively) awaited appearance before the House of Commons. Early in the morning Scot and Robinson, who were still playing their watchdog part, called on him at his Whitehall quarters and escorted him to the Chamber. There a special chair had been placed for him, but with a gesture of humility he declined the honour, preferring to stand behind the chair and rest his arms on the back.

Speaker Lenthall welcomed him in a flowery speech, likening him to the little cloud that Elijah's servant saw on Mount Carmel, which in an instant spread to the refreshment of the whole nation. Monk replied with an account of his march to London and of what he had observed during his progress. He had noticed, he said, that all the people were ardently looking for stable government. Many addresses had been delivered to him with numerous signatures, asking for a full and free Parliament or for the admission of the secluded members without any oath or pledge. He had told the petitioners that the Parliament now sitting was free and that none had ever been convoked in England without an oath beforehand for the security of the Government.

So far, so good; but what followed was less pleasing to the Rump. Monk asked the members to consider his words deeply; and he then added that, in spite of what he had said to the petitioners, he thought that the less in the way of oath or pledge was imposed the easier it would be to establish a quick settlement of some permanent form of government. And he urged them to keep not only cavaliers but fanatics out of power. Concluding with some recommendations on the administration of Scotland and Ireland, Monk then left the House.

Mrs Monk played her part in sugaring the pill her husband administered to the men of Westminster. Ludlow sourly records that she 'took especial care to treat the wives of the members that came to visit her, running her self to fetch the sweetmeats, and filling out wine for them; not forgetting to talk mightily of self-denial, and how much it was upon

her husband's heart that the government might be settled in
the way of a Commonwealth'.

Tuesday, February 7. Heartened by Monk's presence, the
merry citizens of London were vying with each other in
pouring ridicule on the Rump. Pepys noted a particularly
indelicate placard posted at the Exchange. He also recorded
that boys in the streets were crying 'Kiss my parliament' in
place of the more orthodox version.

Wednesday, February 8. The City of London's leaders decided
that the time had come to strike a blow at the Rump.
Having received a deputation calling for a free parliament,
the Common Council passed a resolution refusing to pay
public taxes until the House of Commons was filled up with
equal representatives.

This was a deadly blow, coming as it did from the greatest
financial stronghold in the country. The Government could
not ignore such a challenge, and the Council of State met
in urgent conclave. Led by Haslerig, Council members hit
on a plan which would, they hoped, not only subdue the
recalcitrant citizens but break the power that Monk had
established for himself. In the previous December, when
anarchy was at its worst, the Lord Mayor and aldermen had
ordered chains and posts to be set up at the gates and
principal places in the City for protection against the
undisciplined soldiery. The Council of State now ordered
the General to march his troops eastwards on the following
morning and to overawe the citizens by not only destroying
the posts and chains but even pulling down the very gates
and portcullises of the City. He was also to arrest eleven
members of the Common Council.

Monk was in a difficult position. To carry out his orders
would be to antagonise his most ardent, his wealthiest and
his most influential supporters. Yet he was still the servant
of the Commonwealth; to defy the Council of State would
be to proclaim himself a rebel. As the tension rose in the

City, the General sat up till 2 a.m. in consultation with his advisers.

Since the beginning of the year little had been heard of Lambert. Now he was reported to be living in hiding in London. The Council of State ordered that he should be summoned to appear before them, to give security for his peaceful behaviour, and afterwards to retire to his house at Holmby. A summons was drawn up accordingly.

Thursday, February 9. Monk had made up his mind. His creed was obedience to the civil power, and he would faithfully carry out his orders. Into the City he marched and, while the citizens looked on with sullen bitterness at the actions of the man they had thought their friend, ordered his troops to break down the posts and chains. At the same time he seized nine aldermen and councillors and committed them to the Tower; the other two whose arrest had been decreed escaped out of the City. Monk himself took up his quarters at the Three Tuns in Guildhall Yard.

But at this point the General came up against opposition from his own officers. In all the eventful days that had passed since he left Scotland he had met with nothing but complete loyalty from those under his command; but this outrage committed against respected friends struck at the roots of the officers' feelings. A deputation under Colonel Hubblethorn waited on their commander at the Three Tuns, and with deep emotion its members offered to resign their commissions rather than do what was required of them. They had ventured their lives and honour in his service, they told him, and would never willingly dispute his orders; but if violence were to be done to the City, which was the home and *alma mater* of many of them, he must get others to do it. If they were to be made City scavengers, Hubblethorn added ominously, 'they desired to begin at Westminster, and make that House clean'.

Monk was moved by his officers' words. His own feelings were akin to theirs, but he was not yet ready to defy his masters. He tried to pacify the delegates and, hinting at his sympathy as far as he felt able, assured them that they should yet find that all was as they would have it. But they remained adamant. Monk pressed them no further. Without accepting the resignation of their commissions, he agreed to allow the work to proceed under the command of junior officers who were prepared to obey.

So the destruction went on; but Monk, increasingly disturbed in mind, sent a message to the Council of State asking permission to stop. He had confined himself to breaking the posts and chains; the gates and portcullises were left intact. Surely, he wrote, this was enough. The City was subdued; there was no need for sheer vindictiveness.

But the rulers would not listen. They were on the crest of the wave, and the more unpopular Monk made himself in the City the stronger would be their own position. So they proceeded to tighten the noose which, unfelt as yet, was being placed around their own necks. Haslerig, entering the Commons Chamber, exclaimed with glee: 'All is our own, he will be honest.' A curt note from the Council required Monk immediately to proceed to the destruction of the gates and portcullises.

In the midst of all this turmoil a voice from the past made itself heard. Praise-God Barebones, the lugubrious puritan fanatic who had given his name to one of Cromwell's ephemeral parliaments, arrived at the House at the head of a deputation of sectaries. They appealed on behalf of the 'good old cause' of republicanism against the rising tide of royalism; they called on the Parliament to resist all agitation for the return of the secluded members, and urged that no person should be admitted to any position in the state who had not taken the oath of abjuration of the King and the house of Stewart. Inspired or not, it was a welcome gesture so far as the Parliament men were concerned. But Barebones had no more than propaganda value; the House took note of the petitioners' sentiments and thanked them politely. Praise-God retired into the obscurity from which he had emerged.

Monk in the City received his new orders in bitterness of soul. The gates and portcullises were destroyed.

1660: The Year of Restoration

Friday, February 10. All was quiet in the City; the Common Council, which had been officially dissolved by the Council of State, made a half-hearted effort to meet, but soldiers kept the hall closed. In the afternoon Monk returned to Whitehall, leaving a garrison behind him.

The North was seething with discontent. An important meeting took place at York, attended by Lord Fairfax and many other great landlords of Yorkshire, and letters signed by them were sent to the Parliament and to Monk, calling for the filling up of the House and threatening to refuse to pay taxes until this was done.

London was full of rumours. Monk was to be deprived of his commission; Lambert was to be recalled, Ludlow restored to his command in Ireland, and Vane re-established in authority; the sectaries were going to be put in power in Whitehall (an echo of Barebones's visit to the House).

In this highly charged atmosphere Thomas Clarges decided to take the initiative. In the evening he went privately to his brother-in-law, the General, at Whitehall. He represented to him the ill-will he had caused by his actions in the City, and pointed out how easily the inflamed passions there could spread throughout the country. The only way he could redeem his reputation, urged Clarges, was by marching back into the City with his troops the following morning and publicly declaring for a free parliament.

The General at first played for time. He would do nothing, he said, before Tuesday morning. But Dr Barrow and others joined Clarges at Whitehall, and all urged on the reluctant commander the danger of delay; if he did not act at once, they assured him, his enemies would deprive him of his power. At last Monk was convinced. Barrow was sent off to spy out the lie of the land, and the General and his officers drew up plans for the morning's march. It was decided that a letter should be sent to the Parliament, demanding that writs should be issued by next Friday for filling up the House, and that then a dissolution should be decreed, to give place to a full and free parliament.

Part I: February

The letter was to go in Monk's name. Leaving his officers to draft it, and arranging for a further meeting at 6 a.m., the General retired to bed.

Saturday, February 11. At the six o'clock meeting the letter was signed by Monk and fourteen of his officers, and Clobery and Lydcott were deputed to carry it to the Commons. Among the signatories was Hubblethorn, now fully reconciled with his commander. Without more ado Monk marched back into the City, drew up his forces in Finsbury Fields, and himself repaired to Alderman Wale's house in Throckmorton Street. Clarges had gone ahead to let the Lord Mayor and others know what was afoot.

The Commons received the letter with dismay. But there was little they could do; dissembling their rage as best they might, they passed a resolution of thanks to Monk for his services and sent Scot and Robinson to take the message to him. Private instructions enjoined them to get him to leave the City if possible. As Haslerig left the House in a fury he was accosted by the Quaker Billing, who took him by the arm and cried: 'Thou man, will thy beast carry thee no longer? Thou must fall!'

Meanwhile Monk had not had an easy passage. The City was naturally distrustful of his intentions and in particular the Lord Mayor, Thomas Allen, was not disposed to welcome the man who had committed such ravages only two days before. Clarges had his work cut out to ease the way, but with the help of the amiably disposed Alderman John Robinson he persuaded Allen so far to relent as to invite the General to dinner at his house in Leadenhall Street. At the meal the Lord Mayor told his guest that he was welcome to his house, 'but that the City was full of fears and sad apprehensions of his sudden return, after such violent actions as his soldiers had been employed in'. Monk replied that he hoped to make them of another mind in a few hours; he asked the Lord Mayor to summon a Common Council to meet at Guildhall at four o'clock (thus openly defying the Government), when he would acquaint them with his real intentions.

Monk had been unwilling to disclose further details without knowing the reactions of Parliament to his letter. But before the Guildhall meeting Scot and Robinson presented themselves. They got short shrift. When they made protestations of the Parliament's affection to Monk, Colonel Bridges broke in with the scornful comment that no credit could be paid to their fair speeches when Parliament by its actions proclaimed its malignancy. Clobery seconded his colleague, asking how the General could trust those who gave ear to his enemies. Monk silenced his officers, but his own reply to the envoys was succinct: 'If the Parliament will do as they are desired in my letter, they need not fear but all things will go well.'

At Guildhall Monk showed his hand. He told the Common Council how reluctantly he had acted against the City, and explained that he could have refused only by resigning his commission and that thereby he would have lost his chance to save the country. He then announced that he had demanded that writs should be issued for filling up the Parliament, and that the present House should not sit later than May 6.

As soon as the news leaked out from Guildhall, the City threw off all restraint. Never had such sudden joy been shown; nobody doubted that Monk's action meant, sooner or later, a royal restoration, and the King's health was openly drunk. Monk as he came out was greeted with shouts of 'God bless Your Excellence!' Bells were rung and bonfires blazed in every street; Pepys counted fourteen between St Dunstan's and Temple Bar, and at one point could see thirty-one burning at once. Butchers did a roaring trade; rumps of oxen, sheep and even poultry were bought up by the dozen to be roasted and burned at the bonfires in derision of the Parliament. In the Strand the butchers rang a peal with their knives before sacrificing their rump.

The apprentices, ever ready for a bit of rowdyism, were well to the fore. Speaker Lenthall, on his way home late from the House, narrowly escaped their attentions; he got indoors safely, but his windows were broken and a rump roasted

Part I: February

at his gate. Gumble and Price also found themselves in danger. The apprentices had heard that Scot and Robinson were in the City, and went from coach to coach in search of them. The chaplains suffered in an unfortunate case of mistaken identity; with a cry of 'Here they are!' the young men attacked their coach and pelted it with mud and with less savoury material. Price and Gumble protected themselves as well as they could with the coach curtains, shouting at the top of their voices: 'A full and free Parliament!' This *shibboleth* at length did the trick, and they were allowed to proceed on their way.

So the merriment went on. Monk's soldiers were the heroes of the day, and still more of the night; they were plied with drink from dusk to dawn. There was no difficulty in finding them quarters; they were welcomed with open arms.

Sunday, February 12. London awoke dazed, jubilant, and with a hangover. As Monk emerged from St Paul's to the shouts of an admiring crowd, a young man named Bailey was crossing the Channel in a hired bark. He had seen the bonfires and the roasting of rumps, the drinking of the King's health, and had galloped off for Dover, intent only on being the first to take the joyful news to the King. He landed at Ostend and by nightfall was in Brussels, where the Marquess of Ormonde conducted him into the presence. The King was at first sceptical; it seemed impossible that the messenger could have reached Brussels so quickly. But Bailey seemed an honest enough young man, and he brought credentials from Sir John Stephens, a trusted royalist agent. Both the King and Ormonde came to the conclusion that his story was true, and hopes soared in Brussels.

Monday, February 13. The Parliament invited Monk to attend the House. He curtly refused; so they turned their attention to lesser game. Neither Vane nor Lambert had taken any notice of the orders against them. The Serjeant at Arms was ordered to carry the former to his house at Bellew, in Lincolnshire. A proclamation was issued to the effect that,

71

unless Lambert surrendered to the Council of State by the following Thursday, his estates would be confiscated.

The rump fever had spread to Oxford. The Warden of All Souls, Dr John Palmer, was a dying man; but he was a known supporter of the Parliament, and his condition did not prevent a rump of beef being thrown at him through his bedroom window.

Tuesday, February 14. The Commons had surrendered to Monk, but for the moment he held his hand, preferring to let events develop under their own momentum. The issue of writs had been agreed in principle, and meanwhile the oath of abjuration was dropped. An amendment transformed it into an 'engagement', in the form: 'I, A.B., do promise and declare, that I will be true and faithful to the Commonwealth of England, and the Government thereof, in the way of a Commonwealth and Free State, without a King, Single Person, or House of Lords.'

Thursday, February 16. Petitions were now pouring in from the counties. The Fairfax letter from Yorkshire had arrived; so had one from Oxfordshire, and now another from Lincolnshire. The theme of all was the same: until the Parliament was filled up, no taxes would be paid. The Rump was doomed; so long as it remained a rump it faced death from starvation. The men of Westminster sought legal advice on their right to fill the secluded members' seats; but the judges were not to be drawn, and refused to express an opinion.

Friday, February 17. The time limit for the issuing of writs was up, but not a writ had been issued. Monk, however, was unperturbed; he was now working along a different line. His new aim was to bring the rumpers and the secluded members together; the former, he hoped, had learned their lesson and could perhaps be brought to agree to the admission of their former colleagues. He invited ten of each party to meet him at Alderman Wale's house. Among those on the Rump side were Lord Chief Justice St John, Sir Arthur Haslerig, Colonel Morley, Sir Anthony Ashley Cooper and Colonel Hutchinson; the secluded members included Colonel Popham, Sir William Lewis, Sir John Holland, Sir Gilbert Gerrard, Sir John Temple and Arthur Annesley. They met in the evening, and after a long discussion adjourned until next day.

The news of the doings of February 11 was not everywhere received with equal enthusiasm. The Rev. Henry Newcome, a Manchester Presbyterian minister, recorded in his journal that 'some odd people would needs have bonfires made'. He told the officer 'that if it were true that we heard, it would be true the next post, and we might do it then; and if it should not be true, the town might sadly smart for the forwardness of the rabble'.

Saturday, February 18. Ringleaders of the mutinies in London and at Gravesend at the beginning of the month had been tried by court martial; a sergeant and eight private soldiers had been sentenced, four of them to die and the other five to be tied to a gibbet with halters about their necks for half an hour, then to be whipped by the executioner. So this day they were taken to Charing Cross, where two gibbets had been erected. At the last minute the Commissioners of the Army decided that the four condemned to death should be allowed to draw lots, two to die and two to be spared. The losers were strung up then and there, while the two lucky ones were reprieved until further order. The other five were whipped as ordered; the sergeant received forty lashes, one soldier twenty-one, and the other three thirty-nine. All were dismissed from the Army.

Monk sent off an answer to Fairfax's letter. He told his old comrade-in-arms that the House had agreed to its numbers being filled up; writs were to go out, and there would be no such qualifications as would hinder the secluded members from being chosen again. This was not, Monk admitted, exactly what Fairfax had propounded, but it was so near to it that he hoped it would give satisfaction.

In point of fact the Engagement Bill, laying down the qualifications for the new members, was passed this same day. The qualifications were defined as follows:

> No person who hath been concerned in the Irish rebellion, or who are the professors of the popish religion, or who have married a wife of the same, or brought up his children therein, or have been in arms against the Parliament since Jan. 1, 1641, unless restored by Commission since May 7, 1659, and continued faithful since; or such as have been concerned in any plot for Charles Stuart since 1648, or that have advised or promoted a single person since Jan. 1, 1659; nor any person disabled by Act 17. Car. intituled, an Act disabling Persons in Holy Orders; neither any person who denieth the Scriptures to be the Word of God, or the Sacrament, Prayer, Magistracy, or Ministry to be the Word of God; nor such as are guilty of any of the offences in the Act bearing date 1650, intituled, an Act against several blasphemous and execrable Opinions, derogatory to the Honour of God, and destructive to human society; no common prophaner of the Lord's Day, no common prophane swearer or curser, nor common drunkard; nor the son of a sequestered person (unless such sons as have borne arms for the Parliament, and continued faithful thereto) during the life of his father; nor any that promise or give a reward to be elected, or any entertainment to the electors; also that the elected takes the Engagement before he sits in the House. They who are elected and sit in Parliament, contrary to these qualifications, to forfeit £1,000 to the Commonwealth; and those who elect contrary to the tenor of this Act, to forfeit one part of their real estate, and one part of their personal estate to the Commonwealth.

Monk resumed his discussions with the two parties. No conclusion was reached, because the representatives of the sitting members would not undertake for the rest of the House without their consent; this, they said, could be given only by vote. But the conference passed off amicably enough, and Monk hoped that the secluded members might yet be able to take their seats without acrimony.

While this conference was taking place, Clarges, Clobery

and Gumble were appointed to discuss the same question with the officers of the Army. They found them agreeable to the return of the secluded members, subject to certain conditions.

Monday, February 20. The Commons were at last ready to issue the writs. But now there was a hitch—in the shape of an uncharacteristic assertion of independence by Speaker Lenthall. He maintained that if he signed a warrant for this purpose he would render himself liable to legal action by every one of the secluded members whose place was to be filled. The House argued the point; but the timid old gentleman, who had seldom failed to give in to bullying from any quarter, was adamant. He would have nothing to do with the issue of writs; he would rather be sent to the Tower.

Ludlow was for taking him at his word; but the House eventually decided to by-pass the Speaker. An Act was quickly passed empowering the Clerk of the Parliament, Henry Scobell, to sign the warrant to the Commissioners of the Seal.

As it happened the point was academic; for Monk had decided on his next step. As always he was slow to make up his mind; he followed the advice his chaplain had given him at York. It was his custom to listen to all and sundry while preserving his own counsel; to leave the actual decision till it was safe to delay no longer; then to act with soldierly speed and thoroughness. Now all the long and wearisome conferences had convinced him that nothing was to be hoped for from filling up the House with new members; nor would any agreement between the sitting and secluded members lead to a compromise by which new elections would result in a House similar in composition to that of 1648. The only solution was to force the readmission of the secluded members.

So on this day he invited them to meet him at Alderman Wale's house. When they were assembled he submitted to them four articles to which he asked them to pledge their agreement when they should form a majority in the House of

Commons: first, to settle the conduct of the armies in the three nations so as best to secure the peace of the Commonwealth; second, to provide money for the support of the forces by sea and land, and for their arrears and the contingencies of the Government; third, to constitute a Council of State for the civil government of Scotland and Ireland, and to issue writs for the summoning of a Parliament to meet at Westminster on April 20; finally, to consent to their own dissolution by a time that should be given them.

The secluded members willingly subscribed to the four articles. In addition they promised Monk that they would grant him a new commission as General over all the forces in the three nations by sea and land. He then asked them to meet him on the following morning at his former quarters in Whitehall.

Rumours of the meeting circulated; the Council of State, sitting late, heard that the secluded members intended to force an entrance to the House next morning. On this the Council sent a message to Monk requiring him to prevent such an entrance if it were attempted. He blandly replied that he had no reason to believe that any such project was designed; however, to reassure the Council and the Parliament, he would double the guard at the House. He had in fact, for his own purposes, already arranged for this to be done.

On the same evening Harrington's Rota Club came to an unobtrusive end. Pepys attended, and recorded that 'after a small debate upon the question whether learned or unlearned subjects are the best the Club broke up very poorly, and I do not think they will meet any more'. The times were not propitious for the discussion of political philosophy.

Tuesday, February 21. Early in the morning Monk moved to Whitehall, where his first visitor was Haslerig. The parliamentary leader could get little change out of the General, who, however, apparently convinced him that he was contemplating no violent measures. Haslerig took his place uneasily in the House.

Part I: February

When he had left the secluded members assembled. Monk addressed them at length, reading to them a declaration embodying the articles which they had approved the night before. He told them that the peace of the country depended, after God, on them; he praised their wisdom, piety and disinterestedness, and expressed his confidence that they would show all necessary readiness to repair past evils. He laid great emphasis on the need for a continuance of the republican régime, saying that if the King were readmitted through internal divisions his power would become arbitrary; moreover, a restoration would mean the return of prelacy, whereas a Presbyterian form in religion had been found more satisfactory. He then invited them to go and take their seats, with the assurance that the reinforced guard he had placed at Westminster would ensure their peaceful admittance.

As soon as they had gone he summoned the leaders of the Army, and a letter was drawn up to be sent to all regiments in England, Scotland and Ireland, announcing the return of the secluded members.

Escorted by Adjutant Miller the members, eighty strong, entered the House and took their places. In spite of the rumours of the night before, in spite of Haslerig's visit to Monk that morning, the sitting members appeared to be taken completely by surprise. Babel broke out, and Haslerig was heard crying out that Monk was a traitor. But the secluded members were in their seats; they formed a majority of the House, and the guard was on their side, certain to intervene should their return be resisted. Haslerig, Scot, Ludlow and a few others, acknowledging defeat, left the Chamber in disgust; the rest bowed to the inevitable and remained.

Prominent among the no longer secluded members was William Prynne. This extraordinary man had been a thorn in the side of King Charles I. The most extreme of puritans, he had poured out a stream of invective in pamphlet after pamphlet, denouncing prelacy, frivolity and the vices of the times with all the fury at his command. The theatre, as patronised by the Court, had come in for some of his greatest torrents of wrath, and his literary harangues on this subject had led him to the pillory and lost him his ears. But time had diverted his aim; he was incapable of being long out of opposition, and Cromwell's ascendancy had given him a new target. Prynne did nothing by halves; he was now, at sixty, more royalist than the King. Today he swaggered into the Parliament Chamber wearing a great basket-hilted sword, and prepared to work for a royal restoration with all the zest that no advancing age could diminish.

The restored members lost no time in getting to work. First they revoked all the Acts passed against themselves since 1648, and annulled the resolutions taken to fill up their seats through new elections. Then they fulfilled their promise to Monk; he was appointed Captain-General of all the forces by sea and land in England, Scotland and Ireland, Lawson being confirmed as Vice-Admiral. The appointment of five Commissioners of the Army was revoked. The Council of State was dissolved; a new one composed of thirty-one members, of whom Monk was to be one, was to be appointed on the following Friday.

That night there was a repetition of some of the scenes of February 11. Pepys watched from a window: 'It was a most pleasant sight to see the City from one end to the other with a glory about it, so high was the light of the bonfires, and so thick round the City, and the bells rang everywhere.'

Monk went to bed well satisfied with the day's work. Price arrived at the Prince's Lodgings and was told that his master had retired, but Mrs Monk kept him in conversation and the General, hearing his voice, called him up to his bedside. He asked the chaplain why he had come, and Price replied that his purpose, over and above his normal duty of attendance, was to give him thanks for what he had done.

Monk was not to be put off with this answer; he knew the workings of his faithful servant's mind. 'No, no,' he said; 'this is none of your business; you but dissemble with me; you come now for somewhat else, and I believe I know for what.'

Price asked humbly what he was supposed to have come

for. 'Sit down,' replied the General, 'and I'll tell you. You come for bishops.'

At this point Mrs Monk interrupted. She had of course, being the woman she was, been listening; and she thought Price was going ahead too fast. But her husband silenced her, telling her that it was he and not Price who had uttered the word 'bishops'. Having got rid of her, Monk revealed his thoughts; Price was the confidant with whom he was accustomed to discuss his doubts. He thought, he said, that the bishops could never be restored, 'for not only their lands are sold, but the temper of the nation is against them'.

Price here ventured to suggest that the General could not judge the temper of the nation, since the royalists had not yet thought it prudent to appear openly or make addresses. And he asked his master at least not to commit himself against a restoration of prelacy; he had, he pointed out, refused to be ensnared into abjuring the King and the royal family.

'He paused a while (as his Manner was),' wrote Price of the conclusion of this interview, 'and, taking me by the Hand, *Well, then;* (said he), *so much I will promise you, that I will not be engaged against* Bishops. I thank'd him, and kissed his Hand; adding, that it was best to leave it to God's Providence and the next Parliament, when we should be able to discern the Temper of the Nation, in reference both to Church and State.'

Wednesday, February 22. The House of Commons continued the good work. Sir George Booth, who had led the royalist rising of the previous summer and had been under detention ever since, was set at liberty: a sign perhaps that none of the restored members took Monk's declaration of republicanism very seriously. Those citizens of London who were still under arrest in consequence of the events earlier in the month were also freed, and an order was made that the posts and chains, gates and portcullises, should be restored at public expense. Finally, the agreed resolution was passed for a new Parliament to meet on April 25.

Events in London were quickly reflected in the attitudes of the European powers towards the exiled King. He had been consistently cold-shouldered by the leaders of the Dutch republic. Now the States-General of the Netherlands sent two commissioners to him at Brussels. In a private audience they begged him not to take it ill that they had been in constant correspondence with the English rebels, as the States were obliged to take that course in their own interests and to preserve trade. They hoped His Majesty would think well of them and keep up the ancient friendship and confidence, assuring him on their side of the utmost respect and regard.

At about the same time the Marqués de Caracena, Governor of the Spanish Netherlands, waited on King Charles to assure him of his master's help in recovering his rights. The Duke of York was offered the post of High Admiral of the Spanish Navy.

Thursday, February 23. The new Council of State was set up a day earlier than had been resolved. In addition to Monk, whose inclusion had already been decided, the most important members were Colonel Morley, Lord Fairfax, Sir Anthony Ashley Cooper, Sir Gilbert Gerrard, Lord Chief Justice St John, Sir William Waller, Sir William Lewis, Colonel Edward Montagu, Denzil Holles, Sir John Temple, Sir Harbottle Grimston, John Weaver and Serjeant Maynard. The President was Arthur Annesley. Pepys won a pot of ale on a bet that Prynne would not be a member.

Thomas Scot was deprived of his Secretaryship of State. He was succeeded by John Thurloe, Cromwell's old secretary.

Saturday, February 25. France hastened to join the queue of well-wishers to the English King. Jermyn and Abbot Montagu arrived at Brussels with messages from the French court, and in Paris the great Prince de Condé called on Queen Henrietta Maria to tell her how ardently he hoped to be of service to her son.

There was a minor riot at Durham. Some cavaliers,

celebrating the good times at a tavern, started to distribute sack and beer to all and sundry, soldiers and civilians, who would drink the King's health. There was a merry response, and soon the usual bonfires began to blaze. This was all very well, but the Mayor of Durham was an Anabaptist, and it seemed a good thing to light a fire at his door. This led to an appeal to Captain Richardson, the local commander, who ordered his troops to put out the fires. Discipline was not perfect, and some of the soldiers complied with the order by throwing the blazing wood into the shops. Fighting broke out, and there were a number of injuries as well as damage to property. But at length order was restored.

Pepys was on a trip to Cambridge, where his young brother John was in residence. His father had arrived before him, and the three of them did some good drinking, which included healths to the King. Samuel finished up at supper in Mr Hill's rooms at Magdalene, but he was disappointed at the decline of donnish conversation. 'I could find,' he wrote, 'that there was nothing at all left of the old preciseness in their discourse, specially on Saturday nights.'

Monday, February 27. Accompanied by his friend Blayton, Pepys left Cambridge after a happy week-end. The separation from his wife was not without its compensations, and he was prepared to kick over the traces in a mild way. At the White Hart at Saffron Walden he kissed the daughter of the house, 'she being very pretty', and at Epping, after supper and a game of cards, he had some merry talk with 'a plain bold maid of the house'.

A Bill was introduced for dissolving the Parliament.

Tuesday, February 28. A day of public thanksgiving was celebrated. At St Margaret's, Westminster, the Presbyterian ministers Calamy and Manton preached before the Parliament; at St Paul's the General heard sermons by Dr Reynolds and Dr Gauden, clerics of a more compromising temper.

Later in the day Monk was the guest of honour at a lavish

dinner given by the Grocers Company, destined to be followed by a series of similar City functions. Ludlow had a characteristic comment on these junketings: 'In the meantime the Companies of London made a great entertainment for Monk, where the bargain they had driven with him was ratified and confirmed by dissolute and unbecoming debauchery; for it was his custom not to depart from these publick meetings till he was as drunk as a beast.'

Wednesday, February 29. Once again the end of the month saw calm after the storm. Parliament was preparing for its own dissolution; the only argument concerned the new writs that were to be issued. In whose name should they go out? Eventually the question was shelved for the time being, and the Bill was given its second reading.

MARCH

Thursday, March 1. A great name appeared in the news of the day. *Mercurius Politicus* reported the appointment to the Governorship of Jersey of Carew Raleigh: 'a charge which was borne heretofore by his Father, the most noble and renowned Sir Walter'.

Parliament decided that the day of its dissolution should not be later than March 15. Meanwhile the financial situation was desperate; the Commons had applied to the City of London for a loan, but the commercial magnates, though more friendly to Parliament now that the secluded members were back, were still cautious. Difference arose over security, and a parliamentary committee was appointed to go and plead with the Common Council. This was a far cry from the hectoring attitude of the men of Westminster a few weeks before.

Lambert had written to Parliament and it was decided to take a lenient line. He was dispensed from appearing in person in answer to the proclamation; on providing security he was given permission to live quietly at his own house in the country.

Friday, March 2. Most of the secluded members were Presbyterians, and the party was now well established in power. To consolidate their position they secured the adoption of the Confession of Faith of 1646, embodying the Presbyterian system of theology, as the official doctrine of the Church of England.

Lawson, the naval commander, had lost favour. This too was largely for religious reasons; he was an extreme puritan, an Anabaptist, and was considered dangerous to the Presbyterian ascendancy. He was therefore superseded. He retained the appointment of Vice-Admiral, but Monk, who was officially in command of all forces by sea and land, was given an active naval partner. The man chosen was Edward Montagu, Pepys's patron, who was known to many as a royalist and had in fact for some time past been in secret correspondence with the King. Monk and Montagu were made 'joint Generals or Admirals of the Navy', and Montagu was directed to take up immediate command of the Fleet.

Rumours were, as usual, afloat in London, There was much talk now of 'a single person', but in some minds there was doubt as to who that person would be. The King was of course the favourite, but Monk's reputation and stature had so grown that the possibility of his seizing supreme power for himself was not ruled out. Yet another development was being suggested: Richard Cromwell might return. But there cannot have been many who really believed that this self-effacing person would be willing to emerge from his happy obscurity.

Another rumour was that the Anabaptists were planning a rising, and Monk's troops were on the alert. Meanwhile the City diverted itself with an execution. Richard Marshall, a foot-soldier in Colonel Hubblethorn's company, had been convicted by court martial of the murder of a fellow-soldier, Philip Gooty, in his quarters in Chick Lane, Smithfield; he had stabbed him with a knife after an argument over who should pay for a pot of beer. Marshall was hanged at Smithfield at the time of the market.

The controversy over the writs for the new Parliament continued. The ardent Prynne was for sending them out in the name of King Charles II, but the House as a whole was not ready for this yet.

Sunday, March 4. The Book of Common Prayer, outlawed organ of Anglican doctrine, was openly used at services in the City. At one church the preacher told members of Parliament who were present that, having contributed so much to the ruin of the father, they had nothing now to think of but restoring the son. If they did not do so now that they had the power, his sermon would rise up in judgment against them.

Monday, March 5. Rumours of a plot against Monk, organised by the Anabaptists, Quakers and other sectaries, had been increasing, and the Council of State decided that it was time to take them seriously. Raids were carried out in London and a quantity of arms seized. Scot was closely questioned; it was said that Haslerig was implicated and that evidence had been found against Lambert, who was still in London and who, relying on the vote of four days before, chose this moment to present himself before the Council of State. It was an ill-timed move; the councillors were in a nervous mood, and Lambert was too dangerous to be left at large. His safe-conduct to the country was annulled, and he was sent to the Tower.

The Commons set themselves to the task of safeguarding religious orthodoxy. The Solemn League and Covenant of 1643 was revived, republished and ordered to be set up in the House and to be read in all churches once a year. This famous document, the religious manifesto of the parliamentarians, had officially imposed Presbyterianism on the Church of England. It had also, however, expressly declared the Government of England to rest in King, Lords and Commons; so the royalists saw no cause for alarm in the new move.

Next the Parliament turned on its favourite prey, the Catholics. On the pretext that they had been in correspondence with the sectaries (a most unlikely alliance at this time) a proclamation was issued putting all statutes against popish recusants and priests into execution. Catholics were to be confined to their houses, and a £20 reward was offered to anybody who should reveal the whereabouts of a priest.

From Paris came a report that the Duke of Anjou, younger brother of King Louis XIV, had fallen in love with Princess Henrietta and that a marriage was mooted.

Tuesday, March 6. Admiral Montagu was preparing to take up his command at sea. He was related to the Pepys family and had long honoured Samuel with his patronage. On this day he asked his young cousin to call on him at his house in London; then he took him into the garden and, after a few preliminaries, asked him if he would be willing to go to sea as his secretary. He would want somebody, he added flatteringly, whom he could really trust; would Samuel think it over? Pepys was delighted, and still more so when his patron proceeded to confide in him his views on affairs of state. Wires were being pulled, Montagu told him, to bring Protector Richard back, but if this happened he did not think he would last long. Nor, added the Admiral, would the King unless he carried himself 'very soberly and well'. However, it was the general view now that the King would be restored.

Monk, with his wife and son, was the guest of the Mercers Company.

Wednesday, March 7. Some of the Army officers were getting restive. They presented a remonstrance to Monk, demanding the definite renunciation of rule by any single person, in particular King Charles or any member of his family. Monk was not responsive. He told them sharply that, as he was resolved to support the Parliament and accept its decisions, so he expected that all under him should do the same. If the officers were not prepared to follow him in this, he would find others who were.

Parliament was doing its best to probe the ramifications of the recent suspected plot against Monk. Haslerig, believed to be deeply involved, was called upon to answer charges. As he made his way to the House he was beset by a crowd of boys who chased him with shouts of abuse and cries of 'No Rump, no Rump, Sir Arthur!' and he was obliged to run for sanctuary. In the House he heard the report of the charges against him; then he stood up in his place and asserted his innocence. There was little evidence against him, and nothing much that the Commons could do; they referred the business back to the Council of State, asking for a further report. The names of Scot and Robinson were also mentioned, but here again there was nothing concrete to get hold of.

The French Ambassador, Antoine de Bordeaux, had officially announced to the British Government the peace declared between the Crowns of France and Spain, and had celebrated the event with a *Te Deum* and a lavish reception. The other envoys followed suit, and Giavarina of Venice gave a party. It cost him £35 and he anxiously wrote to the Doge's Government asking to be allowed to put this down to his expense account.

Thursday, March 8. The officers were still dissatisfied, and Monk granted them another interview. Again he spoke with harshness and authority. He had brought them with him from Scotland, he said, on the understanding that they should obey Parliament and submit to military discipline; now they were meddling in affairs that had nothing to do with them. He was the servant of Parliament, and as such he submitted to what it decided for the benefit and quiet of the nation. He advised them all to do the same and not commit themselves to remonstrances. However, since he realised that their anxiety was genuine and that there might be merit in their case, he would authorise a discussion between them and the Parliament men.

Part I: March

Accordingly he arranged that ten members of Parliament should confer with ten representatives of the Army officers. The conference met in the afternoon and lasted some hours; but no agreement was reached and no announcement made.

A Bill for calling the new Parliament on April 25 was introduced and read a first time. Prynne made a long and challenging speech, moving that there should be no dissolution. The House of Lords, he argued, should be recalled, and the King invited to take his place at the head of the Government without more ado.

Friday, March 9. The soldiers having failed to agree with the politicians, Monk would brook no further insubordination. He issued a curt order that all officers with commands in the country should proceed at once to their quarters.

In the House the vexed question of the writs for the new Parliament was at last resolved. In spite of royalist protests it was decided to send them out, according to the established republican formula, in the name of 'the Keepers of the Liberties of England'.

Colonel Robert Whitley, writing to Secretary Nicholas, told a story illustrating the paramount influence in the Monk family. A certain lord, he said, had dined at St James's that week and had asked Monk's seven-year-old son for whom he stood: a King, a Protector or a free state. 'He answer'd that he was for ye King and soe was his mother; and ye truth is she hath contributed very much to ye bringing matters to this passe.'

George Fox's Society of Friends had complained that Monk's soldiers were being rude and troublesome at their peaceful meetings. The General was sympathetic to their grievances, and he issued an order requiring all officers and soldiers 'to forbear to disturb the peaceable meetings of the Quakers; they do nothing prejudicial to the Parliament or Commonwealth of England'.

The City handed over £27,000 to the Parliament in response to the request for a loan. 'The amount is insignificant in view of what is required,' commented the Venetian

Resident, 'but as London will not supply more they have to be satisfied with the little they can get.'

Pepys accepted Montagu's offer of a secretaryship, and wrote to his employer, Downing, asking for leave of absence.

Monday, March 12. Now that the recalcitrant officers had been put in their place, little of importance was happening. An Act was passed confirming the declaration for putting the laws against Catholics into 'effectuall execution'. Having seen to this the Commons adjourned, and Speaker Lenthall proceeded to Whitehall for the christening of his grandson, the infant son of Colonel Sir John Lenthall. The baby was named William, 'as an Omen', reported *Mercurius Politicus*, 'that when he shall be grown up, he will be an imitation of his Grandfathers example, to continue the honor acquired unto the Family'.

Tuesday, March 13. The tide of royalism was flowing ever more strongly. The Commons ordered that the Engagement to be taken by members of Parliament to be 'true and faithful to the Commonwealth of England, as the same is now established without King or House of Lords', should be removed from the file and made null.

Wednesday, March 14. The qualifications to be insisted on for members of the new Parliament were finally decided. All who had been in arms against the Parliament, and their children, all papists, and those who had joined in the Irish rebellion, were excluded. Monk was appointed Major-General of the City of London Militia.

A very young lady named Anne Denton wrote to her uncle, Sir Ralph Verney, of a minor domestic tragedy: 'Youre furmity had broght forth a very fin keten for you, but by ill fortuin sumthing kiled her ketens & she proved very unnatureall & eat them up, which is a gret greve to hir that is your duty full god daughter A.D.'

Part I: March

Thursday, March 15. Pepys's appointment as Admiral Montagu's secretary was settled, and he expected soon to be sent for to the fleet. He packed his belongings and sent them to Montagu's house, paid a round of farewell visits, and took his wife out to dinner at the Sun Tavern. He promised to give her all that he had in the world, except his books which were to go to his brother, in the event of his dying at sea.

For the moment, however, the fleet was held up, chiefly through lack of seamen and of the money to pay them. Parliament passed an Act for the impressment of men, but, as the Venetian Resident commented, 'as the people here do not love violence it may lead to some disturbance in the present crisis'.

The dissolution of Parliament had been expected this day, but although the Commons sat till 10 p.m. they rose without concluding their business. One Act passed gave additional powers to the Council of State during the coming interval; another empowered the Council to discharge Lambert from imprisonment on parole should it see cause. All was then ready for the final act; but John Crew, member for Brackley in Northamptonshire, unexpectedly rose to move that the Commons, before they dissolved themselves, should bear their witness against 'the horrid murder of the King'. An acrimonious debate developed; there were still regicides in the House, and they were not all prepared to lie low and hide their heads. Scot in particular showed conspicuous courage, considering the prevailing temper of the House and country. One of his colleagues protested anxiously that he 'had neither hand nor heart' in the killing of the King, whereupon Scot jumped up and proclaimed that 'he durst not refuse to own that not only his hand but his heart also was in it'. He argued at length in favour of the justice of what had been done, and concluded that 'he should desire no greater honour in this world than that the following inscription might be engraved on his tomb: "Here lieth one who had a hand and a heart in the execution of Charles Stuart late King of England".'

It may have been more than coincidence that this same

evening saw the last of an inscription similar in spirit to that which Scot desired as his epitaph. In the quadrangle of the old Royal Exchange stood a row of statues of all the monarchs of England from Edward the Confessor; on the day King Charles was beheaded his statue was removed and broken in pieces, and in its place the following words were inscribed: 'EXIT TYRANNUS REGUM ULTIMUS RESTITUTAE ANGLIAE LIBERTATIS ANNO PRIMO DIE XXX JANUARII MDCXXXXIIX'. So it had remained to this day, but now, at about seven o'clock, a man appeared carrying a ladder, paint and brushes, and advanced boldly to the statues; some soldiers were close at hand, and it was noticed that they made no attempt to interfere.

The man set up the ladder and climbed it. Very deliberately he washed and cleaned the statue of Queen Elizabeth; then that of King James. Then, to the plaudits of the crowd that had gathered, he painted over the offending inscription, obliterating it completely. That done, he came down and shouted: 'Long live King Charles II!' The cry was taken up; the enthusiasm was tremendous, and before long the City was once again a mass of bonfires.

Friday, March 16. At long last the life of the most protracted and most eventful Parliament in English history came to an end. The Long Parliament had first assembled nearly twenty years before. It had sat throughout the civil war, directing hostilities against the royal forces until leadership was taken out of its hands by the military clique. It had been involved in all the turmoil of the captivity and trial of Charles I, being truncated in the process and surviving only as an obsequious rump subservient to a soldier dictator. It had suffered indignity, humiliation and finally obliteration under Oliver Cromwell, to be revived with fluctuating fortunes amid the anarchy that followed his death. Now in its last few weeks it had been restored to its full strength with the object of leading the way both to its own demise and to a restoration of the monarchy, to the temporary extinction of which it had so largely contributed.

Part I: March

The end came quietly. The Act for dissolution, which could take place only by the House's own consent, was carried unanimously at seven o'clock in the evening. The new Parliament was to meet on April 25, and the Act carried a proviso that 'the single actings of this House, enforced by the pressing necessities of the present times, are not intended in the least to infringe, much less take away, that antient native right which the House of Peers, consisting of the lords who did engage in the cause of Parliament against the forces raised in the name of the late king and so continued to the year 1648, had and have to be a part of the Parliament of England'.

'We are now at liberty,' wrote one of the members, Sir Roger Burgoyne, 'though much against some of our wills: after many sad pangs and groanes, at last we did expire, and now are in another world.'

Sir John Grenville, who had in the summer of the previous year approached the General (without much success) through his brother, the Rev. Nicholas Monk, was in London. It was urgent that he should make contact with Monk on the King's behalf, but access to the great man was not easy, even though he was his cousin. However, another cousin was William Morrice, the General's most trusted adviser. Grenville called on Morrice at St James's and asked him to arrange an interview.

Monk, when approached on the subject, at first showed caution; he was not sure if it would be wise to see Grenville at this stage. He would not receive him, he said, unless he would give some indication of the purpose of the proposed interview. To this Morrice replied that he had already asked him to do this; but Grenville had insisted that the nature of his business was for the General's ear alone. This impressed Monk; the young man was at least discreet. So he changed his mind; if Grenville would come to St James's on the following evening at nine o'clock, he told Morrice, he would speak with him.

A gentleman living in Covent Garden was in trouble with the bailiffs, eleven of whom arrived at his house to arrest him. But the debtor was a tough customer, and so were his friends. He resisted arrest to some purpose; one bailiff was killed and eight wounded before the gentleman was safely lodged in a cell.

Saturday, March 17. Cardinal Mazarin, all-powerful in France, had allowed events to outpace him. Great changes were pending in England, and French influence had no part in them. The French Ambassador, Bordeaux, was instructed to take what steps he could to secure the initiative for his Government.

Bordeaux sought out Clarges as the man most likely to have the General's ear. He spoke persuasively. It was obvious, he said, that Monk was on the verge of some great design, and he concluded that his intention was either to make himself King or to restore Charles II. In either case, this supple diplomatist indicated, the General could count on his good offices, and for this offer he had the full authority of his master the Cardinal. Clarges must see the advantages. If Monk aimed · at the Crown for himself it would be dangerous to trust an Englishman in such an intrigue; if the plan miscarried, evidence could be produced to destroy him. But Bordeaux was a foreigner with diplomatic immunity, and could not be questioned. Moreover, if the worst came to the worst, Monk was assured of honourable exile in France. If on the other hand his design was to restore the King, he could not do better than put the whole execution of the plan into the Cardinal's hands. Mazarin would so manage it that Monk would have the credit of success and no discredit in the event of failure; the King would be given the hospitality of France, with a retinue worthy of his position, until he could sail for England.

Clarges must have smiled inwardly at these Machiavellian proposals. He was certainly not deceived; Mazarin's attitude to the King throughout the dark days of exile had shown how much his protestations of friendship were worth. He told Bordeaux that this was far too deep a matter for him to be involved in. He was willing to arrange an interview with

Monk; but he dampened his visitor's ardour by assuring him 'that the General did not intend to take upon him the Government, but submit all to the determination of the next Parliament'.

Clarges went straight to Morrice and then to Monk. All were agreed in refusing to consider any offer from the Cardinal or the Ambassador. Rather than appear uncivil, Monk said he would receive Bordeaux, but only on condition that he should not propose anything to him concerning the public affairs of government. The interview took place that same evening, and the French Ambassador departed unsatisfied.

Bordeaux having been dismissed with polite generalities, Monk turned to the much more interesting matter of Grenville's visit. The young man arrived secretly at St James's at the appointed hour, and was admitted to Morrice's quarters. There Monk came to him, and, Morrice having been posted at the door to ensure privacy, asked him his errand. Grenville came to the point at once. He was grateful to His Excellency, he said, for giving him this opportunity to discharge himself of a trust, of great importance both to Monk and to the kingdom, which had long before been placed in his hands; and he was happy to be able to perform his duty in obedience to the commands of his master, the King. He thereupon handed to Monk a letter from the King and showed him another addressed to himself, giving him authority to treat with the General on his behalf.

Monk affected astonishment and indignation. He stepped back, holding the offending paper in his hand, and demanded with a frown how Grenville dared to speak to him in such a manner without considering the danger into which he was putting himself. Grenville was ready with his answer. He had long ago considered the matter, he said, with all the danger that might attend it; this could not deter him from the performance of his duty, any more than could all other dangers which he had cheerfully faced at his master's command. But he was the more encouraged to undertake this 'in regard that his Excellency could not but remember the message that he had received in Scotland by his brother'.

This was enough for Monk. There was no need to dissemble any longer. He embraced his visitor and addressed him as 'dear cousin'. 'I thank you with all my heart,' he said, 'for the prudence, fidelity, care and constancy you have showed in this great affair. And I am much pleased also at your resolute secrecy in it; for, could I have understood that you had revealed it to anyone living since you first trusted my brother with it, I would never have treated with you; which now I shall most willingly, and with you the rather because you are one of my nearest kinsmen and of a family to which I owe many obligations.'

The General read the King's letter and the commission he had given to Grenville. Then he said: 'I hope the King will forgive what is past, both in my words and actions, according to the contents of his gracious letter; for my heart was ever faithful to him. But I was never in a condition to do him service till this present time. And you shall assure his Majesty that I am now not only ready to obey his commands, but to sacrifice my life and fortune in his service. To witness this I call this honest man from the door.'

So Morrice was called in, and the three men settled down to discussion of the means of bringing about a restoration. Monk emphasised that it was still necessary to proceed with the utmost caution. The people had long been seduced by seditious propaganda; the Army still contained many republicans in the higher ranks. One slip, and it would be out of his power to serve the King; 'there would not be room for two errors'. He then made a practical proposal. Let the King forestall disaffection and anticipate the people's fears by declaring a free and general pardon, and engaging himself to give it under the Great Seal, to all his subjects who should submit to his authority, except such as should be exempted by Parliament. Further, let the King consent to the settlement of landed estates by Act of Parliament and declare toleration of liberty of conscience for all his subjects.

Grenville's commission did not go to the length of empowering him to agree to such weighty proposals. He therefore suggested that Monk should send a messenger of his own, one fully in his confidence, to the King. Monk agreed, but said that the messenger could be nobody but Grenville himself. Moreover, he would write no letter; it might be intercepted. The message to the King must be delivered by word of mouth.

So the momentous interview ended. Grenville was to come again in a couple of days to receive his detailed instructions.

Morrice, level-headed and unobtrusive, was becoming a power in the land. His increasing influence had been brought to the notice of the King, who on this same day wrote him a singularly friendly letter from Brussels:

> I am assured by a person, through whose handes this will come to you, that you have more than ordinary affection to promote my service and interest, and that you have much credit with those who can contribute very much towards it: all which I believe, and am therefore very willing to give you my thankes, and to assure you, that as your frindes shall have all the reason to rejoyce in the service they shall do for me, that my kindness and power can give them, so you shall finde your particular accounte in it; and that I will be alwayes, Your affectionate frinde, Charles R.

Monday, March 19. Grenville came again to St James's for his instructions. These had been prepared by Morrice in consultation with Monk, and Grenville was now told to take them down in writing. The main heads concerned Monk's advice to the King as revealed in the previous discussion; there was, however, one important addition. It was time, Monk said, for the King to leave the King of Spain's dominions; England was still technically at war with Spain, and, should the negotiations for the restoration get under way with the principal figure still in Flanders, King Philip might take it into his head to detain him there. Grenville was to advise the King to leave Brussels immediately and make for Breda or some other place within the United Provinces.

Having taken down his orders, Grenville read them through carefully and then repeated them from memory to the General. Satisfied with his messenger's competence and discretion, Monk took the paper from him, tore it in pieces and threw it into the fire. The same night Sir John Grenville, speeding secretly through the City, began his journey towards Dover.

The Council of State, now the sole organ of government, issued three proclamations. All royalists and Catholics were to repair to their ordinary places of residence, and all Army officers to their quarters. 'The first two,' commented the French Ambassador, 'seem to have been framed only with a view to give a colour to the last, as it is not a great mortification to send the nobility back to the country, whither they are moreover summoned by the election of the members of the Parliament, which now occupies all minds.'

Tuesday, March 20. Grenville arrived at Dover. There he met Lord Mordaunt, who was also on his way to the King and had already hired a vessel; he was delighted that Grenville should share it. The two were old friends, but Mordaunt, bravest and most dashing of King Charles's followers, was not renowned for discretion. Grenville gave him no inkling of the business he was on.

Thurloe, the new Secretary of State, received a quaintly spelt letter of warning from one of his informants:

Honoured Sir,
My humble servis presented unto you, giving you mani thanks for the favor you did me, for which I am bound to serve you with my lif. Sir, the last night ther cam a gentleman to take his leave of me, whom this day is gon for Flanders with a message from Morden, Massi, and Brown, and divers of the cheefe officers of London, to the King, wherein they do declare, that generall Monk hath vowed to them, he will bring in the king; yet they say, they will not trust him, for he will play fast and loos. The ould members towld my friend, that they and sum of the armi would sudenly agree. They towld him, the day the hows

broke up, the generall sent them a letter they showld not go on to setle the malisha, but withall sent them a private message. The leter was sent only to pleas his officers; and when he hath pickt and culd his army, and put new officers in, he tells them he then will declare for the king; but my friend tells me, they do not beleev him, and ar resolved to goe on with the design, which I fear is nought; for he towld me, if sum know half so much as he, Brown would not be at liberti six days. They will do all they can to invite the generall to stai at London: but what ends they hav, I know not. Sir, I have takne the bowldness upon me to truble your patiens with thes scribled lines, you being concerned in it as much as others; I mean in danger, for they say you are the only head-peece. So, with my daily praers to the Lord for you, I rest

Your most humble servant,
ELIZABETH EINZY

After heavy rain and an east wind the Thames overflowed its banks. Boats were rowed in King Street, Westminster, and Axe Yard, where Pepys lived, was flooded.

Wednesday, March 21. Johnston of Wariston had come out of hiding. He went to Whitehall to see how the land lay, but got little encouragement. His wife actually approached Monk with a request that her husband should have a hearing in the Council pertaining to his lost post. But the General had no love for Johnston; he replied angrily that if he had a hearing it would be the worse for him.

Thursday, March 22. Giavarina's request that his junketings on behalf of the Franco-Spanish peace should be included in his official expenses was debated in the Venetian Senate. Either the envoy had an enemy there or there was one lone champion of economy. The motion was carried by a hundred and fifteen votes to one.

Friday, March 23. At last Montagu, having been put off by the bad weather, took over command of the fleet. He boarded the *Swiftsure* in the Long Reach, off Greenhithe, and as he did so was greeted with a salvo from all the ships. Vice-Admiral Lawson, whom he had superseded, came on board and saluted him with the greatest respect. Pepys, taking up his post as the Admiral's secretary, found his cabin 'the best that any had that belonged to my Lord'. He was also relieved to find that he was not sea-sick.

Johnston of Wariston saw Monk at Whitehall and made an unsuccessful attempt to speak to him. 'The guard pulled me awaye,' he recorded in his diary, 'and his guard went so throng about him and would suffer non to com neare to him that I thought strange to see it.'

Mordaunt and Grenville arrived at Ostend, and now, safely across the Channel, Grenville wrote down all that had passed between him and Monk for the King to read.

Saturday, March 24. News of the first elections to the new Parliament was coming in. Sir Anthony Ager and Heneage Finch were elected for Canterbury.

At Brussels the King was waiting impatiently for news. He wrote to Jermyn in Paris lamenting that the rough weather had held up the post from England. He had heard a report that the Parliament had passed a vote in favour of King, Lords and Commons. Did Jermyn know anything about it? 'Pray hasten all you can my coming to you,' he concluded; 'for, besides the passion I have to wait on the Queen, I think it is the properest place for my public concerns. There is a gun which I bespoke of the Turennes; if it be finished pray send it to me, and I return you what it costs. God keep you.'

Johnston at last managed to present his petition to Monk; but he might have saved his labour. Monk refused to read or discuss it, saying curtly that Johnston had had £600 as compensation for his loss of place ('wherof I never had a penny,' wrote the victim dolefully). Lady Johnston got in a word with Mrs Monk, but to no avail. Johnston walked in an adjoining room while they talked, 'and two things came to my mynd—the one that this tyrannical mans reigne would not last (but Lord keepe my hand even of prayer from

stretching itself out against him). . . . The uther was that he
so kindled when he saw me or heard of my place that he
eyther had som response and som feare of my being in any
place, or he had som privat desseigne and interest in
reference to my place.'

Monday, March 26. Lord Fairfax, who as a Scottish peer was
ineligible for the House of Lords, was elected member of
Parliament for York.

Tuesday, March 27. Elections to Parliament were announced
for the City of London. The members chosen were Mr
Recorder Wilde, Major-General Browne, Alderman Robinson and Alderman Vincent.

Mordaunt had sent a letter ahead of him to Brussels, in
which he assured the King that he was now convinced of
Monk's support for his restoration. On receiving this King
Charles decided to write to Monk himself. He had still no
knowledge of the success of Grenville's mission.

'If this be the first letter you have received from me,'
wrote the King, 'it is only because some of your friends have
not found a convenience of delivering one to you, which they
have had long in their hands. And you cannot but believe,
that I know too well the power you have to do me good or
harm, not to desire you should be my friend. And I think
I have the best ground of confidence that can be that you
will be so, in believing you to be a great lover of your
country and that you desire to secure the peace and happiness and to advance the honour of it, and knowing very well
that my heart is full of no other end, which I am sure you
will know yourself as soon as you know me. And whatever
you have heard to the contrary, you will find to be as false
as if you had been told that I have white hair or am crooked.
And it is upon this confidence only that I depend upon you
and your assistance to the bringing that to pass which I may
say can only with God's blessing bring peace and happiness
to the nation and restore it to its just reputation and honour,
and secure all good men in the possession of what belongs to

them.' The King assured Monk that he had complete trust in him 'and as much kindness for you, as can be expressed by Your affectionate friend, Charles R.'

Johnston of Wariston, despairing of justice in London, set out for Edinburgh with his wife.

Wednesday, March 28. With a restoration in prospect, those whose loyalty was suspect were getting nervous. The following notice, signed by Henry Scobell, Clerk of the Parliament, appeared in *Mercurius Politicus*:

> Whereas mention hath been made in several printed Books, that *John Fowke* Alderman, was one of those persons that did actually sit as Judges upon the Tryal of his Majesty, with the Council and Attendants of the Court, and was in the number of the Judges at the Kings sentence of Death: These are to give notice to all men that the same is most false and scandalous . . .'

Dr Thomas Clarges was elected to sit as member of Parliament for the City of Westminster.

Thursday, March 29. A lively newspaper and pamphlet war, in which Prynne had taken his inevitably prominent part, had been raging between royalists and republicans. The publications had become daily more scurrilous; the Lord Mayor and Court of Aldermen now stepped in and prohibited the printing of all pamphlets and 'books of intelligence' within the City and Liberties of London without lawful authority.

Friday, March 30. Mordaunt and Grenville, the former now fully informed of developments, arrived in Brussels and made their way secretly to the Chancellor's quarters. Here they were joined by the King, and Grenville imparted his highly welcome news. Monk's advice was eagerly examined, and a long conference took place between the King, Ormonde, Hyde, Nicholas, Grenville and Mordaunt.

The way ahead was not entirely easy. In particular

Part I: March

Monk's suggestions on land settlement gave the King and his advisers food for thought. Land had changed hands on a vast scale; crown and church estates, and the property of those who had fought for the King, had been confiscated and disposed of as the republican authorities saw fit. Monk proposed a general settlement which would in general leave the present owners in possession. This would obviously be grossly unjust to those who had forfeited their estates by their loyalty to their King.

Again, the question of an amnesty and a declaration of religious toleration presented difficulties. No man was less bloodthirsty than King Charles; as for religion, he was to spend most of his reign in unwearied endeavour to subdue his subjects' passion for persecution. But he held it incompatible with his filial honour to consent to the pardon of those responsible for his father's death. And religious toleration, however desirable in itself, could not be brought about without amending the laws of England.

At length it was decided that a declaration should be drawn up containing such points in Monk's proposals as the King could conscientiously endorse; those on which he had reservations were to be left to Parliament to decide. In particular the question of the murderers of his father was to be referred to Parliament, 'yet with such expressions and descriptions, that they could not but discern that he trusted them in confidence that they would do themselves and the nation right, in declaring their detestation of, and preparing vengeance for, that parricide.'

In addition to the declaration letters were to be drawn up to Monk, the House of Commons and the Common Council; and, since it was still uncertain whether Parliament was to consist of one House or two, one was to be prepared for the House of Lords as well. As soon as they were ready, Grenville was to take them to England.

Next came consideration of Monk's advice that the King should leave Spanish territory. All agreed that this was sound, and it was decided that no time should be lost. Plans were put in hand for a quick getaway during the next few days.

APRIL

Sunday, April 1. A boy 'in a white stuff suit, the collor of his doublet too big for him, his hair all cut off his head, with a black hat, of a sallow complexion, about 17 years of age, and very little of stature', stole a sum of money from his master, a shoemaker named John Pye, living in Petty France, Westminster. Mr Pye offered a reward of forty shillings for his apprehension.

Soldiers at Dunkirk were reported to be drinking the King's health openly in the streets.

Monday, April 2. The revolution in power that took place when the secluded members returned to Parliament was reflected in the press. The two official newspapers, the *Publick Intelligencer* and *Mercurius Politicus*, one appearing on Mondays and the other on Thursdays, had for some time been both edited by Marchamont Nedham. He was a journalist with a shady record, who had changed sides with shameless regularity during the various conflicts of the past twenty years; but he had recently been too closely identified with the republican régime to be able to do so any longer. He was now dismissed, and his place was taken by Henry Muddiman, the pushing and enterprising journalist who had introduced Pepys to the Rota Club, and Giles Dury. To signify the change the papers were renamed the *Parliamentary Intelligencer* and *Mercurius Publicus*.

Tuesday, April 3. The declaration and letters were ready, and it was time to put into operation the plan for the King's departure from Brussels. The Dukes of York and Gloucester rode out of the city, and the King called on the Spanish Governor and casually informed him that he intended to pay a visit of two or three days to his sister, the Princess Royal; his brothers had gone on ahead to tell her to expect him. Caracena apparently suspected nothing; he merely suggested that the Duke of York should go to Spain as soon as possible to take up his naval command. In reply King Charles remarked that he hoped that, by the time he returned, the forces the King of Spain was always promising him would be available. He might need them at any moment.

Wednesday, April 4. But either Caracena had guessed more than King Charles supposed or his suspicions were aroused when he thought it over later. In the very early hours of the morning a breathless young Irishman, William Galloway, presented himself at the Chancellor's lodgings. He was, he said, page to Don Alonzo de Cardinas, a former Spanish Ambassador in London, who was now living in Brussels and advising Caracena on English affairs, and he must see the Chancellor immediately; he had something to tell him that concerned the King's life. Hyde was roused from his sleep, and the young man, trembling with fear, told his story.

On Tuesday evening Caracena and Cardinas had been long in conference together, and Galloway had overheard them saying something about sending a guard to attend the King. At length they parted, and a little later the Governor sent Don Alonzo a paper. The latter went to bed not long after, laying the paper on a table in his bedroom. This was Galloway's chance. His own bed was in his master's ante-chamber, and when he was sure that Don Alonzo was asleep he crept into his room and took the paper. It was, he found, an order for a Spanish officer to attend the English King with a guard of horse wherever he went, but not on any account to suffer him to leave the town. Galloway regarded his first loyalty as being to King Charles; taking the paper, he ran at top speed to find the Chancellor.

There was only one thing to be done; the King must leave Brussels before the order could be carried out. He was aroused in his turn, and he gave prompt orders to his equerry, Sir William Armourer, to have everything ready for him to leave by 3 a.m. Soon he was away, with Ormonde, Grenville, Armourer and a couple of servants. As for the gallant Galloway, he got back to his quarters and replaced the paper on the table where he found it, with Don Alonzo none the wiser.

Between eight and nine in the morning an officer arrived at the royal residence, only to find that the King had left some hours before. Galloway's loyalty, aided by the Spanish capacity for sleep and the spirit of *mañana*, had saved the day.

The royal party made for Antwerp. On the way Grenville took the opportunity to broach a matter which had been on his mind since he left England. He told the King of the excellent qualities of Mr William Morrice; of his influence with General Monk; of how helpful he had been and how his co-operation was smoothing the way to restoration. Apologising for his temerity, Grenville ventured to make a suggestion: if he could be empowered to promise Morrice one of the Secretaryships of State, the good cause might yet be further assisted. The King thought the idea excellent, and authorised Grenville then and there to give such an assurance to the General when he reached England.

At Antwerp Mordaunt was waiting, and from there the party made for the Dutch frontier. As soon as they were across it, the King produced the declaration and the letters, all dated from Breda, and handed them to Grenville to take to England. The letters were addressed to the Speakers of both Houses, to the Lord Mayor of London, and to General Monk. With each letter was a copy of the declaration.

The Declaration of Breda, the manifesto of the Restoration, had been drawn up by Hyde. It was addressed in the name of the King 'to all our loving subjects of what degree or quality soever'. It began by describing the troubles through which England had passed and the King's longing to contribute to the healing of his country's wounds: 'So we do make it our daily suit to the Divine Providence, that He will in compassion to us and our subjects, after so long misery and sufferings, remit and put us into a quiet and peaceable possession of that our right, with as little blood and damage to our people as is possible. Nor do we desire more to enjoy what is ours, than that all our subjects may enjoy what by Law is theirs, by a full and entire administration of justice throughout the land, and by extending our mercy where it is wanted and deserved.'

The document proceeded on the lines decided on at Brussels. The King promised a free and general pardon to all who should, within forty days of the publication of the Declaration, publicly declare their loyalty, 'excepting only such as shall hereafter be excepted by Parliament'. Liberty for tender consciences in religion was declared, and the King proclaimed his willingness to assent to such an Act of Parliament as should be passed for granting that indulgence. The settlement of the land question would be left to Parliament.

Sir John Grenville took from his King the document which was to usher in a new era of English history. Then he and Mordaunt made for the coast and England. That night the King and Ormonde arrived at Breda.

Thursday, April 5. Hyde, with the rest of the royal retinue, joined the King at Breda.

Alderman Atkins followed Fowke in getting a disclaimer printed of his having had any part in the trial of the King. Giavarina was caustic about these self-justifications. 'Many of his Majesty's enemies,' he wrote to the Doge, 'are now trying to curry favour with him by excuses and justifications. Two aldermen of London who were judges and signed the king's death warrant now defend their impious action by unsubstantial pretexts. Although their names appear in all the sheets which make mention of this horrid spectacle they are not ashamed to put into the Gazettes which come out every Monday and Thursday, that they are not entered in the parliament Journal and deny that they had a hand in that innocent blood, thus endeavouring to establish their blamelessness. All these things tend to show that there is no reason for doubting the king's return.'

Friday, April 6. A game of football in York developed into a riot. Some of the rowdy players were committed to custody by the Mayor, whereupon their comrades tried to break into the prison. But the troops were called in and the mob dispersed.

Sunday, April 8. The English Fleet was at sea. Montagu had transferred his flag from the *Swiftsure* to the *Naseby*, which passed two East India merchantmen outward bound; and Pepys and the lieutenant spent some time looking through the lieutenant's glass at the women on board, 'being pretty handsome'. Later Pepys had a theological discussion in the lieutenant's cabin, 'the parson for and I against extemporary prayers, very hot'.

Monday, April 9. Marchamont Nedham was going down fighting. In spite of his dismissal he had continued to publish a paper under the old title of *Mercurius Politicus*. Now the Council of State issued an order 'that the Master and Wardens of the Stationers Company, London, be, and are hereby required to take care, that no Books of Intelligence be Printed and Published on Mundayes or Thursdayes weekly, other than such as are put forth by Mr Henry Muddiman, and Mr Giles Dury, who have an allowance in the behalf from the Council of State.'

Tuesday, April 10. Just when everything appeared to be proceeding smoothly towards the return of the King, a sensation of the first magnitude burst upon London. Lambert escaped from the Tower.

Wednesday, April 11. Nobody knew quite how it had happened. The most picturesque story was that a lady had smuggled into Lambert's room a ladder of silk, down which he had climbed from his window to the river, where six of his friends were waiting with a barge. Meanwhile the girl who waited on him put on his nightcap and tucked herself up; when the warder looked in to say good night it appeared that his prisoner was in bed. But when he unlocked the door in the morning he got a bit of a shock. 'In the name of God,

Joan, what makes you here?' he exclaimed. 'Where is my Lord Lambert?' To which he received the reply: 'He is gone; but I cannot tell whither.' Joan was said to have received £100 for her pains, but to be now in close custody.

Whether there was anything in this story or not, the stark fact was that Lambert was at large. And the Government was thoroughly alarmed. The republicans were desperate; their cause was at its lowest ebb, but they would clutch at a straw. There was one man capable of rallying them, and that man was Lambert. Should he succeed in raising the banner of revolt, all the carefully laid plans for a royal restoration might yet be jeopardised.

The Council of State issued a proclamation calling on Lambert to surrender within twenty-four hours; anybody harbouring him was to be subject to all the penalties to which he himself was liable. All officers, civil and military, were required to help in tracing him, and a £100 reward was offered for his capture. At the same time Monk wrote to all his subordinate commanders ordering them to see that no officers were absent from duty; if any agitators were detected among the men they were to be secured and sent at once to headquarters. The danger of disaffection in the Army was only too obvious.

Nothing of this was known on board the *Naseby*, where Montagu again took Pepys into his confidence. He now saw his way clear, he told his secretary, to bring in the King. But he was not sure of some of his captains, including Cuttance, the commander of the *Naseby*.

Thursday, April 12. With Lambert's movements a mystery, nerves were on edge in all quarters. The City of London set up their chains and put three regiments on guard.

Monk, however, preserved his habitual imperturbability. Continuing his round of City entertainments, he dined at Vintners' Hall. On the same day he was chosen unanimously as member of Parliament for his native county of Devon.

Monday, April 16. Lambert was lying low. It was nearly a week since his escape, but no authentic news of his whereabouts had reached the authorities. There were, of course, plenty of rumours; one was that he had appeared at Uttoxeter with a small company of horse. There were signs of unrest in the Army; at Hull a seditious petition had been presented to the officers. The ringleaders were arrested, given thirty-one lashes each, and turned out of the city gates. Clearly Monk had imposed sound discipline on the Army. There might be local disorders, but the Captain-General was in command of the situation.

Wednesday, April 18. There was news at last. Colonel Streater, in command of troops at Northampton, reported that Lambert was believed to be hovering in the northern parts of the county. How he had got there was unknown, but another picturesque story was being retailed in London. Lambert, it was said, had a few days before been hiding in a house at Millbank, Westminster, where his presence was suspected. Soldiers surrounded the house, whereupon Lambert dressed himself in women's clothes and a mask, gave £10 to a neighbour to break down a wall in his house, and so got away to where a coach was waiting. Thus he had escaped northward.

The strength of his force in Northamptonshire was unknown, and Streater reported that he was himself short of cavalry. Monk took prompt action. He sent for Colonel Richard Ingoldsby, a regicide who had changed his allegiance and been in correspondence with Charles II, and who was trusted by Monk as a tried soldier, and ordered him to be at Northampton with his regiment by Saturday. There he was to take over command; he would have Streater under him and also Colonel Rossiter, who was in the neighbourhood, with as many of their troops, now widely dispersed, as could be quickly concentrated.

Thursday, April 19. Intrigue was clouding the bright hopes of the English court at Breda. Hyde had always been unpopular in some circles, where his overbearing manner and modest origin were resented, and rumours were being industriously circulated that he had lost the royal favour. The King vigorously defended his Chancellor in a letter to Sir Alan Apsley. 'The truth of it is,' he wrote, 'I look upon the spreaders of that lie as more my enemies than his, for he will always be found an honest man, and I should deserve the name of a very unjust master if I should reward him so ill that hath served me so faithfully. Therefore I do conjure you to let as many as you can of my friends know the falsehood and malice of that report, and I shall take it as a service.'

Friday, April 20. It was Good Friday, and the Venetian Resident reported to the Doge that his chapel was thronged with Catholics, 'who pray for the Senate as much as for themselves'.

Ingoldsby, making good time, reached Cambridge.

Saturday, April 21. Ingoldsby had carried out his orders to the letter. On this day he rode into Northampton, where he was met by Streater. The Earl of Exeter had recruited a hundred gentlemen of the county as volunteers, and the Trained Bands of the town were in arms. Streater, in addition, was preparing to remedy his lack of cavalry by requisitioning, should it prove necessary, the horses that would be brought into Northampton for the fair on Monday, and mounting four hundred of his foot with them.

More was known now about Lambert's movements. He had called on his followers to meet him at Edgehill, where the first great battle of the civil war had been fought in 1642. Doubtless he hoped that the good old cause would be rallied by the memories of battles long ago, and that his mind was working on these lines was suggested by the fact that he himself went first to Naseby, scene of the decisive rebel victory of 1645. But the good old cause was moribund, and only a few troops of horse, with a handful of officers, assembled at Edgehill.

In London a new proclamation was issued. Lambert was declared guilty of high treason, and those who had rallied to him were ordered to leave him at their utmost peril. Any who should fail to do so within twenty-four hours, and likewise any who should join him after the issue of the proclamation, would themselves be guilty of high treason and their estates forfeited. The Militia and all other forces were required to give all assistance in suppressing Lambert's revolt.

The fleet in the Downs was the scene of great activity. Distinguished visitors were coming and going, received with honour by Montagu, who this day sent a message of loyalty to the Council of State and the new Parliament. Pepys, seeing Sir John Boys and others welcomed by the Admiral and given convoy in the direction of the Dutch coast, was in a high state of excitement, convinced that they were carrying messages to the King. Samuel was having the time of his life. As Montagu's trusted servant he was treated with a respect he had never known before. On this day the captain of the *Naseby* invited him up to his cabin, where he presented him with a barrel of pickled oysters and opened another which they sampled then and there with a bottle of wine.

Sunday, April 22. On Easter Sunday took place the last military skirmish of the civil wars. Early in the morning news was received in Northampton that Lambert was at Daventry, whereupon Ingoldsby decided to march out to meet him. Ingoldsby's forces were not impressive. He had his own complete regiment, Captain Linley's troop of Rossiter's regiment, and two companies of Streater's, commanded by the colonel himself. Lambert for his part had four troops of horse commanded by Colonel Alured, Major Nelthorpe, Captain Haslerig (Sir Arthur's son) and Captain Clare. The rest of his troops consisted of a motley and hastily armed mob of Anabaptists and other sectaries. With Lambert at his headquarters were two of the most notorious regicides, John Okey and Daniel Axtell.

By the time Ingoldsby reached Daventry Lambert had

left the town, but the two forces came face to face in a ploughed field nearby, separated by a small brook. During his advance Ingoldsby had his first success, Captain Elsmore with a small party surprising young Haslerig and taking him prisoner. Haslerig was released on parole on condition that he should bring his troop over to Ingoldsby: a condition he fulfilled soon after, sending his men over under his quarter-master while himself keeping in the background.

Neither of the miniature armies could feel confident of victory, and for four hours they faced each other. During this time Lambert sent out a number of scouts, apparently in the hope of spreading disaffection in the opposing forces. His ruse recoiled on himself. Ingoldsby took care to see that no unauthorised person should talk to the enemy, but went himself in the guise of a private soldier to talk to the scouts. His arguments were so effective that a further twenty-five troopers came over to him.

At last Lambert proposed a parley. This was agreed to, and a delegation of his officers appeared before the Government commanders. They were asked what Lambert was in arms for, and gave the somewhat surprising reply that, for the security of the country, he demanded the restoration of Richard Cromwell to the Protectorship. This sudden resurrection of the fallen ruler's claim exposed as nothing else could the hollow nature of Lambert's case. In this final crisis of his fortunes he could find no better symbol for his cause than a man discredited, uninterested and almost forgotten. The officer delegates were briefly answered by a spokesman of Ingoldsby's; they were only trying, he told then, to set up one whom they themselves had pulled down. He advised them to submit at once and obey their superiors as soldiers.

As soon as Lambert's officers had returned to their lines Ingoldsby advanced, Streater leading with six files of musketeers; their orders were not to shoot till they came within push of pike. There was hardly a pretence of resistance. A few shots were fired and one or two of Lambert's horse were wounded; then Nelthorpe's troop surrendered,

Clare's disintegrated, and Lambert's men pointed their pistols at the ground in token of submission.

Ingoldsby rode up to Lambert and told him he was his prisoner. Thereupon Major Creed and one or two others of the rebel officers tried to intercede, asking Ingoldsby to do what he would with them if he would only allow Lambert to escape. Ingoldsby contemptuously refused the offer; he would not be so treacherous to his superiors, he said, as to let the chief enemy go. At this point Lambert turned his horse and made a bolt for it, but Ingoldsby rode after him, caught up with him and vowed he would pistol him on the spot unless he yielded immediately. Lambert's spirit was broken, and he whined pitifully: 'Pray, my Lord, let me escape, let me escape.' When that was of no avail he submitted. With him surrendered his officers; only Okey, Axtell and Clare escaped.

Lambert's final act of defiance thus came to an ignominious end.

Monday, April 23. In the general enthusiasm for old ways an attempt had been made to reopen the London theatres. Such unbridled debauchery was going too far; puritanism was far from dead. The Council of State ordered 'that the stage-players in the several playhouses in and about London be required to forbear acting at their peril'.

Life was perhaps easier at sea. Pepys gave a party in his cabin to broach the barrel of pickled oysters. Then he and his guests fell to singing and Montagu, who had been playing skittles on deck, heard them and came down to join in. Together they sang a ribald song about the Rump to the tune of 'Green Sleeves'.

Tuesday, April 24. Lambert with two of his officers, Cobbet and Creed, was brought up to London by coach. As a reminder of their probable fate the coach was driven, to the accompaniment of ribald shouts from the multitude, close under the gallows at Tyburn. The three officers were taken immediately before the Council of State and invited to make

Part I: April

their defence. They acknowledged that they had taken up arms on the pretext of opposing the royalists, but added that if those who had pledged themselves to help them had performed their promises a considerable army would have been on foot in a few days. They were committed to the Tower, and a proclamation issued commanding the escaped officers to surrender on pain of being declared traitors.

To celebrate the victory of order and tradition a magnificent parade was held in Hyde Park of the Militia of the City of London. Six regiments of the Trained Bands and four of Auxiliaries took part, twelve thousand men in all. Men of high standing were in the ranks of the volunteers; the Earl of Winchelsea trailed a pike in Alderman Robinson's company. The Lord Mayor in his collar of 'esses' and with sword, mace and cap of maintenance, the aldermen in scarlet and the commissioners of the Militia in full uniform, added colour to the scene. 'The Regiments were all so gallantly accoutred,' commented *Mercurius Publicus*, 'as did sufficiently speak both the strength and wishes of the City, there being little visible difference betwixt the Trained Bands and Auxiliaries, but only in their Age.'

At the end of the parade the Auxiliaries drank the King's health on their knees.

The Rev. Hugh Peters did not like the way things were going. He sent a somewhat rambling letter to Monk, starting: 'I take it indeed as an act of much love and tenderness that your honour sent this bearer to see an old decrepit friend. The Lord God—who is able—requite all respects to his unworthy servants. Truly, my Lord, my weak head and crazy carcass puts me in mind of my great change, and therefore thank God that these twelve months—ever since the breach of Richard's Parliament—I have meddled with no public affairs more than the thoughts of mine own and others presented to yourself.' Peters went on to hope that sobriety and religion would prosper in the nation, and he concluded:

;.. my hearts duty to your Excellency bids me say that since

113

all Europe is in fear and shaken exceedingly, Geneva besieged—as I hear—and Orange demolished, Holland perplexed, the popish enemy triumphing everywhere, how glorious could it be if in your days the Protestant churches might be comforted, who hang so much upon England, witness Queen Elizabeth's time. But I forget myself and leave with my most hearty thanks and assuring you that I have no design nor business in this world but what you know; opinions and whimseys I loath, but am orthodox through mercy.

Wednesday, April 25. The new Parliament assembled at Westminster. The Presbyterians were well represented in the Commons, but were far from their old ascendancy. The qualification rules proved a dead letter; at least a hundred openly declared royalists, many of whom had borne arms against the Parliament, had been elected, and no attempt was made to exclude them. After hearing a sermon from Dr Reynolds at St Margaret's, Westminster, the members settled down to work. Monk took his place as member for Devonshire, and he and Fairfax entered the House together.

Little was done on this first day. The opening business was to elect a Speaker, and Sir Harbottle Grimston, a moderate Presbyterian who had been a secluded member, was chosen. His first duty, in accordance with a vote of the House, was to express the thanks of the Commons to General Monk, which he did with grace and dignity. He praised the General for his great services and his wisdom, his achievement in conquering the country's enemies and bringing peace to church and state 'without a bloody nose'; he addressed him as 'our physician' who 'hath cured us with his lenitives'; he assured him that he had his monument in the hearts of all well-wishers in England, and he doubted not that he had too a crown of glory laid up for him in heaven. Finally he returned thanks in the name of the House, adding, 'he was sure his lordship would believe it if he had not said so'.

It had long been tacitly assumed that the Lords would sit once more in the new Parliament; and now they took their seats almost casually, no public announcement being made.

Part I: April

The only doubt had concerned who should sit. Was the House to be composed only of the Parliament supporters who had sat up to 1648, or were the old cavalier peers to be admitted? The General had inclined towards the former alternative. He felt that a mainly cavalier House of Lords at this stage would antagonise the Army, some of the leaders of which were still hopeful that the restoration would include terms to which the King must subscribe. Events were making an unconditional restoration virtually certain, but Monk still moved with characteristic caution. So in accordance with his views only a handful of peers, survivors of 1648, took their seats; but nobody regarded this as a permanent arrangement. A number of young peers who had succeeded since the civil war wanted to enter the House, but were dissuaded by the General for the moment.

In the absence of a Lord Chancellor the peers chose the Earl of Manchester as their Speaker. Their first act was to confirm the appointment of Monk as Captain-General of all the Land Forces of England, Scotland and Ireland.

Thursday, April 26. The House of Lords proposed April 30 as a fast-day, and sent the proposal down to the Commons for ratification. The Commons agreed, and by so doing recognised the House of Lords as part of Parliament. At the same time General Monk, still acting as an unofficial dictator, signified his willingness that the young peers should take their seats in the Lords. It was arranged that they should enter the House next day.

The Commons voted thanks to Colonel Ingoldsby for his feat in capturing Lambert without bloodshed.

Among the books advertised in *Mercurius Publicus* was *A Character of Charles the Second. Written by an impartial hand, and exposed to the publick view, for information of the People.*

Friday, April 27. The young peers, cavaliers to a man, took their seats. They were about thirty in number, quite enough to swamp the old Parliamentarian lords even had the latter not largely changed their tune. Those who had fought against the Parliament still did not press their claims, but the character of the House was plain. There would be no more talk of admitting the King on terms.

Mordaunt was jubilant. He wrote ecstatically to Ormonde: 'The Cabal Lords are quite defeated, and his Majesty is like to be restored on honourable terms. My dear Lord, I am so full of joy, I can scarce write sense: but you will pardon all my defects.'

To Hyde Mordaunt wrote: 'Concerning Monk there can be no more scruple, for all he does is from his heart, or I am most extremely deceived; and if he errs, it is for want of consulting more persons than he does trust, for he has bound himself up in Mr Morrice, who is questionless a most singular person for piety, loyalty and parts, and one who is indefatigable, else his business would destroy him, all passing through his hands.'

Since Sir John Grenville had parted from the King on the road to Breda on April 4, his movements had been obscure. His instructions had been to go straight to England, and he must have arrived some time before this. Yet nothing had been heard of him. It may be conjectured that he had been in secret communication with Monk, and it was perhaps on the General's advice that he delayed further action until Parliament was sitting.

Be that as it may, on this day Grenville presented himself before Monk with the documents he had received from the King. The General expressed his humility and respect, but as Parliament stood adjourned till after Monday's fast he advised Sir John to attend the Council of State on the following morning and produce the King's letters there.

Saturday, April 28. Accordingly Grenville presented himself before the Council. But not yet were the contents of the momentous letters to be made public. The Council would not presume to open them without the authority of the Parliament. Grenville was instructed to attend the House at its next sitting on May 1.

Part I: April

Sunday, April 29. An unruly mob invaded the Anabaptists' meeting place on St Dunstan's Hill near Thames Street, pulled down the pulpit and broke up the seats. Some arrests were made, but it was feared in some quarters that this was a bad augury for liberty of conscience under the monarchy. One of Ormonde's agents wrote to him suggesting that it would make a good impression if the King would indicate his disapproval of such hooliganism.

Monday, April 30. The fast-day was duly observed. Richard Baxter aroused some controversy by the theme of his sermon at St Margaret's. It was not possible, he proclaimed, that a man should be true to protestant principles and not be loyal, while it was impossible to be loyal while adhering to papist principles.

The newspaper war was in full swing. Nedham had dropped out of the running, but his colleague John Canne was still in the field. Muddiman denounced his rival's insolence and inaccuracies in a majestic leading article in the *Parliamentary Intelligencer*:

> The Reader is desired to take notice that since this Order [suppressing *Mercurius Politicus* and the *Publick Intelligencer*], a certain person hath presumed, to publish two idle Pamphlets, under the titles of the *Publick Intelligencer*, on Mundaies, and *Mercurius Politicus*, on Thursdaies, in the last of which (for, unless upon this occasion, I should not have troubled myself with him) he hath informed us, that the House of Lords had chose the Lord *Say* (a person indeed of great merits and parts, and one that doth very well deserve what Honours may be conferred on him) Speaker, *pro tempore*, detracting thereby from that respect and sentiment of the former services which that Honourable House had for the Earl of *Manchester*, who with so much prudence managed that great work before, and was therefore desired to take the same burthen on him again, which he was pleased to accept of.

After detailing 'another great error our News-monger hath in his information concerning the House of Commons',

Muddiman drew attention to a piece of misreporting of the Lambert campaign:

> The Printer, in the last page of Monday book, in a Letter of *Apr.* 31. [Was this Canne's error or Muddiman's?] had by over-sight omitted the place where that letter was dated, *viz. Oxon,* which made our new *Politicus* write the Lord *Howard* lying that night at *Northampton,* the place from whence a former Letter was dated; whereas his Excellency had ordered him to march by *Oxon,* and Colonel *Ingoldsby* by *Northampton,* to pick up the Renegado Officers, and the rest of their Fraternity on both sides, and in case they had not been dispers'd before, to have met and joyn'd Forces at *Edge-hill,* to give them battel.

At some past date Monk, in a moment of jocularity, had assured Sir Arthur Haslerig that, if his life was ever in danger, he would save it for twopence. Things were looking black now for republicans, and Haslerig wrote to Monk assuring him that he had never done anything in opposition to the present authority settled by Parliament and the Council of State. Neither was he in any way involved in Lambert's insurrection. He had always acted with the authority of Parliament and never against it, and held it his duty to submit to the authority of the nation and not oppose it. He hoped now to spend the remainder of his days in peace and quiet. And he enclosed two pennies.

MAY

Tuesday, May 1. 'Our Chronicles make mention of an *Ill May day;* Let this of 1660, henceforward be called the *Good one* for ever, as having produced the most desired, the most universally satisfactory, and the most welcom News that ever came to these three Nations since that 29. of *May* which was the Birthday of our Sovereign *Charls* the Second, whom God preserve.'

In these words *Mercurius Publicus* opened its ecstatic account of the doings of this first day of May, 1660, the day the nation declared itself to be once more a monarchy.

It all began with the appearance of Sir John Grenville in the Lobby of the House of Lords and the announcement that he had a letter from the King to be presented to their lordships. He was called in, and he handed to Lord Manchester the letter the King had written to the Lords, together with a copy of the Declaration of Breda. The letter asked for the support of the peers and expressed confidence that they would be zealous for the rights of the Crown and the re-establishment of government on its ancient basis.

The letter and declaration were read with traditional ceremonial and every mark of respect, the Speaker referring to the King as 'our sovereign lord'. Then three votes were passed:

> That the Lords do own, and declare, that, according to the ancient and fundamental Laws of this Kingdom, the Government is, and ought to be, by King, Lords and Commons.
>
> The Lords having a deep sense of the Miseries and Distractions that this Kingdom hath been involved in, since the violent Attempts to dissolve the established Government; and conceiving that the separating the Head from the Members hath been the chief Occasion of all our Disorders and Confusions; they desire that some Ways may be considered, how to make up these Breaches, and to obtain the King to Return again to his People.
>
> That a Committee of the House of Commons may be appointed, to meet with a Committee of the Lords, to prepare such Things as may be in order to these good and necessary Ends; and to frame a Letter of Thanks and Acknowledgement to His Majesty, for His gracious Letter and Declaration.

Grenville next repaired to the House of Commons, where a similar scene was enacted. In his letter to the Speaker the King affirmed his trust in parliaments, his zeal for Protestantism and his readiness to leave to Parliament the question of the punishment of transgressors. A second letter was also laid before the House: that to General Monk, who had hitherto refused to open it, preferring to submit it to the House of which he was a member.

Members vied with each other in declaring their loyalty and their enthusiasm; the first to speak was Luke Robinson, whose republican sentiments had waned since the days when he harried Monk on his march to London. Monk himself made a dignified speech, and was followed by many others. Then the House made a practical gesture. Taking into consideration 'that his Majesty, having been deprived of his revenue, could not but be in want of monies', the Commons voted him a gift of £50,000, with £10,000 for the Duke of York and £5,000 for the Duke of Gloucester.

The conference between the two Houses took place in the afternoon. It was resolved that England should be governed as in former times and that means should be found for arranging the King's return to his country as quickly as possible.

Monk, having received back his letter from the Speaker, called a meeting of his officers and read it to them. Here again there was no opposition; the revulsion in favour of monarchy was complete, and even the diehard republicans in the Army dared not oppose it. A declaration was drawn up recognising the King and promising him the Army's obedience.

Lastly came the City. Grenville and Mordaunt presented the royal letter and Declaration to the Common Council, which promptly ordered that the arms of the Commonwealth should be taken down in all places and those of the King set up in their stead. Then, not to be outdone in generosity, the Councilmen voted £10,000 to the King, £1,000 each to the Dukes of York and Gloucester, and £300 each to Grenville and Mordaunt.

That evening there were rejoicings that put the previous celebrations in the shade. The usual bonfires lit London from end to end, and another sign of joy made its appearance. The Maypole, immemorial accompaniment of an English May Day, had been banished by the puritans as a symbol alike of paganism, popery and frivolity. Now the poles were set up in all parts of the country, as fast as the news spread from Westminster. At Deal, where the fleet was now at anchor, the King's flag was hoisted on top of a maypole, while the guns of the Castle fired a salute out to sea, in the direction from which the King of England would soon be welcomed. As for the sailors in the port, 'as many as had money or credit for drink', recorded Pepys, 'did do nothing else'.

Wednesday, May 2. The Army leaders had drawn up an address of loyalty to the King, which was immediately sent out to all regiments and garrisons in England, Scotland, Ireland and Dunkirk, with the instruction that all should endorse it and that the names of dissenters, if any, should be sent to the Captain-General. Monk himself presented the address to the House of Commons, and when it had been read he asked and received the House's permission to send Clarges over with it to the King. At the same time the Commons voted £500 to Grenville to buy himself a jewel.

The next business was the choice of Commissioners to wait on the King with messages of loyalty. The Lords chose the Earls of Oxford, Warwick and Middlesex, Viscount Hereford and Lords Brooke and Berkeley; the Commons Lord Fairfax, Lord Bruce, Lord Falkland, Lord Castleton, Lord Herbert of Worcester, Lord Mandeville, Sir Horatio Townsend, Sir Anthony Ashley Cooper, Sir George Booth, Sir John Holland, Sir Henry Cholmeley and Mr Denzil Holles. To represent the City of London the Common Council appointed Aldermen Langham, Reynoldson, Brown, Thompson, Frederick, Wale, Adams, Bateman and Robinson, Mr Recorder Wild, Sir Nicholas Crisp, Mr Vincent, Mr Biddulph, Mr Foord, Mr Bloodworth, Sir James Bunce, Mr Lewis and Mr William Bateman. All were ordered to prepare for the journey as quickly as they could and 'to desire his Majesty to make a speedy return to his Parliament, to the exercise of his kingly office'.

Thursday, May 3. Next it was the turn of the Navy. With the

King's main letter to Monk had been enclosed another to him and Montagu as joint commanders at sea. This had been sent on to the fleet and was now in Montagu's hands.

This was Pepys's big day. Montagu summoned a council of war aboard the *Naseby*, and while the ships' captains were being assembled he dictated to his secretary the vote of loyalty he wanted the council to pass. When all were ready Pepys was deputed to read the King's letter and the Declaration of Breda to the commanders. Then, while they discussed the contents among themselves, he sat down and went through the motions of drafting the motion which had already been decided on. All went well; 'not one man seemed to say no to it,' he commented, 'though I am confident that many in their hearts were against it.' The principal hurdle surmounted, Pepys went up with the Admiral and the captains to the quarter-deck and there read the papers and the vote to the seamen. Asked for their opinion, the men cried out with enthusiasm: 'God bless King Charles!'

All was now plain sailing; the remaining proceedings were a formality, but for Pepys a delightful formality. He visited every ship in turn, overjoyed at the honour and respect with which he was received on board: still more so by the delight expressed by the men when he read them the Declaration. As he returned to the *Naseby* in the evening the guns of the fleet boomed forth, Montagu firing the first himself and shouting as he did so: 'God bless his Majesty!' Guns from Deal and Sandwich Castles answered the fleet, and with pennants flying and loyal toasts echoing from one ship's company to another the Navy proclaimed its loyalty. To cap it all the Admiral gave two pipes of canary to the ship's company of the *Naseby*.

When it was all over Montagu called his secretary to his cabin and favoured him with one of those confidences which Pepys so treasured. He showed him private letters he had received from the King and the Duke of York, in which the former asked his advice on how to arrange his coming return to England and the latter, now designated as the future Lord High Admiral, offered 'to learn the seaman's trade of him, in such familiar words as if Jack Cole and I had writ them'. Pepys also learnt for the first time that Montagu had long been in direct and secret communication with the King.

The United Provinces were anxious not to be left behind. The States of Holland and West Friesland appointed Commissioners to wait on the King of England at Breda to congratulate him on his coming restoration to the throne of his ancestors (of which they did not yet know officially) and to invite him to come as soon as he pleased to The Hague in preparation for his passage to England. Compliments were expressed to the Duke of York, the Duke of Gloucester and the Princess Royal. Mention was also to be made of 'a firm and indissoluble alliance for the mutual conservation of the common interests of his Estate and of this Republick'.

In London Sir John Grenville received the thanks of the House of Commons. The Speaker addressed him in a gracious speech and presented to him the £500 voted the day before, 'due to a person whom the King hath honoured to be the messenger of so gracious a message'.

The House of Lords ordered that all statues of King Charles I should be put up in the places where they had been pulled down, and likewise the arms of the Crown.

Friday, May 4. Clarges set out from London with Monk's answer to King Charles's letter, together with the address subscribed by the officers of the Army. And on the same day, aboard the *Naseby*, Montagu wrote to the King and read the letter to his secretary 'to see whether I could find any slips in it or no'. Montagu advised Scheveningen, the port of The Hague, as the best place from which the King could sail for England. There was nothing in the world, he added, of which he was more ambitious than to have the honour of attending His Majesty. Meanwhile, at Breda, the first news reached the King of the events of May 1.

The Earl of Manchester, Speaker of the House of Lords, was appointed by both Houses a Commissioner for the Great Seal.

Saturday, May 5. When Clarges arrived at Deal the towns-people strewed his path with herbs in honour of his mission. In London and Westminster, and on board the ships of the fleet, the clergy prayed for the King by name.

Murmurings had been heard that the new Parliament had no legal existence. The Commons therefore passed a Bill 'for removing and preventing all Questions and Dispute, concerning the Assembling and Sitting of this present Parliament', and sent it up to the Lords. It was read twice in the Upper House, but then the Lords adjourned them-selves into a committee and decided to submit the Bill to the consideration of the judges.

Monday, May 7. Preparations for the King's reception were proceeding feverishly. The royal arms were set up in the courts of justice and the statue of Charles I restored to its place in Guildhall Yard; orders were issued for the supply of standards and flags to the fleet. Montagu himself toured his ships to see what alterations were needed, and later directed his secretary to write for silk flags and scarlet waistcloths, 'a noise of trumpets and a set of fidlers'. Pepys, presented by Captain Cuttance with a dozen bottles of Margate ale, made merry till one o'clock in the morning.

Prominent in organising the domestic side of the King's return was Mrs Monk. One of the Lord Chancellor's in-formants wrote of her activities:

> She is an extremely good woman, far from vanity, and full of zeal to his Majesty, for whose person she is providing linen, and because it was (as she saith frankly) her old trade, she will save the King one half in laying out the other, for the chambers, tables, etc. Of his bed she takes as much care as if she were young again; and on all occasions interposeth for his party.

The most important decision of the day was on proclaim-ing the King. The Lords passed a resolution that His Majesty should be proclaimed 'King of England, Scotland, France and Ireland, and all the Dominions and Territories thereunto belonging', and appointed a committee of four to discuss time and place with the House of Commons. Later it was decided that the Proclamation should take place on the following day.

Nathaniel Brooks, at the Angel in Cornhill, advertised a cookery book in the *Parliamentary Intelligencer*:

> The Accomplisht Cook, the Mystery of the whole Art of Cookery, revealed in a more perfect method than hath been publisht in any Language; expert and ready wayes for dressing Flesh, Fowl, and Fish; the raising Paste; the best direction for the manner of Kick-shaws, with other *A la mode* curiosities; approved by the many years experience of *Robert Man*, in the time of his attendance to several persons of Honour.

Tuesday, May 8. With all the traditional pageantry lovingly restored, the capital put the seal on the decision of Parliament. 'Let this day in its Order,' commented *Mercurius Publicus*, 'as well as the first, never want a distinguishing mark in the Kalender, for signal Joy and Felicity, in which his Sacred Majesty, with an universal testification of Loyalty from all degrees, was solemnly Proclaimed by the Lords and Commons, the Lord Mayor, etc., in the Cities of London and Westminster.'

The Lords adjourned early in the afternoon and proceeded to the Painted Chamber, where they formed up in procession: Lord Manchester leading, followed by the Duke of Buckingham and the Earl of Oxford. The Commons met them in Palace Yard, and there the members of both Houses stood bare-headed while William Ryley, Clarenceux King of Arms, read the Proclamation. As King Charles was recognised as having reigned since his father's death, special wording had had to be devised:

> Although it can no way be doubted, but that his Majestie's Right and Title to his Crowns and Kingdoms, is, and was every way Compleated by the Death of His most Royal Father of glorious Memory, without the Ceremony or

solemnity of a Proclamation: Yet since Proclamations in such Cases have been alwayes used, to the end that all good Subjects might upon this occasion testifie their Duty and Respect; And since the armed violence, and other Calamities of many Years last past, have hitherto deprieved Us of any such Opportunity, wherein we might Expresse Our Loyalty and Allegeance to His Majesty: We therefore the Lords and Commons now assembled in Parliament, together with the Lord Mayor, Aldermen, and Commons of the City of *London,* and other Freemen of this Kingdome now present, do according to our Duty and Allegeance, heartily, joyfully, and unanimously Acknowledge and Proclaime, that immediately upon the Decease of our late Sovereign Lord King CHARLES, the Imperiall Crown of the Realme of England, and of all the Kingdoms, Dominions, and Rights belonging to the same, did by inherent Birthright, and lawful and undoubted succession, Descend and come to His most Excellent Majesty, *CHARLES the Second,* as being Lineally, Justly and Lawfully next Heire of the Blood Royal of this Realme; and that by the Goodnesse and Providence of Almighty God, He is of *England, Scotland, France,* and *Ireland,* the most Potent, Mighty, and undoubted King: And thereunto We most humbly and faithfully do Submit, and Oblige Our Selves, Our Heires, and Posterities for ever.

God save the KING.

The Proclamation read, the Lords and Commons took coach and the procession started. First rode the Head Bailiff of Westminster and servants with white staff to prepare the way. Then followed a troop of Army officers and other gentlemen with trumpets before them; then the Lifeguards; then six trumpets and three heralds; then a herald between the serjeant to the Commissioners and the Mace of the Council; then Clarenceux King of Arms between Serjeant Norfolk and Serjeant Middleton; then the Usher of the Black Rod. The Lords and Commons followed: Manchester first in his coach and six; next Speaker Grimston, and then Monk. At the rear of the procession rode a troop of horse.

Part I: May

In Whitehall the King was proclaimed a second time, and the procession then proceeded along the Strand. At Temple Bar there was a halt while the ancient ceremonial of admittance to the City was enacted. The gate was closed in the face of the procession, whereupon Ryley, with trumpets before him, advanced, knocked and demanded entrance. Alderman Bateman came to the gate and asked who it was that knocked; the reply was that if he would open the wicket and desire the Lord Mayor to come to the gate the King of Arms would deliver his message. Thomas Allen, the Lord Mayor, rode up to the gate with his principal officers to receive the message; the trumpets sounded, and then Bateman asked Ryley who he was and what was his message. Ryley, on horseback and with his hat on, replied: 'We are the Heralds at Arms, commanded by the Lords and Commons in Parliament assembled, to demand entrance into the famous City of London, to proclaim Charles the Second King of England, Scotland, France and Ireland; and we expect your speedy answer to this demand.' The wicket was shut again while the City magnates conferred; then Bateman came forward again and told Ryley that his message was accepted and the gate would be immediately opened. The King of Arms entered with trumpets sounding before him and was joyfully received by the Lord Mayor in his crimson velvet gown and hood, the aldermen and sheriffs in scarlet, and the officers of the Militia gallantly accoutred on horseback.

The Lord Mayor and aldermen joined the procession. From Temple Bar to the Old Exchange the streets were lined by the City Militia with drawn swords; citizens watched from every window. At Chancery Lane the King was proclaimed a third time, and when Ryley raised his voice at the words 'Charles the Second' the people took up the cry, which echoed all the way to the Old Exchange, so that it was nearly a quarter of an hour before the rest of the Proclamation could be read. The fourth proclamation was in Cheapside, where the shouting was so great, *Mercurius Publicus* reported, that, though all the bells in the City were rung, Bow Bells could not be heard. Last came the proclamation at the Old Exchange; the guns at the Tower fired a salute, and the ceremony ended with bells and bonfires.

Thus Great Britain became a monarchy again. 'This day, Sir,' wrote Mordaunt to the King, 'ought to be hallowed as an anniversary jubilee, since this day is the first day of our temporal redemption from tyranny and oppression, and from this day we may count our entrance into Canaan, England before being more severe to us than Egypt to the Israelites.'

At Breda King Charles received important visitors. First came the delegates of the States-General of the United Provinces. They were received with ceremony and paid their respects to the King, the Dukes of York and Gloucester, and the Princess Royal. Best of all, they brought to the needy monarch a gift of £6,000 sterling.

Next came Clarges, who had travelled with great speed from the coast. He was met outside the town by Lord Gerard and conducted to the King to present the papers from Monk. King Charles greeted him with affection and knighted him on the spot.

Richard Cromwell, in a final gesture of renunciation, resigned the Chancellorship of Oxford University.

Thursday, May 10. The King was proclaimed at Oxford with due ceremony and magnificence. The conduit at two places ran claret for three hours; hundreds of bottles of wine were given away by the Mayor, barrels of beer were put in the street for all and sundry, and a hundred dozen loaves of bread were distributed to the poor.

King Charles wrote to Monk in answer to the papers Clarges had brought. He told the Captain-General that he would make good any promises Monk had found it necessary to make to his officers. He expected, he went on, that the Commissioners from Parliament would soon reach him, and he intended early in the following week to accept the States' invitation to The Hague. From there he would sail for England. He wrote also to Morrice, thanking him for his services and promising that he would henceforth write to him 'with that freedome as is due to such a servante'.

In London a day of thanksgiving was held, and the clergy in all churches were officially instructed to offer prayers 'for his most Excellent Majesty, and for the most Illustrious Prince James Duke of York and the rest of the Royal Progeny'.

The Parliamentary Commissioners were about to set out, and received their instructions from Parliament. They were to tell the King of the great joy which had greeted the Proclamation; to present him with a copy of the Proclamation itself, and to acquaint him with the desire of both Houses that he should come back to his kingdoms at the earliest possible moment. Finally they were to ask him where he proposed to land in England and whether he wished to come to London by road or by river.

Meanwhile the Commons busied themselves with details of the royal household needs. A committee of the House, which had doubtless received unofficial advice from Mrs Monk, presented a list of requirements; they included for the King's bedroom in Whitehall Palace 'a rich bed, to be of velvet, either embossed with gold or laced and lined with cloth of silver or sattin as shall be best approved of, with a high Chair of State, two high stools, one foot stool and two cushions, all suitable to the bed; two great quilts or mattresses of sattin, suitable to the lining of the bed; two thick fustian quilts, to lie under the sattin quilts; one down bolster; one pair of fustian blankets and one pair of Spanish blankets; and one close stool, suitable to the bed.' Similar, but slightly less luxurious, fittings were recommended for the two royal dukes and the great officers of the household. A second list dealt with coaches, staff and liveries for the King's travels, and a third with flags and decorations for the fleet; Montagu's cabin in the *Naseby* was to be 'new glazed with square glass'.

Late that night Sir John Grenville arrived aboard the *Naseby*. He was on his way to the King and had been entrusted with the money voted by Parliament. But he also had a message for the Admiral. The King's friends, he told him, thought it absolutely necessary in the present state of feeling that the King should come to England at once; would Montagu therefore sail for Holland at the earliest possible moment and expedite the voyage? Montagu promised to do so, and in the meantime sent Grenville on in the *Speaker* to complete his journey and tell the King what was proposed.

The pent-up emotions of the English were indeed causing some anxiety; unless they were given the outlet they craved, the excitement might lead to trouble. 'I pray, my Lord,' wrote Henry Coventry to Ormonde, 'hasten his Majesty over as soon as may be, to prevent the town's running mad; for betwixt joy and expectation the people hardly sleep.'

Friday, May 11. The possibility of disorders mounted as the Proclamation was read in town after town throughout England. At Hull, under the eye of Fairfax, the celebrations were held with due solemnity and decorum, but at Boston in Lincolnshire some sprightly youths seized the Commonwealth arms as they were taken down, dragged them through the town, bound them to the whipping post and had them scourged by a 'beadle'. They then subjected them to more unseemly indignities.

Mindful of his promise to Grenville, Montagu set sail from the Downs. But he was overtaken by a Scottish gentleman who told him he had heard that the Parliamentary Commissioners were just setting out and would have to be taken over to Holland. Montagu wanted to sail on, but felt he could hardly ignore the Commissioners. He anchored off Dover and held a conference with his senior officers; finally it was decided to send Rear-Admiral Stayner to confer with Lord Winchelsea, Constable of Dover Castle, on what was best to be done.

Saturday, May 12. In conformity with the spirit of the Declaration of Breda a Bill for a general pardon, indemnity and oblivion was introduced in the House of Commons and given first and second readings. The debate raised tricky issues; some of the regicides were still sitting in the House, and many members had fought in the parliamentary army against Charles I. Among those who took the opportunity to justify themselves was the captor of Lambert, Ingoldsby, who made what was described as a 'whining recantation' of his conduct at the trial of the King. With many tears he protested his repentance, and then told a story of how he had been unwilling to subscribe to the death sentence, but Cromwell had held his hand and forced him to sign. Nobody believed the story, and Ingoldsby slunk out of the House in ignominy.

As he did so Colonel John Hutchinson entered the House. He too had been a regicide, and found himself expected to make a speech of justification. He did so with more dignity than Ingoldsby had shown. If he had erred at the time of the civil wars, he said, it was through inexperience and defect of judgment; his heart had ever prompted him to pursue the good of his country rather than his own advantage. If the sacrifice of his life would conduce to the public peace he would gladly submit to the disposal of the House; as for the killing of the King, he asked his fellow-members to believe that 'he had that sense of it that befitted an Englishman, a Christian and a gentleman'.

Opinions differed on whether these submissions were acceptable. One member protested that the colonel seemed to be much sorrier for the events and consequences than for the actions; but another represented that, when a man's words admitted of two interpretations, it befitted gentlemen to accept the more favourable. In the end Hutchinson was suspended from sitting in the House.

But it was young John Lenthall, son of the former Speaker, who raised the greatest storm. He boldly threw a bone of contention among the members by declaring that 'he that first drew his sword against the King committed as high an offence as he that cut off the King's head' and that he did not believe that any distinction would be made between the two. This was too much. The old soldiers of the republic protested in horror at such a reflection on their new-found loyalty, and Lenthall was called upon to withdraw his remark. He did so, but the House was not satisfied. A vote of reprehension was passed, and Lenthall was called to the Bar to receive a rebuke from the Speaker. Grimston told him that there was 'much of poison in the words' and that they were spoken out of design to set the House on fire. He warned him that, had not the subject of the debate been mercy and indemnity, he would have received a much harsher punishment than a mere rebuke. Lenthall was duly chastened; but some who listened to the Speaker's words may well have wondered if the representative of the people was not protesting a little too much.

Report had reached the Government that Mrs Oliver Cromwell had secreted goods that were properly the property of the King at a warehouse in Thames Street. A raid was carried out, and goods 'of great worth and value' were seized.

Sunday, May 13. Dr Gauden preached in Westminster Abbey. After the sermon he gave the sacrament to members of the House of Lords; they received it kneeling according to the old reverence of the Church of England.

Monday, May 14. When the debate was resumed on the Bill of Indemnity, the Commons showed themselves more concerned with vengeance on the guilty than on the mercy that was the ostensible purpose of the measure. An order was made that all who had sat in judgment on Charles I should be secured, together with the two executioners if they could be found, Cornet Joyce who had seized the King at Holmby House in 1647, and a few other named individuals. Seven of the judges (though no names were mentioned) were to be excepted, as regards life and estate, from the provisions of the Act of Pardon and Oblivion.

Ludlow had wind of what was afoot. He was never lacking in courage, but his friends implored him to escape while the going was good. He knew the roads out of London would be watched; the safest place was in the back streets of the town. He slipped out of his house under cover of darkness and went into hiding.

Montagu had finally left four ships to escort the Commissioners and sailed with the rest of the fleet for Scheveningen. He arrived early in the morning and sent officers to convey his respects to the Queen of Bohemia and her great-nephew, the nine-year-old Prince of Orange, who were in residence at The Hague. Pepys had a happy day ashore, thrilled with the sight of a foreign city. With his friend Creed he went on a coach tour, and in the same coach were two pretty ladies, who sang all the way and were very free to kiss the two blades that were with them. Later Pepys and Creed went for a walk and were much impressed by the neatness of The Hague. In the evening they called on the Prince of Orange, being surprised at the smallness of his entourage and the ease with which they were admitted. They found the Prince's tutor a fine man 'and himself a very pretty boy'.

Meanwhile the King had left Breda. His last journey had been from Brussels, where he had taken horse before dawn and galloped as a fugitive to the Dutch border. Now he moved in the highest state. The deputies of Holland and of the States-General, who had waited on him at Breda, went on ahead early to prepare the way, and the King was seen off by the Burgomaster and worthies of the town. Magnificent coaches had been provided for the King, the two dukes and the Princess Royal, and the route was lined by soldiers.

At Moerdijk they were met by a fleet of yachts that were to take them to Rotterdam and Delft, and the royal party divided. King Charles and his sister went together, and the King, who loved sailing and took a keen interest in ships and boats, was so pleased with the yacht allotted to him that he declared his intention of having one built like it as soon as he was settled in England. A splendid dinner had been prepared on board, astonishing the English stewards by its lavishness. Unfortunately the water was rough and the Princess Royal was sea-sick as soon as the yacht set sail;

so dinner, which was planned for noon, had to be postponed till the fleet anchored off Dordrecht between three and four in the afternoon.

The plan had been to spend the night at Dordrecht; but the programme was upset by the unexpected arrival of Sir John Grenville. He brought the money from England, and the King, never having seen so large a sum before, excitedly called his sister to come and look at it. But Grenville also brought the news that the King's presence was urgently needed in England, and while the situation was being discussed a messenger arrived to say that Montagu had anchored off Scheveningen. Obviously it would still be many days before the journey to England could be organised, but the King decided he must push on at once. By nightfall the little fleet was at Rotterdam. At about the same time the *Hampshire*, the *Yarmouth* and the *Norwich*, carrying the Commissioners from the House of Commons and the City, caught up with the remainder of the Navy at Scheveningen.

At home many more towns proclaimed the King, among them Dublin and Edinburgh. From the latter a grim incident was reported. A republican gunner announced that he would not obey the order to fire his cannon in salute, and further expressed the hope that the devil would 'blow him in the air that loosed any cannon for that purpose'. Under direct orders from his commanders the man finally carried out his duty. The cannon misfired, and he was blown to pieces.

The Dubliners had a joyous time. A funeral was staged of 'a certain Monster they called *The Commonwealth*, represented by an ugly mis-shapen body without an Head, but with an huge insatiable belly, and a prodigious Rump'. The corpse was carried to the grave and 'buried without expectation of Resurrection'.

The people of Sherborne, where the celebrations were on a particularly grand scale, similarly let themselves go. Effigies of Cromwell and Bradshaw (the presiding judge at the trial of King Charles), their hands smeared with blood, were formally tried at the sessions bench and sentenced to be dragged to the place of execution and hanged on gibbets forty feet high. On the way to the gallows the conducting officers suffered badly from blows from fists, swords, halberds and pikes which were intended for the inanimate victims; but they apparently endured these philosophically in so good a cause. Eventually the corpses were so hacked and mutilated that they were hardly worth burning; but the Commonwealth arms were dragged down to help make up the funeral pile.

From Kidderminster a witch-ducking was reported. Widow Robinson, her two daughters and a man had been arrested for witchcraft; their offence was aggravated by the pronouncement by the elder daughter that 'if they had not been taken the King should never have come into England, and though he now doth come yet he shall not live long, but shall die as ill a death as they'. The four were ducked in the river, where 'they would not sink but swam aloft'. These sorcerers were strangely made. 'The man had 5 teats,' recorded an observer, 'the mother 3, and the eldest daughter had one, and when they went to search the women none were visible. One advised them to lay them on their backs and keep open their mouths and they would appear, and so they presently appeared in sight.'

Tuesday, May 15. The voyage by river ended at Delft, and the royal family and their attendants again took coach. The progress to The Hague was one long triumph. They seemed to pass through one continuous street, wrote Hyde, 'by the wonderful and orderly appearance of the people on both sides, with such acclamations of joy, as if themselves were now restored to peace and security.'

At the capital the King was received in state and conducted to the House of Prince Maurice of Nassau, which had been specially prepared for him. There he was greeted by his radiant aunt Elizabeth of Bohemia, most colourful of royal exiles, and by the elder members of the House of Orange. The King was tired after his journey, and his seasick sister still more so. They asked to be allowed to dine in private; only the family were present at the meal, and as soon as it was over the Princess went off to her own house to rest. The brothers had a little time to themselves, and then King Charles once more addressed himself to official business, in the shape of a visit from the States-General.

The peers' Commissioners arrived at Scheveningen in the *Centurion* and were the guests of Admiral Montagu at dinner. All the Commissioners were now assembled and ready to wait on the King.

In London the House of Commons ordered the arrest of Mr Secretary Thurloe on a charge of high treason. The next business was to provide for the Coronation. The royal regalia had been scattered during the interregnum, and there was little hope of assembling all the items. A committee was appointed to trace them, but in the meantime Alderman Thomas Vyner, the City's leading goldsmith, was commissioned to provide a new crown and sceptre. The cost was estimated at £900.

The debate on the Indemnity Bill went on. It was resolved to pass a posthumous attainder on Cromwell, Bradshaw, Ireton and Pride for the murder of the King, to take effect from January 1, 1649.

Wednesday, May 16. Now the Commissioners for the Lords, the Commons and the City of London presented themselves before the King, made their obeisance, and formally requested that he should go at once to England and take possession of his kingdoms. The King received them graciously, letting them know that he was only too anxious to do what they asked; he hoped, indeed, to embark for England on the following Monday, May 21. Sir Thomas Clarges was deputed to leave at once for London to tell General Monk of the decision.

As the Commissioners left the presence Lord Fairfax stayed behind and, in private conversation with the King, asked his pardon for his past offence in bearing arms against his Sovereign.

The next to claim audience were a party of Presbyterian

ministers, Reynolds and Calamy among them, who had come over to Holland with the Commissioners. The King listened to their expressions of loyalty with his customary grace, but the reverend gentlemen had not come solely to pay their respects. After preliminary courtesies they came to the point. They were concerned about the forms of worship to be used in future and about the example the King would set. The Book of Common Prayer had been long out of use in England, and many of the people had never seen it. It would cause great bewilderment if the King were to revive its use in his own private chapel, where people would throng to see him; they therefore asked him not to use the Anglican rite, or at any rate not in full but mixed with 'other good prayers' more acceptable to the Presbyterian element.

This was too much for King Charles. He was not going to have these people dictating to him the form of his own private worship. He told them with a sharpness they little expected that, while he gave them liberty, he had no intention of sacrificing his own; that he had always used the form of service which he thought the best in the world and had never discontinued it in places where it was more disliked than he hoped it was by them; that when he was in England he would not inquire how far it was used in other churches, though he was sure it would be in many, but that he would have no other used in his own chapel.

In face of this rebuff the ministers raised another point: the use of the surplice. The sight of this priestly garment, they urged, would give scandal and offence. They hoped the King would not allow his chaplains to wear it. His Majesty's reply was again downright. The use of the surplice had always been held to be a decent custom of the Church of England, constantly practised till the recent evil times; he was bound for the present to tolerate a certain amount of disorder in the exercise of God's worship, but never would he by his own practice discountenance the good old order of the church in which he had been bred.

That was that. The Presbyterians, finding the new

monarch was not as pliant as they had supposed, withdrew disconsolate.

The King's last visitor was more welcome. He was the captain of the ship which had taken him from the Sussex coast to safety in France after his escape from Worcester in 1651.

Thursday, May 17. Clarges left for England in the *Norwich*, carrying with him a letter from King Charles to Monk. 'I have thought the best I can of the place where I should disembark,' the King wrote, 'and have resolved, God willing, to land at Dover. You can hardly imagine the impatience I have to see you, for, till then, I shall take no resolution of moment. I pray bring Mrs Monk with you, and believe me to be very heartily your affectionate friend.'

The royal residents of The Hague were caught up in a round of ceremonies and entertainments. The whole family were the guests of the States-General at dinner, and the Duke of York attended a parade of the Guards between The Hague and Scheveningen.

Saturday, May 19. The Duke of York, now appointed Lord High Admiral of England, went to Scheveningen with the intention of receiving the sailors' oath of fidelity. But the wind was contrary and the sea rough, and Montagu found it impossible to send boats ashore. The Duke tried to get the local fishermen to take him to the *Naseby*, but they knew the sea there and flatly refused. He had to return to The Hague with his mission unfulfilled.

Pepys was enjoying himself. He had been staying ashore the last few days, and today he had a riotous time with Charles Anderson, an old Cambridge friend. They went to a tavern, where they were much taken by an exceeding pretty lass; she was 'right for the sport', Pepys confided to his diary, but it was Saturday night and the house was crowded, so they could not enjoy much of her company. Nevertheless they stayed drinking till midnight, when Anderson saw Pepys back to his lodging. Charles was in high fettle by this

time and announced his intention of going back to lie with
the girl, 'which he told me he had done in the morning'.

Sunday, May 20. In spite of his night out Pepys was up early
and off to Scheveningen. But like the Duke of York the
day before he was unable to get aboard the *Naseby*, so he
retired to an inn to rest. The house was free and easy in its
customs, and in the room allotted him Samuel found a pretty
Dutch girl in bed. But he was still timid in such matters, and
he 'had not the boldness to go to her'; he lay down and slept
for an hour or two on the other bed. At length the lady,
evidently deciding there was nothing doing, got up and
dressed. Pepys watched her and talked to her as best he
could; then contented himself with kissing her hand. After
this not very satisfying adventure he returned to The Hague.

King Charles had arranged to attend service at the chapel
used by the French Protestants in the Dutch capital; as soon
as their service was finished Mr Hardy, a minister who had
come over with the Commissioners, was to take the chapel
over. But the plan was frustrated by the French congregation.
They wanted to see the King of England and they refused
to leave. The entreaties of neither their own pastor nor
Hardy had any effect on them; they sat immovable in their
pews. Tempers began to rise; the English could not get in,
and the service could not start. The King decided it was
best to call the whole thing off; he retired and made his
devotions in the Princess Royal's private chapel.

Afterwards came a crowd of victims of scrofula to be
touched by the King. Since the days of Edward the Confessor
England's monarchs had been believed to have the power
of curing 'the King's Evil' by touch. Charles II's services
were especially in demand; the return of kingship after so
long an interval was perhaps held to have enhanced his
healing powers. From the time of his arrival in the Netherlands onwards the number of suppliant invalids constantly
increased.

In the evening came the climax of the visit to The Hague:
a state banquet given to the royal family at Prince Maurice's

House by the States of Holland. All the magnificence this wealthy province could muster was in evidence. The walls were hung with cloth of gold, and crystal candlesticks stood on the tables. One of the courses was served on gold plate, the whole of which was afterwards presented to King Charles. In the centre of the high table, under a gilded crown, sat the King. On his right was the Queen of Bohemia, on his left the Princess Royal. At the end beyond Queen Elizabeth were the Dukes of York and Gloucester, and opposite to them, next to his mother, the little Prince of Orange. Opposite to the King, on both sides of a long table, were the nobles and deputies of Holland in order of rank.

As soon as the King's health was drunk a torch was shone from one of the windows, and at this signal a volley of great and small guns was fired, to be taken up from one post to another throughout the whole of Holland. Music and fireworks completed the entertainment, with squibs and rockets fired from boats in the river till dawn dispersed the crowds.

Monday, May 21. It was still blowing hard in the Channel, and Clarges had a rough passage. At last he was put safely ashore at Aldborough in Suffolk; from there he made his way to Ipswich, where he was entertained at the public expense of the town. A messenger was sent off to Monk in London.

But the rough weather also affected the King's programme. It was useless to try to embark in such high seas, and a postponement of two days was decided on. Perhaps it would be calmer by Wednesday.

The House of Commons received the news of two important captures. Thomas Harrison, one of the more notorious regicides and a fanatical Fifth Monarchy Man, had been brought prisoner to London; he was sent to the Tower. An even more interesting prisoner was Desborough. He had not been concerned in the trial of the King, so was not among those proscribed. But he had evidently decided that the new England was no place for him and endeavoured to leave the country. He was seized on the coast by the sheriffs of Essex and sent up in custody to London. It was decided that the Council of State should examine him and decide whether or not proceedings should be taken.

Tuesday, May 22. At last the wind dropped and the sun shone; a calm sea and a fine morning gave promise of a gay voyage to come. But the next day had now been fixed for the embarkation; in the meantime it was possible for the Duke of York to pay his promised visit to the fleet.

With him were his younger brother and the Dutch Admiral Opdam; Montagu went in a boat to meet them and escorted them to the *Naseby*. As they reached the ship's side the men on board gave a great shout, and many hurled their caps into the sea. The guns boomed out, and the salute was taken up by all the ships of the fleet.

On board the Duke got down to business. The officers and men were disengaged of the oath they had taken to the last Parliament, and took a new oath to the King. Then the Duke and Montague had a long conference, allotting each ship its duties after the return to England. Duke James was already showing that he intended to be by no means a figurehead in his capacity of Lord High Admiral.

The dukes dined in the *Naseby*, and then James visited the other flagships to administer the oath. Finally Montagu saw his visitors ashore. As he returned to the *Naseby* the news came that the King, who had been paying farewell visits to his various hosts, had come to meet his brothers at Scheveningen. A salute was fired, the first King Charles had received from the ships of his own navy.

Meanwhile Monk set out for the coast. With him were a great company of the nobility and gentry of England, divided into troops to be billeted in various centres in the region of Dover. As they marched crowds thronged about them, acclaiming the Captain-General with an enthusiasm that bordered on idolatry. He humbly disclaimed their plaudits, 'knowing' (in the words of Gumble) 'he was but a Morning-Star to usher in a rising Sun, which though it had set in

Clouds, yet now would shine with the greater Splendor and Glory, and the Brightness would not eclipse but much Augment his happiness'. Clarges met him at Rochester and handed over the King's letter.

Captain Anthony Belcham was called to the Bar of the House of Lords, charged with having spoken treasonable words against His Majesty. He had been heard to say that 'the Queen was a whore, the King a bastard, and the whole generation whores and rogues'. He was committed to Newgate.

Wednesday, May 23. At last everything was ready for the voyage. It was a glorious morning; the wind had quite dropped and the clouds had vanished, 'dispelled to farthest corners of the sky'. In the bay at Scheveningen the fleet had been augmented day by day by new arrivals, and thirty-eight great ships stood ready to escort their monarch home.

Long before dawn thousands of Dutch sightseers began to take up their places on the sandhills along the coast. By the middle of the morning it was estimated that there were a hundred thousand people there, and The Hague was almost deserted. At two o'clock in the morning the drums beat to summon the troops who were to line the route.

At eight o'clock the States of Holland went in a body to Prince Maurice's House to pay their final compliments to King Charles through the mouth of Grand Pensionary John de Witt. The King made a gracious reply; then, when the deputies had left, he went to the Princess Royal's house for a few minutes' conversation with his sister. On coming out he took horse, with his brothers and the Prince of Orange, and set forth for Scheveningen. The Queen of Bohemia, the Princess Royal and the Princess Dowager of Orange followed in coaches, and the procession was joined by the States of Holland and the foreign ambassadors.

As soon as the King appeared on the hill above Scheveningen the Dutch cannon thundered out, answered by the great guns of the English fleet. From then on there was a continuous roar; the Dutch fired twenty-nine guns, and all the guns of the fleet saluted six times over. 'The Citizens and the Guards,' wrote an eye-witness, 'answered thereunto with their volley of Musket shot, and the Cavallery with their Carbines, and invited thereby the Fleet to make all their artillery to thunder, which after having lightened the air, filled it with so thick a smoak, that those great floating Castles, disappeared in a moment to the eyes of those that were on the land.'

The King dismounted at the waterside and took his leave of all but those of his immediate family, who were to accompany him on board. And now Admiral Montagu, who had hitherto kept in the background, arrived in his barge to take his sovereign aboard his flagship. Here there was a slightly embarrassing situation. The States had themselves provided a barge, richly furnished with tapestries and flying the royal flag. King Charles solved the problem by going first aboard the Dutch boat and greeting the officers and crew; then, leaving his brothers, sister and nephew there, he and his aunt Elizabeth transferred to the Admiral's barge so that an English boat should take him to the ship. The King greeted Montagu with the greatest affection as one of the most powerful instruments of his restoration.

It was past eleven when the royal party arrived on board the *Naseby*. There was little more in the way of ceremonial, and the royal family sat down together for a farewell dinner before going their several ways. It was a memorable meal: 'a blessed sight to see', said the admiring Pepys. Only Queen Henrietta and her younger daughter were absent from the family scene.

After dinner came the intimate farewells. King Charles gave his little nephew his blessing and took leave of his brave old aunt, who, buoyant as ever, was overjoyed to see one of the family enjoy the good fortune that had never come her way. But the Princess Royal broke down. She had been her brother's loyallest supporter, fighting for his rights and encouraging him in the darkest days of depression. She had lived for this day; now it had come it was almost too much to bear. She clung to the King in a torrent of tears and could hardly be persuaded to leave him. But the time had come, and the signal had to be given for the ships to set sail. Only the King remained in the *Naseby*. The Duke of York embarked in the *London* and the Duke of Gloucester in the *Swiftsure*; the royal ladies and the little prince set out for the shore.

Now the King turned his attention to his navy. It would never do for him to return in a vessel bearing the name of a battle that had been the crowning disaster to his father's cause. So he renamed the *Naseby* the *Charles*. Then he set about rechristening other ships whose names now commemorated the Cromwellian régime. His own family had first consideration; the *Richard* became the *James*, the *Speaker* the *Mary*, the *Dunbar* the *Henry* and the *Lambert* the *Henrietta*. Other names chosen were *Happy Return*, *Richmond* and *Success*.

It was four o'clock when the fleet set sail. The King was now in the highest spirits; he was never happier than when he was at sea, and all the afternoon he walked up and down, examining every detail of the ship. Then he settled down on the quarter-deck, and his mind went back to that other, so different, voyage when he had left the Sussex coast for France after the six weeks of hairbreadth escapes that followed his defeat at Worcester. His friends were gathered round him and he told them the full story of those extraordinary adventures: of how he had travelled four days and three nights on foot, dressed in a country coat and breeches and country shoes that made his feet so sore that he could hardly walk; how some people who had known him recognised him in his disguise, but none betrayed him; how at one place servants had challenged him to drink to prove he was not a Roundhead, a challenge he joyfully accepted; how in another a man had knelt down privately and kissed his hand, saying he would not ask who he was, but prayed God to bless him wherever he was going; finally of how difficult it was to find a boat to take him to France, and of his adventures on the other side. When he arrived at Rouen he looked so unkempt that the innkeeper searched the rooms to see that he had not stolen anything.

So the evening passed. Charles supped privately in his cabin, glad to be alone after all the crowded days that had gone before. Then he watched for a while on deck as the Dutch coast disappeared from view.

After all the years of exile the King of England was on his way home.

Thursday, May 24. As the *Charles* sailed towards Dover, Colonel Morley, who had neglected John Evelyn's advice to take the lead in restoring the King, went to his friend and begged his intercession in procuring a pardon for his republican activities. Evelyn, vexed at a good chance thrown away, could only recommend him to the good offices of Lord Mordaunt.

Friday, May 25. Monk was at Canterbury, where at three o'clock in the morning he was roused from his sleep and told that the fleet had been sighted off Dover. He took horse and rode for the coast.

The fleet anchored soon after dawn. The Dukes of York and Gloucester boarded the *Charles*, and the three royal brothers settled down happily to a hearty ship's breakfast of pork, boiled beef and peas: the seamen's rations. After breakfast the Duke of York sought out Pepys, whom he addressed by name, promised him his future favour, and discussed the business of the Navy with him. Meanwhile the King, some talk having arisen about tall men's heights, measured his own against the wall of his cabin, marking the spot with his knife. Later, when sightseers swarmed aboard the *Charles*, a number of tall men stood under the mark, but none came up to it. William Blundell of Crosby found himself five inches shorter than the King.

At about one o'clock in the afternoon the King and his brothers, accompanied by Montagu and steered by Cuttance, left for the shore in the Admiral's barge. Pepys, with some of the royal train and one of the King's favourite dogs, followed in another boat. The dog was not boat-trained, and its misbehaviour made Pepys reflect that 'a King and all that belong to him are but just as others are'.

The King's first act on reaching the beach was to kneel down on the sand and give thanks to God for his home-coming. Then he turned to General Monk, who was waiting on his knees to kiss his hand; he raised him up, embraced him and addressed him as 'Father'. The two central charac-ters in the Restoration talked privately for a few moments, while the air resounded with shouts of 'God save the King!' In the midst of it all one cry was heard of 'God bless General Monk!' It came from the Duke of Gloucester.

As the guns on shore and in the ships fired their salutes, and the huge crowds at last set eyes on their King, the enthusiasm was tremendous. John Dryden afterwards des-cribed the scene. Apostrophising the King, he wrote:

> Methinks I see those Crowds on Dovers Strand
> Who in their hast to welcome you to Land
> Choak'd up the Beach with their still growing store,
> And made a wilder Torrent on the shore.
> While spurr'd with eager thoughts of past delight
> Those who had seen you, court a second sight;
> Preventing still your steps, and making hast
> To meet you often where so e're you past.

A canopy was held over the King's head as he walked up from the beach to the town. There he was met by the Constable of Dover Castle, the mayor and aldermen and the minister, Mr Redding. Redding presented him with a large Bible with gold clasps, which King Charles declared with admirable solemnity was the thing that he loved best in the world. The mayor surrendered to him his white staff of office, which the King handed back to him in confirmation of his authority.

As Dover could not accommodate anything like the number of people who now surrounded the King, it had been arranged that he should go straight on to Canterbury. Accordingly, after a brief halt for refreshment, he took coach with his two brothers (the Duke of Buckingham sat in the boot), and the whole procession moved off. Two miles outside Dover the King left his coach and rode the rest of the way, with the royal dukes on his right and Monk on his left. On Barham Down troops of horse of the nobility and gentry were drawn up, together with the Kentish levies on foot. The King reviewed them, riding to the head of each troop and company to the sound of trumpets and the shouts of the crowd. And so on to Canterbury, where the mayor presented His Majesty with a gold cup that had cost £250.

The rest of the day was spent in receiving a seemingly endless stream of visitors at St Augustine's, where the King was to stay as the guest of Lord Campden. Among the foreign diplomats who paid their respects was the Venetian Resident, who was gratified when the King talked to him in Italian. But here King Charles had a foretaste of some of the trials that would vex the opening months of his rule. Visitor after visitor took advantage of the occasion to retail his sufferings in the royal cause, the sacrifices he had made and his present indigent condition. So gracious a prince would, of course, put all right now, and there was a particular post at court that would just suit so loyal a servant. After a succession of such importunacies even King Charles's abundant good nature began to be somewhat strained; however, he managed to put a pretty good face on it, and to escape with non-committal expressions of goodwill.

Monk's behaviour also caused him embarrassment. At the first opportunity the General put into his hands a list of seventy names, with the suggestion that all those listed should be appointed to the Privy Council. Not wishing to discuss the matter, Charles put the list unread into his pocket; but when he and Hyde perused it later they found that many were included who had been zealous for the republic or were otherwise undesirable. The King was furious, but it would be the worst possible thing to begin the new era with a quarrel with the man to whom he owed his throne. Hyde was therefore deputed to approach the tactful Morrice, who looked into the matter and succeeded in clearing the air. It seemed that Monk, like the King, had been the victim of importunate suitors; to get rid of them he had weakly promised to put up their names to the King. Having fulfilled his promise, he did not care in the least what His Majesty did about it. He did, however, take the opportunity to point out a few of the names which really did merit consideration. So peace reigned at Canterbury.

Saturday, May 26. General Monk now received his reward; with Mordaunt and Winchelsea he was made a Knight of the Garter. The King put the George about his neck, and the Dukes of York and Gloucester adjusted the Garter as a mark of especial respect. At the same time Morrice was knighted and given his appointment as joint Secretary of State with Sir Edward Nicholas; and he and the Earl of Southampton were sworn of the Privy Council.

The King wrote to the two Houses of Parliament, giving them formal notice of his arrival in England and invoking God's blessing on their labours. He hoped, he told them, to reach London on the following Tuesday, his thirtieth birthday.

Later he wrote to his sister 'Minette' to tell her of the wonderful welcome he had received. 'My head is so prodigiously dazed,' he wrote, 'by the acclamation of the people and by quantities of business that I know not whether I am writing sense or no.'

Sunday, May 27. The Garter had also been conferred on Montagu, and Sir Edward Walker arrived on board the *Charles* at Dover to perform the ceremony on the King's behalf. Montagu summoned all the captains in the fleet to come and see him invested.

King Charles attended service in Canterbury Cathedral. He was shocked to find the nation's premier church so dilapidated and neglected, but the people seemed glad to hear the Common Prayer again.

Monday, May 28. Before leaving Canterbury the King held

one more Garter investiture. The recipients were the
Marquess of Hertford and the Earl of Southampton, who
had been nominated for the honour when they had been with
the King in Jersey ten years before.

A more sinister figure to be honoured was Sir Anthony
Ashley Cooper, long afterwards to be pilloried by Dryden as
'the false Achitophel', who was made a Privy Councillor.
He had been prominent in the moves leading up to the readmission of the secluded members, and his name had now
been put forward by Monk. He had recently married a niece
of Lord Southampton; 'it was believed,' wrote Hyde, 'that
his slippery humour would be easily restrained and fixed by
the uncle.'

And now it was time to begin the march to London. The
King advanced to Rochester, and from there took the
opportunity to pay a visit to Chatham and inspect the
Royal Sovereign and other ships. At Rochester he was the
guest of Colonel Gibbons, whose regiment was quartered in
the town.

The royal route was lined with cheering crowds, and the
streets of Rochester were hung with garlands made up of
costly scarves and ribbons, decked with spoons and bodkins
of silver and small plate. It was the same wherever the King
passed. 'Never were seen such numbers of people of all
Degrees and Conditions,' wrote Gumble, 'thronging all the
Road from *Dover* to *London*; many Women and Children
came many miles, and placed themselves upon hillocks in the
way, and many men upon trees (like *Zachaeus*) to see this
blessed sight, and all with the greatest joy, blessing God
that they had lived to see that day of his Majestie's Restauration, and were ready to sing their *Nunc Dimittis*, even willing
to depart in peace now their eyes had seen the Salvation of
their Countrey.'

John Dauncey, assiduous chronicler of royalty, had been
quick off the mark. On this day was published his 'History
of his Sacred Majesty, *Charles* the Second, King of *England*,
Scotland, *France*, and *Ireland*, *Defender of the Faith*, etc., begun
from the horrible murthering of his Royal Father, of happy

memory, and continued to this present year 1660, by a person of quality.'

Tuesday, May 29. The promised hour was come at last. On this most momentous day of the century, the thirtieth birthday of King Charles II, the English summer for once played its part to perfection; the sun shone clear and bright as the great procession started from Rochester, bringing the King to his capital after the long years of exile. Crowds had been gathering all night, and long before dawn troops were in position along the road His Majesty was to take.

The King himself was astir before five in the morning. The mayor and corporation of Rochester waited on him, presenting him with a basin and ewer of silver-gilt; the Kent Militia lined the route, and girls strewed flowers and herbs before the royal coach as the journey began.

Amid shouts of joy and the ringing of bells the King arrived at Blackheath. There the Army was drawn up: fifty thousand men, horse and foot, in good order and equipage, ready to declare their loyalty. Monk introduced his chief officers, who kissed the King's hand, and Colonel Knight presented a paper expressing the soldiers' joy at the honour of having His Majesty among them. Then King Charles took horse, leaving his coach to follow empty.

The next halt was at St George's Fields. Here the Lord Mayor of London and the aldermen were waiting in their scarlet robes, with the principal citizens in black velvet, wearing chains about their necks ('not improperly', commented Ludlow). Allen presented his sword on his knees to the King, who returned it to him and then knighted the Lord Mayor, aldermen and sheriffs. A large tent had been erected and a banquet prepared; and here the King dined before the final stage of the journey.

It was half past four in the afternoon when the procession crossed London Bridge and entered the City of London. Major-General Brown led the way with a troop of three hundred horse, all in cloth of silver doublets, their drawn swords flashing in the sunlight; then came other troops of horse and companies of foot, in various uniforms. After these were two trumpets with His Majesty's. arms; the sheriffs' men in red cloaks, richly laced with silver, to the number of eighty; then six hundred men of the City Companies on horseback, each company having footmen in livery attending.

A kettledrum and five trumpets followed; then the Life Guards commanded by Lord Gerard, followed by more trumpets; the City Marshal with eight footmen; the City Waits and all the City officers in order; the sheriffs and aldermen in their robes, with footmen in livery; the heralds and maces, and then the Lord Mayor with drawn sword. Next to him rode Monk and the Duke of Buckingham, and then came the King, dressed in a plain suit of dark cloth and with a plume of scarlet feathers in his hat, between the Dukes of York and Gloucester. More troops brought up the rear of the procession.

The streets of London, hung with tapestry, were lined by the Trained Bands and members of the City Companies. Conduits ran claret; stands for spectators had been erected wherever possible, and ladies watched from every window. As the King passed, smiling and waving his hat to his adoring subjects, the shouting was almost deafening. Among those watching was John Evelyn. 'I stood in the strand,' he wrote, '& beheld it, & blessed God: And all this without a drop of blood, & by that very army, which rebell'd against him: but it was the Lords doing, et *mirabile in oculis nostris*: for such a Restauration was never seen in the mention of any history, antient or modern, since the returne of the *Babylonian* Captivity, nor so joyful a day, & so bright, ever seene in this nation: this hapning when to expect or effect it, was past all humane policy.'

At the end of the Strand had stood, until seventeen years before, a precious relic of English history: Charing Cross, the final memorial that King Edward I had built in 1290 as testimony of his love for his dead Queen. Puritan vandalism had destroyed the cross, and there was an open space where it had stood. In this space a company of six hundred pikemen, all veterans who had fought for King Charles I, were on parade under the gallant Sir John Stowell to acclaim the long-awaited triumph of their cause. The King saluted them as he passed.

And so on to the Royal Palace of Whitehall. Here the members of the two Houses of Parliament were waiting, and speeches of welcome and loyalty were made by Lord Manchester and Sir Harbottle Grimston. The King replied briefly; it was after seven o'clock now, and he had been on the move for more than fourteen hours. He told the Lords and Commons that he was so disordered by his journey and by the noise still sounding in his ears, which he confessed was pleasing to him as expressing the affections of his people, that he could not speak as he would have wished. But he rejoiced in his restoration only because it gave him the opportunity, by the advice of his Parliament, to advance the freedom and happiness of the nation. Next to the honour of God he would study the welfare of his people and would be not only a true Defender of the Faith, but a just assertor of the laws and liberties of his subjects.

One more ceremony had been planned: a service of thanksgiving in Westminster Abbey. But the King was exhausted; it was decided that the public service would be too much for him to bear, and he made his oblation privately in the Presence Chamber of the Palace.

Tired out as he was, his ironic sense of humour still showed itself. When at last the various officials had departed, he turned to those about him and said with a smile that it was evidently his own fault that he had stayed away so long, for he had met nobody in England who did not protest that he had always wished for his return.

When, late at night, Price sought out Monk to congratulate him on the happy outcome of his labours, the reserved, taciturn General burst into tears. 'No, Mr Price,' he said; 'it was not I that did this; you know the jealousies that were had of me, and the oppositions against me; it was God alone who did it. To him be the glory, Whose is the kingdom and the power over this and all governments.'

Part I: May

For many years royalists had been singing in exile the rousing ballad written by Martin Parker:

> Though for a time we see Whitehall
> With cobwebs hanging on the wall,
> Instead of silk and silver brave
> Which formerly it used to have;
>> With rich perfume
>> In every room,
> Delightful to that princely train;
> Which again you shall see
> When the time it shall be
> That the King enjoys his own again.

Now the prophecy had come true; Whitehall was restored to its former glories, and London was drinking itself into a state of happy insensibility in an orgy of bonfires and fireworks. Abraham Cowley, most passionately loyal of royalist poets, penned his paean of joy:

> All England but one *Bonefire* seems to be;
> One Aetna shooting flames into the *Sea.*
> The *Starry Worlds* which shine to us afar,
>> Take *ours* at this time for a *Star.*
> With Wine all rooms, with Wine the *Conduits* flow;
> And *We*, the Priests of a *Poetick* rage,
>> Wonder that in this *Golden Age*
> The *Rivers* too should not do so.

The King was enjoying his own again.

PART II

———————— ◇ ————————

SUMMER

Wednesday, May 30, to Saturday, June 2. The wild revels of Restoration night came as something of a shock to the staider spirits among the royal train, with the result that the first recorded act of the restored monarchy was one singularly uncharacteristic of the régime as it was to develop. A royal proclamation issued on May 30 denounced those whose idea of loyalty was to 'spend their time in taverns, tipling-houses, and debauches, giving no other evidence of their affection to us but in drinking our health, and in inveighing against all others who are not of their own dissolute temper'. Mayors, sheriffs and justices of the peace were required to be vigilant in the discovery of dissolute and prophane persons and such as cursed and swore and reviled or disturbed ministers.

Ludlow, lying low in London, was unimpressed with this display of virtue. The King, he commented, 'publickly violated his own order in a few days, at a debauch in the Mulberry Garden; and more privately at another meeting in the City, where he drank healths to the utmost excess till two in the morning'.

It was hardly to be expected that this staunch old puritan would take any other view; but his censure of the King in the first flush of Restoration rejoicing was almost certainly unjust. King Charles, though appreciative of the good things of life, was not at any time of his life a heavy drinker. His tastes in dissipation ran rather to women than to wine. Nevertheless, the proclamation savoured of Hyde's views rather than the King's; it was also a sop to the Presbyterians who feared that the return of monarchy would usher in an orgy of unbridled licence.

No immediate effect was apparent. For three days and

nights the revels went on, effigies of Cromwell and others being burned in the innumerable bonfires. The foreign envoys played their part; Giavarina kept a fountain of wine going at his door, 'according to the custom of the country', and put in a bill for £97 to the Venetian Senate for special expenses.

On Thursday the Dukes of York and Gloucester took their seats in the House of Lords, and at the same time those cavalier peers who had as yet absented themselves claimed their places, bringing the House to completion. The next day the King himself went to the Lords and gave the royal assent to three Bills; the first gave official recognition to the Convention Parliament, the second authorised a £70,000 a month tax for three months, and the third regularised the continuance of judicial proceedings. One thing was causing him some displeasure: the Bill of Oblivion was still hanging fire. The King gave a strong hint that their lordships and the Commons would be doing a service to their sovereign if they would kindly get a move on.

The Lords resolved that His Majesty be moved 'that he would be pleased that an Act be passed for the keeping of the 29th day of May as a Holy Day and Thanksgiving Day, in commemoration of his Majesty's happy return into this Kingdom, and the day of his Majesty's nativity'.

The King was having a busy time, receiving endless streams of visitors and taking all his meals in public so that his subjects could gaze upon their long-absent sovereign. But on Saturday night he relaxed. He and his brothers, with General Monk, dined with the Countess of Devonshire at Roehampton; after dinner the three royal visitors danced with the ladies for an hour, and, as a fellow-guest noted, 'danced rarely well'.

Queen Henrietta wrote her congratulations to her son from Colombes: 'You may judge of my joy, and if you are torn in pieces over in England, I have had my share here in France. I am going this moment to Chaillot to have a *Te Deum* sung there, and on to Paris to light our *feux de joies*. We had them here yesterday. I think I shall have all Paris to congratulate me. Indeed, you would never imagine what joy there is here.'

Sunday, June 3, to Saturday, June 9. The King was caught up in a round of receptions. Visitors were innumerable, and they came from all parts of the country. Evelyn, who was one of them, recorded that His Majesty hardly had leisure to eat during the first few days. But he bore it all with a buoyant good humour which added to his popularity. When William Prynne came to kiss his hand and prayed God to bless him, King Charles smiled, slapped him on the shoulder, and said heartily : 'And so you also, Mr Prynne.' Among other visitors came a deputation from the much abused Quakers. Charles promised them on the word of a King that nobody should molest them provided they lived peaceably.

Such a programme left little time for recreation. But the King was an active man, of seemingly inexhaustible physical energy, and he snatched what moments he could. He walked in St James's Park, where Pepys, back from Dover, saw him 'gallantly great'. He also found time to play tennis. This was his favourite game, and he was an excellent player. There was a court in Whitehall Palace, besides the venerable one at Hampton Court (still in use three hundred years later) in which Henry VIII had played. Charles made a habit of getting up at five o'clock in the morning for an hour or two in the tennis court. On Friday he managed to get out to Hampton Court, returning in time to touch for the Evil and to receive a parliamentary deputation in the Banqueting House.

Princess Henrietta had got her brother's letter written from Canterbury, and she replied happily :

> I have received the letter you wrote me by Mr Progers which gave me no little joy, for to know that you were arrived in England and at the same time that you had remembered me gave me the greatest joy imaginable, and in truth I would I were able to express what I think and you would see that it is true that nobody is more your servant than I.

Parliament spent the whole week discussing the Indemnity Bill. On Tuesday the Commons decided to except seven persons by name from 'for life and estate'. They were Thomas Harrison, William Say, John Jones, Thomas Scot, Cornelius Holland, John Lisle and John Barkstead. Most of these, like the rest of the regicides, were out of Parliament's clutches, and a proclamation was issued calling on forty-four men by name to surrender within fourteen days on pain of being excepted out of the Bill.

One of the mysteries that Parliament was most anxious to solve was the identity of the masked executioner who had actually cut off the King's head. A committee formed to investigate the matter had recourse to the astrologer William Lilly, who affirmed that the culprit was Cornet Joyce. Whether this information came from the stars or from more mundane sources is not clear, but Joyce was ordered to be secured. So at the same time was Hugh Peters.

Colonel Hutchinson sent a penitent letter to the Speaker, lamenting his former offences and promising to dedicate the remainder of his life to the King's service. He was expressly promised the benefits of the Indemnity Bill, but was deprived of his seat in Parliament and barred from any position of public trust.

Sunday, June 10, *to Saturday, June* 16. The dreary, interminable debates on the Indemnity Bill went on. It had been decided to except a maximum of twenty, and Hugh Peters and William Hewlett, one of those suspected to have been King Charles I's executioner, were added to the list. Eight others, including Haslerig and Desborough, were excepted for punishment short of death. Later Lambert's name was added.

The Commons next turned their attention to John Milton. Two books of his against monarchy were cited, together with one by the Rev. John Goodwin, and the two authors were ordered to be taken into custody. In addition the King was petitioned to issue a proclamation ordering the books to be burnt by the common hangman.

The King was getting tired of all this, and he sent a

sharp letter to the Commons requiring them to delay no longer, but to get the Indemnity Bill passed. It was read in the House by Morrice as Secretary of State, but it would take more than letters to divert the members from underlining their loyalty in blood.

For all this the King continued to find time to amuse himself. He had taken up river bathing; a Londoner wrote that he and the Duke of York went every evening as far as Battersea, Putney and Barn Elms, to swim, and that they both swam excellently. On Saturday the King and his brother were the guests of the Lord Mayor, Sir Thomas Allen, who provided a magnificent dinner at his house.

Monk had lost a dog. The following notice appeared in *Mercurius Publicus*:

> A White Greyhound Bitch, belonging to his Excellency, was lately lost from the Cockpit, if any one bring her thither, he shall be well rewarded for his pains.

Sunday, June 17, to Saturday, June 23. By Wednesday the list of the twenty excepted from pardon was complete; among those excepted for punishment short of death was Fleetwood. But the arguments still went on. It was urged that Sir Richard Onslow should be excepted on the ground that he had, in a speech during the civil war, compared the King with a hedgehog, saying he had wrapped himself up in his own bristles. Meanwhile Thomas Scot had been arrested in Flanders and was brought prisoner to Westminster.

It was reported that Queen Henrietta, after taking the waters at Bourbon, would be coming to England in a few weeks. The House of Commons, pending the settlement of a revenue for her, voted her £20,000 for her immediate needs.

Edinburgh celebrated the Restoration. A banquet was held at the Cross, fountains ran wine, and fifteen hundred bonfires blazed on Arthur's Seat.

On Saturday King Charles touched more than six hundred people for the Evil in the Banqueting House, putting round the neck of each a white ribbon with an angel of gold on it.

1660: The Year of Restoration

Sunday, June 24, to Saturday, June 30. Admiral Montagu had been promised an earldom and proposed to take Portsmouth for his title. In the midst of his triumph he did not forget the interests of his faithful servant and kinsman, and Pepys heard with delight that he was being proposed for the post of Clerk of the Acts, one of the four principal officers of the now revived Navy Board. This would be a wonderful advancement for one who a few months before had been a minor clerk at the Exchequer, but the way to fame and fortune was not all plain sailing. Montagu was not an entirely free agent; Monk still had a say in naval affairs. Moreover, there were plenty of aspirants for this as for every office. Relations between Monk and Montagu were not of the best, and Pepys heard with dismay that Lady Monk was preparing to interfere. However, his patron was firm. Meeting Sir Thomas Clarges at Whitehall, he told him plainly that, whatever his sister and brother-in-law might have to say, he intended to press Pepys's appointment. How would Monk like it, he asked, if he, Montagu, were to attempt to select officers for posts in the Army? It was surely not too much to ask that he should be granted the naming of one official for the Navy.

So Pepys got his appointment, refusing an offer of £500 from another aspirant for the job if he would turn it down. But there was further trouble in store. To his horror Pepys discovered that a forgotten old gentleman named Barlow, who had been Clerk of the Acts under Charles I, was still alive and was coming up to London to claim the post. Samuel could only await his arrival with trepidation.

The poets were coming back into their own. In one and the same issue of *Mercurius Publicus* were advertised three poems on the Restoration. The first, *Astraea Redux*, was by John Dryden; the second, *An Ode upon the Blessed Restoration and Return of His Sacred Majesty Charles the Second*, by Abraham Cowley; the third, *Poem upon His Sacred Majesties most happy Return to his Dominions*, by Sir William Davenant, who had been appointed Poet Laureate after the death of Ben Jonson in 1637.

Part II: Summer

Thursday, June 28, was observed as a day of thanksgiving for the Restoration. There were services in all churches in the morning and bonfires at night, with the ringing of bells and firing of the guns at the Tower.

There were evidently dog thieves about. Monk was not the most exalted person to suffer, and another advertisement appeared in *Mercurius Publicus*:

> A Smooth Black Dog, less than a Grey-hound, with white under his breast, belonging to the Kings Majesty, was taken from *Whitehal*, the eighteenth day of this instant June, or thereabout. If any one can give notice to *John Ellis* one of his Majesties Servants, or to his Majesties Back-stayrs, they shall be well rewarded for their labor.

On Friday John Thurloe was set at liberty, on condition that he should attend the Secretaries of State when they should require him to do so.

Sunday, July 1, to Saturday, July 7. The royal dog had not been found, and the King's patience was exhausted. A second notice appeared in *Mercurius Publicus*, bearing the unmistakable mark of His Majesty's personal authorship:

> *We must call upon you again for a black Dog, between a Greyhound and a Spaniell, no white about him, only a streak on his breast, and his taile a little bob'd. It is his Majesties owne Dog, and doubtless was stolen, for the Dog was not born nor bred in England and would never forsake his Master. Whoever finds him may acquaint any at Whitehall, for the Dog was better known at Court than those who stole him. Will they never leave robbing his Majesty: must he not keep a Dog? This Dogs place (though better than some imagine) is the only place which no body offers to beg.*

So great were the crowds of those wanting to be touched for the Evil that a limit had to be imposed. On Monday the King touched two hundred and fifty in the Banqueting House, but it was then announced that the ceremony would in future take place only on Fridays. Not more than two hundred would be admitted on each Friday, and they were to apply to the royal surgeon, Mr Knight, in Russell Street, Covent Garden, for tickets. Should any persons of quality wish to apply, Mr Knight undertook to wait on them at their lodgings upon notice given.

The House of Commons, putting the Indemnity Bill by for the moment, turned to the urgent business of raising money. The chief drain on the country's finances came from the armed forces; Lord Falkland pointed out that the cost of the Army and Navy came to £6,000 a day. Moreover, he urged, it was inconsistent for Parliament and an army to exist together, and now that the troubles were over the Trained Bands were all that was needed. Colonel Birch added that the people's liberties were not safe with a strong army in being, and urged that it should be paid off. At length it was decided to devote every Tuesday, Thursday and Saturday to devising means of raising money for this purpose.

Meanwhile important appointments were announced. First and foremost, General Sir George Monk was raised to the peerage as Duke of Albemarle; he was at the same time appointed Master of the Horse. Ormonde was made Grand Master of the Royal Household, and Sir John Robinson Lieutenant of the Tower in succession to Morley. The Bishop of Salisbury, Dr Brian Duppa, who had been the King's tutor when he was Prince of Wales, was made Lord Almoner.

More arrests took place. Among the victims were Haslerig and Vane.

On Thursday the King and his brothers, with both Houses of Parliament, were entertained at Guildhall with all the pomp that the City of London could muster; the cost was said to come to £5,000. Unfortunately the splendour was dulled by continuous rain throughout the day. The English summer, which had smiled so graciously on the Restoration, had now returned to normal.

Sunday, July 8, *to Monday, July* 16. At last the Indemnity Bill was passed by the House of Commons and sent up to the Lords. The Commons were now able to take up the vexed question of the religious settlement. Was the Church of

Part II: Summer

England under the restored régime to retain some of its Presbyterian guise, or were the bishops to be restored to full authority? This was the most difficult of all the Restoration problems, and the Commons found themselves quite unable to solve it. The Grand Committee for Religion sat on Monday, July 9, and the debate went on till night; the committee sat for an hour in the dark before candles were brought in, and then they were twice blown out. Speeches were cautious, and little mention was made of the bishops. Finally it was resolved 'that the King's Majesty be desired to call such a number of divines as his Majesty shall think fit to advise concerning matters of religion, and that the Grand Committee do forbear to sit until the 23rd of October next'.

The bishops, however, were unobtrusively emerging from retirement. On Sunday, July 8, Henry King, Bishop of Chichester, preached before the King in Whitehall chapel. Pepys was present, and recorded that King 'made a great flattering sermon, which I did not like that Clergy should meddle with matters of state'.

Pepys had taken up his new post and spent a lot of time conferring with Montagu, who had changed his mind about his title and decided to be Earl of Sandwich. On Friday he sat late at his patron's quarters in Whitehall writing letters, and after a time he heard 'great doings of music at the next house, which was Whally's'. Greatly excited, he found that the King and his brothers were 'there with Madame Palmer, a pretty woman that they have a fancy to, to make her husband a cuckold'. This was Barbara Palmer, a lady of great loveliness, uncertain temper and complete lack of morals, who was to fill the limelight as King Charles's principal mistress in the opening years of the Restoration.

On Wednesday a great fire broke out in the City of London, several houses in Threadneedle Street being destroyed. On Thursday Scot and Axtell were lodged in the Tower, joined twenty-four hours later by Haslerig and Vane. On Friday Monk took his seat in the House of Lords as Duke of Albemarle.

On Saturday the restored régime was installed in one of King Charles's most distant possessions, the colony of Barbados. On that day a commission arrived from the last Council of State for a local planter, Colonel Thomas Muddiford, to take over as Governor. He received the island's complete support, his republican predecessor offered no resistance, and two days later he proclaimed the King. A banquet was held and four butts of sack were given to the soldiers to drink His Majesty's health. Muddiford in his speech addressed his guests as 'dear friends and fellow-planters, a name which none of my predecessors could so truly own as I do, for though divers of them having (by the advantage of their places) gotten plantations and so become planters, yet none of them from being first planters became Governors'. He went on to say that though he was the first planter-Governor 'there is hopes I shall not be the last, but that by the clemency of our gracious King he will continue this dignity among yourselves'.

Tuesday, July 17, to Saturday, July 21. Barlow, the old Clerk of the Acts, arrived in London and called on Pepys, who found him 'an old consumptive man, and fair conditioned'. They had a long talk, and finally struck a bargain. Barlow would renounce his claim provided Pepys agreed to pay him £50 a year, to be increased to £100 if Pepys's own salary was raised. Both parties were satisfied; at least Pepys had not lost his newly-won honour. Still, it would be a drain on his income, and he was just moving into a fine new house in Seething Lane near the Navy Office. There was no saying how long the consumptive Barlow might live.

Next day Pepys was presented with half a buck from Lord Sandwich's country estate at Hinchingbrooke, in Huntingdonshire. But it smelt a bit strong, so he gave it to his mother.

The Commons had finished with the Indemnity Bill, but the Lords were only just beginning. A committee of the House reported its opinion that all who had passed sentence on the late King, or signed the death warrant, should be excepted from pardon. The House of Commons was asked to pass up all documents connected with the trial.

Sunday, July 22, to Tuesday, July 31. The Lords were proving more vindictive than the Commons. There were few of them whose families had not suffered in some way during the interregnum, and they were not disposed towards mercy for their persecutors. Two lists were read in the House: the first of those who sat in judgment on King Charles I, the second of those who signed the death warrant. The Lords voted that all named in either list, with the single exception of Colonel Hutchinson, should be excepted absolutely out of the Act of Indemnity and Oblivion.

But the King was becoming more and more exasperated. He had agreed to leave the matter of punishment to Parliament, but if the Lords were allowed to go on making exceptions they would nullify the promises he had made in the Declaration of Breda. After consultation with his Chancellor he went down to the House and addressed their lordships in no uncertain terms. He had, he said, already called on the Commons to hasten the passing of the Bill; now the Lords were holding it up. He wished the Act to become law without further delay, and so establish a solid foundation of peace and security. As for himself, he thanked God that he had the same intentions and resolutions that he had had at Breda; he had then promised that his subjects should not live in fear of what might happen to them, and he intended that that promise should be kept. If the peers did not join with him in extinguishing that fear, they would be forcing him to break his word. He thanked them for insisting on justice upon those who had been the immediate murderers of his father, but he assured them that he had never thought of excepting any other from pardon. He demanded that their lordships should now go ahead and pass the Bill without any exceptions other than of those immediately guilty of the murder.

The executioner of the King was still being sought. Another

suspect, one William Giffen, was committed to the Castle of Edinburgh.

The King of Portugal staged a bull-fight in Lisbon in honour of the restoration to his throne of his brother of England.

Wednesday, August 1, to Sunday, August 12. The Lords had been slightly shaken by the King's rebuke, but they had not yet finished with the Indemnity Bill. On August 1 they voted that Colonel Francis Hacker, Sir Harry Vane, Sir Arthur Haslerig, Colonel John Lambert and Colonel Daniell Axtell should be wholly exempted from pardon. However, nine days later, they wound up their debates and sent the Bill back to the Commons with their amendments.

On Saturday, August 11, the Commons tackled the matter once again, wrangling over the Lords' amendments. The proposal to except all who had anything to do with the trial and execution led to long debate. Sir George Booth was for pardoning all who surrendered of their own free will. Colonel King agreed with the Lords in excepting the lot. Sir William Lewis wanted to return to the House's former vote, rejecting all the amendments. Sir Heneage Finch and others proposed banishment for those not executed. Sir Anthony Irby suggested a conference with the Lords. So it went on. In the end the vote went in favour of those who surrendered.

But while the Houses of Parliament argued about who should or should not be brought to the scaffold, England was coming to life again. The long night of puritanism was over, and in these summer days traditional pleasures and amusements were revived. The London theatres were re-opened and the King and his brothers became ardent playgoers, to the horror of his Presbyterian chaplain, Dr Edmund Calamy, who implored him in vain to stop lending his patronage to such iniquitous spectacles. The King took his admonition in good part, but no puritan divine was going to dictate to him how he should spend his time. On August 9 he got away to Gravesend to inspect the East India fleet, and on his return watched an entertainment of dancing on ropes at Whitehall.

A spirit of light-hearted enjoyment was abroad this August. Pepys, taking the air in Hyde Park, saw a fine foot-race three times round the park between an Irishman and one Crow, who had formerly been one of Lord Claypole's footmen. Crow won by more than two miles.

All Pepys's amusements were not so innocent. He was becoming a little bolder in his amorous adventures. On Sunday, August 12, he fell in with his old friend Betty Lane, the Westminster Hall stall-keeper. He took her to Lord Sandwich's house, and they cracked a bottle of wine in the garden. Then, his courage increasing, he took her to his own house (Mrs Pepys was presumably out), where he was 'exceedingly free in dallying with her, and she not unfree to take it'. He decided there were possibilities in Betty Lane.

Queen Henrietta's proposed trip to England was still hanging fire. At the beginning of August a young Yorkshire squire, Sir John Reresby, visited her in Paris before returning home and asked if he could perform any service for her. She gave him a letter for her son, making a particular recommendation of Reresby's own services.

Monday, August 13, to Saturday, August 18. High spirits were going too far in some directions; King Charles found it necessary to issue a royal proclamation against duelling. All subjects were forbidden to challenge or cause to be challenged any person or persons to fight a duel, or to carry or accept any challenge, or to fight or act as a second. Anyone who should defy this proclamation would not only incur His Majesty's highest displeasure, but would be held incapable of holding any office in the King's service, besides suffering such punishment as the law provided.

A second proclamation concerned Milton and Goodwin, whose books were declared to be treasonable. All copies of the books were to be delivered up and all efforts made to capture the authors, both of whom were in hiding.

The States of Holland, remembering the pleasure King

Charles had taken in the yacht that took him to Rotterdam, had sent him a stately pleasure boat, richly gilt within and without. Charles was delighted with it; by 5 a.m. on Wednesday he was off to view it below London Bridge. 'The King,' commented Pepys, 'do tire all his people that are about him with early rising since he came.'

On Saturday Pepys saw his first play, Beaumont and Fletcher's *The Loyal Subject*, at the Cockpit. Actresses had not yet appeared and the boy Kynaston acted the Duke's sister, making the loveliest lady Pepys had ever seen, but with not a very good voice.

Queen Henrietta had had a visit from the Queen Dowager of France, Anne of Austria, who came to tell her that King Louis joined her in asking the hand of Princess Henrietta for her younger son, Philip Duke of Anjou, known by the title of 'Monsieur'. The English Queen promptly wrote to King Charles asking for his approval of the match. 'I assure you that your sister is by no means averse to the idea,' she wrote, 'and as for Monsieur, he is very much in love and extremely impatient for your answer.'

The *Parliamentary Intelligencer* advertised a most useful medicine:

> *Sir* Kenelm Digby's *Sympathetical Powder prepared by Promethian fire, curing all green wounds in a short time, that come within the compass of a Remedy; As also the Tooth-ach infallibly, is to be had* at M. Nathaniel Brooks, *at the* Angel *in* Cornhill, *and at* M. Samuel Speeds *at the* Printing Press *in* St Pauls Church-yard.

An epidemic of spotted fever was reported from Scotland.

Sunday, August 19, to Saturday, August 25. On Monday a conference took place between the two Houses in yet another attempt to reach agreement on the Indemnity Bill. The Commons represented that, much as they abhorred and detested the murder of the late King, they felt bound to limit the number of those to be excepted for life; many had surrendered in obedience to the proclamation, and the

King's honour was concerned in the business. As for Vane, Haslerig, Lambert and Axtell, they saw no reason why these four should be held to have merited death. The Lords debated the Commons' views and then proposed another conference for the next day. To give it greater weight it was suggested that the Duke of Gloucester should take part.

This second conference duly took place, and in the presence of royalty a compromise was worked out. The Commons agreed to except Vane, Lambert and Axtell for life, with the proviso that the King should be petitioned to mitigate the severity of the sentence. Haslerig was to be spared in view of the request made by the Duke of Albemarle, who had not forgotten the twopence. On other questions the Lords concurred with the Commons. At last all obstacles seemed to have been removed.

The Commons were able to turn to the question of the Army. It was agreed that it should be disbanded, and commissioners were appointed to discuss ways and means with the Captain-General. As a first step Albemarle issued an order to all regiments that no new officers or soldiers were to be taken in to fill vacancies.

Autumn visits to England were being planned. Louis XIV proposed to send two envoys to England, both to congratulate the King on his restoration and to discuss the question of a marriage between Monsieur and 'Minette'. Another person who was turning her eyes towards England was the Princess Royal. Ever since she had parted from her brother on board the *Naseby* at Scheveningen she had been looking forward to a reunion on English soil. Now she announced her intention to the States-General of the Netherlands. She would be away some time, she said, and she took the opportunity of recommending her young son to their care and of hinting that now would be a good time to confer on him those rights and dignities which his father had enjoyed, and which so far had been withheld from him.

Some lawless elements were taking advantage of the hue and cry for regicides. Seven armed horsemen arrived at the house of Mr William Grove near Wantage, saying that they were soldiers and that they had a warrant to search the house of Cornet Joyce. When Grove demurred they added that they had an order from the Duke of Albemarle to arrest him for high treason. They then raided the house, seized £70 in gold, and forced Grove and his son to go with them in the direction of Oxford, saying their orders were to take them to London. In Bagley Wood they dismounted the two Groves, tied them up, and decamped with their horses.

Sunday, August 26, to Friday, August 31. At long last the Bill of Indemnity was ready, and on Wednesday the King came down to the Lords to give it the royal assent. In its final form it offered a general pardon for all crimes or treasons against the late or present King or the royal house. Excluded by name, and left to be dealt with by the common law, were thirty regicides, plus the two executioners if they could be identified; six others were excepted as regards punishment other than death, and nineteen more were excepted with the proviso that, if they were condemned, the sentence should be suspended for a decision by the King and Parliament. Vane and Lambert were among the excepted, but a petition was to be sent to the King asking that their lives should be spared.

Four other Bills received the royal assent at the same time. The first confirmed all acts of civil justice since 1642; the second restricted the interest on usury; the third declared May 29 a day of thanksgiving, and the fourth introduced a poll tax, the proceeds to be devoted to the paying off and disbanding of the Army. In his speech to Parliament the King welcomed the Indemnity Bill and promised that he would for the future show no severity except where malice was notorious and the public peace disturbed. He thanked the Houses for the Poll Bill as much as if the money were to go into his own coffers; but he took the opportunity to remind them that those coffers were very far from being full. Since coming to England he had lived chiefly on what he had brought with him; the tonnage and poundage granted him were eaten up by the weekly expenses of the Navy.

'Nor have I been able,' he concluded, 'to give my brothers one shilling since I came into England, nor to keep any table in my house but what I eat myself. And that which troubles me most is to see many of you come to me to Whitehall and to think that you must go somewhere else to seek your dinner.'

It was a busy week in Parliament. The Captain-General submitted his plan for the disbandment of the Army, and the Commons considered it in detail. It was resolved that the forces should be disbanded with all convenient speed, that all officers and men who had been in service on April 25 should be paid their arrears, and that a Bill for the disbandment should be drawn up at once.

A Bill was introduced for appointing a Postmaster-General. At about the same time an enterprising Dutchman announced in the press the latest improvements in his postal service:

A New Post having been settled lately at Amsterdam *for* England, *We are desired to give notice, That the long complaints and great prejudice Merchants sustained by the slow Transport of Letters between* England *and* Holland *engaged one* Mr Vander Heyden *of their going round about by* Antwerp, *and that the* Hamburgh *and* Italian *Letters were twice as long upon the way more than was needfull. Therefore on the 22nd of* June *last, he began from* Amsterdam *to bring Letters to* London *in three or four days, and since from* Hamborough *in six, and from* Italy *in eleven days, which before was never practised to the great satisfaction and contentment of the Merchants (who have already found the advantage of it their Letters being come three or four weeks upon every Tuesday, and the last week upon the Monday) as by a general Certificate signed by many of them it appears; – – – And whereas the* German *and* Italian *Letters used to lye at* Antwerp *three or four days before they begun their so tedious passages, he hath taken care that from* Amsterdam *they goe away immediately after receipt; and if the Merchants do desire it, he will ingage to send the said Letters twice a week. The said* Vander Heyden *hath treated with the* Post-master Generale *in* England, *who by his Majesties consent hath agreed to that enterprise. The Pacquet boat that carries his Letters goeth from* Dover *to* Sluice *every Saturday about three a clock in the after noon, and takes in Passengers, for whom he hath all the convenient accommodation.*

In the Lords a Bill was introduced for restoring the Dukedom of Norfolk, void since the fourth Duke had been attainted and executed by Queen Elizabeth in 1572, to Thomas Earl of Arundel. During this week also the Earl of Southampton was appointed Lord High Treasurer.

Sir John Reresby arrived in London, meeting his mother and others of his family who had come up from Yorkshire to see the King. Reresby was presented to the King by the Marquess of Ormonde and was able to deliver his letter from the Queen Mother. King Charles received him genially, asking him a number of questions about the Queen and about his trip.

On the last day of the month the King sent a letter to Parliament. He had been asked by many members, he said, to dispense with their services so that they could go into the country for their health and their affairs; he therefore proposed that both Houses should go into recess on September 8, reassembling on November 6. Before they rose, he hoped, they would see to the raising of such money as was necessary for the debts of the Navy and the disbandment of the Army.

AUTUMN

Saturday, September 1, to Saturday, September 8. The big sensation of the opening days of September was the news of the capture of Hugh Peters. The clerical firebrand was taken at the house of Nathaniel Mun, a Southwark weaver, and *Mercurius Publicus* reported the whole story with a wealth of detail which perhaps owed more than a little to Henry Muddiman's fertile imagination.

According to this account information reached Sir Edward Nicholas at the end of August that Peters was lurking around Southwark, and two officers were sent to arrest him. They traced him to the house of a Quaker named Broad, whose daughter, Mrs Peach, had had a baby two days before, and entered the house to search it. They were too modest to search Mrs Peach's bedroom, however, and this enabled the wily Peters to outwit them. He crept into bed with the young lady ('according to his custom', said *Mercurius*), and when the officers found a passage leading to another house and went to investigate he dashed out, leaving behind a cane with a rapier in it, a small pocket Bible, gloves and a grey cloak.

So Peters for the moment escaped, but on Sunday night he was run to earth at Mun's house. The weaver's wife at first tried to bar the way, but the searchers forced the door and found their quarry in a room upstairs. He hotly denied that he was Peters; his name was Thompson, he said, and he would sue the officers for false arrest. He refused to come down, but when neighbours and the local constable came along to help the Secretary of State's officers he began to change his tune. He promised to go along with his captors, but asked to be allowed to have a drink to raise his spirits. This being granted, he sank two quarts of beer.

Even two quarts hardly seem to have done the trick, for his next request was a piteous entreaty that the officers should not allude to him publicly as Peters. 'For, said hee, if it be known that I am Hugh Peters, the people in the street will stone mee.' He was taken to the constable's house, where he once again denied that he was Peters. Mr Peach, however, was brought to the house and affirmed that the cloak, cane and gloves left in his wife's room belonged to the man before him. Peters said he was lying, and then absent-mindedly picked up the gloves and put them on. Thereupon he was taken to the Tower, where he finally admitted his identity. His final gesture was to accuse his captors of false pretences in arresting him under the name of Thompson.

Parliament settled down to work to get its business done before the adjournment. Finance was the most urgent question. To inquire into the King's revenue a Commons committee had been formed under Sir Heneage Finch, who reported that the total revenue was estimated at £819,398, whereas the expenses of government amounted to at least £200,000 above this figure. It was resolved that the royal revenue should be made up to £1,200,000 a year. At the same time £10,000 was voted to be charged on the receipt of the excise for the use of the Duke of York and £7,000 for the Duke of Gloucester, and £5,000 for the repair of the King's houses.

The petition on behalf of Vane and Lambert was put up to the King and granted. First steps were next taken towards disbanding the Army; it was voted that the regiments should disappear in order by lots.

At the end of the week, however, parliamentary business had still not been concluded, and the Houses had to ask that the adjournment should be postponed till the following Tuesday. This was granted by the Lord Chancellor on behalf of the King.

Meanwhile the promised conference of divines met at Syon College. A draft royal declaration, drawn up by Hyde, was put before them; it aimed at a middle road between the old Anglicanism and Presbyterianism. There was great argument, but no conclusion was reached.

Accompanied by Jermyn, the two French envoys arrived in England. They were the Marquis de Ruvigny from King Louis and the Comte de Vagliac from the Duke of Anjou. They had an audience of the King and then called on the Duke of York; but it was noted that there was no visit to the Duke of Gloucester. Before long it had become known that the young Duke was ill in bed. Later the news leaked out that he had smallpox. There was general anxiety, but by the end of the week it was reported that he was better.

Preparations were in hand for the visit of the Princess Royal, and Sandwich was sent to meet her in the *Resolution*. He embarked at Deal on Friday, September 7.

Pepys had plenty of work to do in arranging for the expedition; but he found time for a gay party with his friends and neighbours in Axe Yard, the Crisps. A great deal of wine was drunk, and Diana Crisp, the daughter of the house,

EXECUTION OF THE REGICIDES

From a contemporary print.
By courtesy of the Trustees of the British Museum

began to be so loving and kind to Pepys that he was led to fear that she was not as good as she should be.

Two days later he was able to put his suspicions to the test. He had not yet disposed of his Axe Yard house, and going over there he fell in with Diana. He took her upstairs and dallied with her a long time, recording in his diary the philosophic conclusion that 'nulla puella negat'. He then went home to give his wife her music lesson.

But the most important event of the week was one of which, for the moment, hardly anyone knew. At about midnight on September 3 the Duke of York was married to Anne Hyde, daughter of the Lord Chancellor, at her father's residence, Worcester House in the Strand.

They had fallen in love the year before, when Anne was

a maid of honour to the Princess Royal. A contract of marriage was made between them at Breda in November 1659, and this was now confirmed by the secret ceremony performed according to the Book of Common Prayer by the Duke's chaplain, Dr Joseph Crowther. Thomas Butler, Earl of Ossory, son and heir of the Marquess of Ormonde, gave away the bride.

Sunday, September 9, to Saturday, September 15. Peace was proclaimed between the crowns of England and Spain. A Spanish Ambassador, the Prince de Ligne, arrived in London, richly attended and with great pomp, and was heartily acclaimed in the streets as he went to call on King Charles. The war was a relic of Cromwell's policy, and since his death had had little reality. Nevertheless, the peace was not entirely popular. Giavarina reported that the news was received with disgust by the Presbyterian party, 'the inveterate and irreconcilable enemy of the Catholic crown and of all the House of Austria'. A discreet silence was maintained in the treaty on the question of Dunkirk, which remained in English hands.

Parliament had still not concluded its business by the second date named, and it was not till Thursday that it finally rose. Before the adjournment an unexpected debate took place in the Commons on the King's matrimonial prospects. Mr Bamfield, seconded by Mr Stevens, moved that the King should be desired to marry, and to marry a Protestant. In answer to this Mr Annesley said he thought that the motion was not timely, and that when Queen Elizabeth had been approached on such a question she told the House to mind its own business. Other speeches followed, but the prevailing opinion was that this was a matter for the King and his immediate advisers, and the motion was withdrawn.

Sandwich arrived at Hellevoetsluis in the *Resolution* on Tuesday, and on Wednesday proceeded to The Hague to conduct the Princess Royal to his ship. On the same day the Duke of York set out for the coast to await his sister, taking advantage of the opportunity to review the fleet. While he was away from London a deep sorrow fell on the nation and the royal family. The Duke of Gloucester had seemed to be recovering; on the morning of September 13 he was reported out of danger. Then came a sudden relapse, and that same evening at nine o'clock, shortly after Parliament had adjourned, he died.

The Duke was only twenty. He had had no time to make his mark on history, but all contemporaries spoke of his bright promise and his death was sincerely lamented. King Charles was deeply distressed; he had been devoted to his young brother, and for several days he refused to see anybody.

Only once had young Henry really emerged into the limelight. That was when, to the consternation of his elder brothers, his mother had tried to make him a Catholic. Ironically enough he was the only one of the three sons of Charles I to die a Protestant.

The senior officers of the Army dined together in King Street and declared their agreement to disbandment. On the same day a foot soldier at Exeter was sentenced by court martial to run the gauntlet of two companies for speaking irreverently of the King. His fellow-soldiers 'did lay it home upon his Ribs, and then kicked him off with much disdain, to teach him and others their duty to their Lord and Sovereign'.

Sir John Reresby's homecoming was worthy of a tough young Yorkshire squire. At Selby on his way to York he had an argument with some fellow-travellers on who should get into the boat first. He was struck on the head with a cudgel, whereupon he launched out with his sword and wounded two of his opponents. A free fight developed, and Reresby had to be rescued by his Moorish servant, finally escaping into the nearest house.

Next he went to Malton, where the fair was on. He dined with Sir Thomas Norcliffe, who had several handsome daughters. One was betrothed to a young gentleman, who was present at dinner and with whom Reresby promptly quarrelled over the girl, throwing a glass of wine in his face as they sat at the table. They arranged to fight next day, but thought better of it and were reconciled. Sir John got home without further misadventures.

Sunday, September 16, *to Saturday, September* 22. It was five days before the Duke of York heard of his brother's death. He was at sea with the fleet, which was cruising in the Downs. Meanwhile there was no sign of the Princess Royal, who was held up by bad weather. So the *Charles* put in to Gravesend, and there the news reached the Duke of his bereavement. He was deeply affected, and left immediately for Whitehall.

Exactly when the storm broke over the Duke's marriage is uncertain, but it was apparently very soon after his return to London. The story could not be suppressed much longer. The Duke and his bride had not waited for the Church of England ceremony at Worcester House, and Anne was now well advanced in pregnancy, though her father, if not her mother, seems to have remained in blissful ignorance of anything amiss. So James went to his brother the King, and, with the fervour of a young man in love, confessed that he was contracted to Anne Hyde, asked leave to acknowledge the marriage, and declared that if this were not granted he would leave the kingdom and spend the rest of his life abroad.

King Charles from the first took the affair calmly. He had had hints of it already; the thought of a marriage between a royal duke and a commoner failed to shock him; he had a great regard for his Chancellor and an affection for Anne Hyde. She was in fact an admirable young lady: not beautiful, but blessed with an abundance of sound sense, great good nature and a sprightly wit. She was the last person to ensnare a prince for her own betterment, and without doubt the passion was genuine on both sides.

What worried the King, however, was the effect the news would have on Sir Edward Hyde. The Chancellor was the most rigid of moralists, and the thought of his daughter in the

Duke of York's bed was liable to blow him sky-high. There was also a more mundane consideration. Hyde was well aware of his unpopularity in certain quarters, and the news that Anne was married to the Duke would be seized on as evidence that he was aspiring to royal honours. His enemies could be relied on to make the best of the weapon thus put in their hands.

In this delicate situation the King had recourse to two old and trusted friends. He summoned Ormonde and Southampton and asked them to arrange for Hyde to meet them in the Palace and there break the news to him as gently as they could. The meeting duly took place. Ormonde warned Hyde that what he had to say might be unwelcome, and advised him to compose himself to hear it; he then told him that the Duke of York had owned a great affection for his daughter to the King, that she was believed to be with child, and that the King required the advice of them and of him on what he was to do.

Even the King can hardly have expected the Chancellor's reaction to be quite what it was. He lost all self-control and burst into a torrent of invective against his daughter. As soon as he went home, he said, he would turn her out of his house as a strumpet, let her shift for herself, and never set eyes on her again. Ormonde tried to calm him. His passion, the Marquess urged, was too violent to be allowed to rule his actions; it was thought that the Duke was married to his daughter, and there were other measures to be taken from those his anger had suggested to him.

The mention of marriage redoubled Hyde's rage. He declared that he would much rather his daughter was the Duke's whore than his wife; in that case nobody could blame him for the resolution he had taken, for he was not obliged to keep a whore for the greatest prince alive. But if he had any reason to suspect marriage he would propose a solution. The King should immediately send Anne to the Tower and put her in a dungeon with a guard so strict that nobody could get to her; then an Act of Parliament should be passed for cutting off her head, 'to which he would not only give his consent, but would very willingly be the first man that should propose it'.

At this point the King entered the room, sat down at the table, and asked how matters stood; whereupon Southampton, staggered by what he had just heard, replied that His Majesty had better consult with soberer men, for Hyde was clearly mad. The King adopted a tone of sweet reasonableness. He assured Hyde that he understood how he felt, but that the matter could not be kept secret much longer, that he must decide what to do before it became public, and that Hyde must therefore lay aside his passion and tell him what he thought was best.

But the King's gentleness had no effect on Hyde. He launched out into another tirade, saying he would rather see his daughter dead with infamy than married to the Duke; and he repeated all he had said about her being sent to the Tower and her head cut off with all possible speed.

It was hopeless to try to reason with him in this mood ; the only solution was to wait till he had come to his senses. The Duke of York now appeared, and the King took him off into another room to tell him what the Chancellor had said. Hyde stumped off home and gave orders to his wife that Anne was to be confined to her room, to receive no visits, and not to appear at meals.

When the Duke heard of this order he was much offended, and complained to his brother. The King thereupon remonstrated with the Chancellor, who replied that as Anne had not discharged the duty of a daughter His Majesty ought not to deprive him of the authority of a father; and he flatly refused to relieve the restraint he had put on her. Lady Hyde, however, was not so harsh; unknown to the Chancellor, the Duke found himself admitted to Worcester House, and was even able to spend whole nights with his wife.

On Friday the Duke of Gloucester was buried very quietly in Westminster Abbey, which the day before was the scene of another ceremony. William Juxon, Bishop of London, the senior and the most illustrious of the surviving bishops who had attended Charles I on the scaffold, had been named for the see of Canterbury, vacant since the death of Laud. On September 20 his appointment was confirmed at a solemn service in the Abbey.

Sunday, September 23, to Saturday, September 29. The Princess Royal had at last been able to put to sea, and the King and the Duke of York went to meet her at Margate. They stayed one night on board the *Resolution,* and on September 25 brought their sister by river to Whitehall. But it was not the happy homecoming she had hoped for. She had learnt on board of the death of her youngest brother, and now she learnt also of her second brother's secret marriage to her former maid of honour. She was not pleased.

At the end of the week a more renowned member of the royal family arrived. With an extraordinary absence of ceremony, and indeed almost unnoticed, Prince Rupert of the Rhine slipped into London.

After the Duke of Gloucester's death a groundless rumour that the Duke of York had smallpox had got around. One Samuel Wildey hastened to send his remedy to the King from Rotterdam:

> Take new laid eggs, three yolks and whites, fry them in fresh butter that was never salted, twelve onces, till the eggs be very hard. Then pour the butter from the eggs into a basson full of fayre cold water. Let it stand till the butter be cold and caked, then take it of from the water and put it into a fayre vessel and beat it with a wooded spatter, continually adding three or four drops of damaske rose water, till the butter with beating come to be white.
>
> Then take of that unguent four onces, added to it *saccarum* sugar-candy, *albi* two drams finely pulverizated misse, *fyat electuarium.*
>
> Be sure to give of this three times a day and so in the night the quantity of a nutmegg upon a knife point. Let it dissolve in his mouth and swallow it down—this by God's grace and assistance—will cure the small pox in the throat which is the cause of most men's death in that disease.
>
> Then take the unguent with out the candy and warme it in a saucer and anoynt the face and eyes with a feather

morning and evening, and this preserves the eyes and keeps the face from pitting.

Now if it please God that his Royall Highness the Duke of York cannot sleep, lett a live pigeon be splitt in two, and one halfe be applyed so soone as it is splitt to the sole of one foot and the other halfe to the sole of the other foot, fast bound with rowlers and so remaine twenty-four houres, and by God help, that will procure sleep and extract the venemous quality of the disease from the heart and vitall spirits.

Sir Abraham Reynardson was chosen to be Lord Mayor of London in succession to Sir Thomas Allen.

Sunday, September 30, to Saturday, October 6. Rumours, mainly garbled, about the relations between the Duke of York and Anne Hyde were beginning to circulate. In court circles a strained silence was maintained; the Duke avoided the Chancellor, and the King decided that nothing more was to be gained from alluding to the matter. But the Princess Royal had expressed her opinion forcibly; feminine pique had got the better of her, and she was furious at the thought of her former maid of honour taking precedence over her. Now a more formidable figure had entered the fray. Queen Henrietta Maria had heard the news and had forthwith written violent letters to both her sons, announcing that she was coming at once to England to prevent so great a stain and dishonour to the Crown.

Beset on all sides, Duke James fell below his usual standard of integrity. He began to think of renouncing the marriage, and the clandestine visits to his wife at Worcester House ceased. His evil genius at this time was his great friend, Sir Charles Berkeley. It is difficult to arrive at the truth of Berkeley's part in the whole obscure affair; but it seems that he put forward the view that the Duke's marriage could not be valid because not approved beforehand by the King. Then, taking the view that his loyalty demanded that he should break the marriage at all costs, he convinced the Duke that he himself, as well as others, had been to bed with

Anne. The unhappy James, in the state of mind he had now reached, was prepared to believe him. ·

The King had other things to think of. He was still taking 'his usual physic at tennis' in the early mornings, and he had found a new interest in remodelling and improving St James's Park. He was engaged in joining up the various ponds to make one large canal or lake, and his idea was to have a variety of boats from different countries there. He had already written to Holland, and he now asked the Venetian Resident if he could arrange for two gondolas to be sent over by an English ship. Giavarina was delighted with the idea, and wrote at once to the Venetian Senate.

The Bishop of Lichfield, who bore the curious name of Accepted Frewen, had been appointed Archbishop of York. On Thursday he was the central figure in another Westminster Abbey ceremony, in the presence of the Bishops of Winchester, Bangor, Rochester, Bath and Wells and Salisbury. Pepys saw them all coming out, and noted how people looked at them as at strange creatures, and few with any love or respect.

The disbanding of the Army was getting under way. Lord Bellasis's, Sir Henry Cholmondeley's and Colonel Charles Fairfax's regiments were paid off in the early days of October, quickly followed by others.

Sunday, October 7, to Saturday, October 13. Royal scandals and all other topics were now pushed into the background by the great event of the autumn, the trial of the regicides. Twenty-nine had finally been rounded up and were arraigned before Sir Orlando Bridgeman, Chief Baron of the Exchequer, at Hicks's Hall, Clerkenwell. They were Sir Hardress Waller, Thomas Harrison, William Heveningham, Isaac Penning-ton, Henry Marten, Gilbert Millington, Robert Tichborne, Owen Rowe, Robert Lilburne, Adrian Scroop, John Carew, John Jones, Henry Smith, Gregory Clement, Edmund Harvey, Thomas Scot, John Downes, Vincent Potter, Augustine Garland, George Fleetwood (not to be confused with his namesake Charles, the former Commander-in-

Chief), Simon Mayne, James Temple, Peter Temple, Thomas Wait, John Cook, Hugh Peters, Francis Hacker, Daniel Axtell and William Hewlett.

The trial opened on Tuesday with the presiding judge's charge to the jury. Bridgeman traced the legal position of the monarchy from the earliest times, showing that no single person or community of persons had any coercive power over the King of England; that the King was supreme Governor, subject to none but God, and could do no wrong, and that if he could do no wrong he could not be punished for any wrong. The court then adjourned till next day.

Wednesday's hearing was devoted to the recording of pleas. All the accused pleaded not guilty except Waller, who confessed his guilt but asked that his petition for mercy should be referred to the King, and Fleetwood, who pleaded that he had obeyed the proclamation in surrendering within fourteen days; he also appealed to the King for mercy. Marten pleaded the Act of Indemnity, and when told that he was an excepted person insisted that he was not because his name was spelt wrongly in the Act; his objection was over-ruled. Carew and Axtell at first refused to plead, but on Sir Heneage Finch, the Solicitor-General, moving that they should be recorded as standing mute they answered not guilty. Peters, called on to plead, lifted up his hands and eyes and said: 'I would not for ten thousand worlds say I am guilty.'

The whole of Thursday was taken up with the case of Harrison. He delayed the proceedings by objecting to thirty-five successive jurymen, but at last a jury was selected and the trial began. He was charged with imagining and compassing the late King's death; evidence was produced to show that he signed and sealed the execution and that, speaking of the King, he said to his fellow-conspirators: 'It will be good for us to blacken him what we can; pray let us blacken him.' In his defence he maintained he had acted by the authority of Parliament, and then declared that he had often prayed God to direct him and that what was done was done in fear of the Lord. The jury found him guilty

without leaving the box, and the Lord Chief Baron pro-
nounced the traditonal sentence for high treason:

> The judgment of this court is, and the court doth award,
> that you be led to the place from whence you came, and
> from thence to be drawn upon an hurdle to the place of
> execution; and there you shall be hanged by the neck, and
> being alive shall be cut down, and your privy members to
> be cut off, your entrails to be taken out of your body, and,
> you living, the same to be burnt before your eyes, and your
> head to be cut off, your body to be divided into four
> quarters, and head and quarters to be disposed of at the
> pleasure of the king's majesty, and the Lord have mercy
> upon your soul.

Next day, Scroop, Carew, Scot, Clement and Jones were
tried. Scroop was convicted largely on the evidence of Sir
Richard Brown, who had just been elected Lord Mayor of
London, Reynardson having withdrawn on grounds of age
and ill-health. Scot found the words he had recently spoken
in Parliament brought up against him; he was said to have
so gloried in the death of the King that he would like his
act inscribed on his tomb; among the witnesses was William
Lenthall. Scot replied that what he said in Parliament was
privileged and should not be brought up in evidence, and he
embarked on a long and able defence, ranging over the whole
course of parliamentary history. But it availed him nothing;
the facts were indisputable. He and his four companions
were all condemned to death.

Cook and Peters received the same sentence on Saturday.
Against Cook it was alleged that at the trial he had particularly urged the execution of King Charles, saying that 'the
King must die, and monarchy with him'. Against Peters a
host of charges was brought. He had plotted with Cromwell
to dispose of the King; he had called His Majesty tyrant and
fool, saying he was unfit to be King and that the kingly
office itself was dangerous and useless; he had marshalled
and encouraged the soldiers on guard at the trial, and commanded them, when the King approached, to cry out:
'Justice! Justice!' He had preached a sermon comparing

King Charles with Barabbas and declaring that 'none but Jews would have let Barabbas go'; he had been on the scaffold just before the King died, and afterwards declared: 'Lord, now lettest thou thy servant depart in peace, for mine eyes have seen thy salvation.'

His conviction was inevitable and he made little defence, merely saying that he stood for religion, for the law and for the poor, and that he had done much good to members of the King's party; to which Bridgman replied that he was not being questioned on the good he had done, but on the evil he was accused of having done.

Harrison was the first to suffer. On Saturday morning he was drawn on a hurdle from Newgate to the place where Charing Cross had stood. As he mounted the scaffold he said that what he and his fellows had done was the cause and work of God, which he was confident God would own and raise up again. He was hanged with his face towards the Banqueting House in Whitehall, where the King had been beheaded; when, the rest of the sentence having been carried out, his severed head was shown to the people, they gave a shout of joy. His quarters were then carried back on the same hurdle to Newgate.

A strange story was reported from Ireland. A wild man had taken up residence in the woods in County Kilkenny; he was naked except for a red cap, and had long reddish hair on his body. He had no arms, but was so fleet of foot that no horse could overtake him. He hunted only when hungry, but had so terrified the people round about that the countryside had become a mass of besieged families.

King Charles again approached Giavarina about the gondolas; would he please arrange for some gondoliers to be sent with them?

Sunday, October 14, to Saturday, October 20. The trials went on; so did the butchery. On Monday Carew was hanged and quartered, and Axtell, Hacker and Hewlett condemned to death. It was Axtell who had been in charge of the guard at the trial of the King, and who had figured in one of its most dramatic incidents. When Bradshaw, the presiding judge, said that the King was being tried in the name of the people of England, a lady in the gallery (generally believed to have been Lady Fairfax) interrupted with the cry that 'it was a lie, and not half nor a quarter of the people', and that Cromwell was a traitor. Axtell gave the order that if the lady said another word she should be shot, and the soldiers trained their muskets on her. This was part of the charge against him; it was also stated that he had struck his soldiers for not calling for 'justice' against the King and that on the day of sentence he ordered them to cry out: 'Execution! Execution!'

Next day it was the turn of Cook and Peters to die. Peters was the most hated man in England, and for both were reserved the extreme refinements of cruelty. When Cook was dragged to the scaffold the head of his friend Harrison was placed on the same hurdle, the face looking towards him. But Cook died calmly and bravely, declaring that as a lawyer he had stood for law and justice and adding a prayer for the present King.

Accounts differ on how Peters met death. Burnet says that 'he had neither the honesty to repent of it [pressing for the King's death] nor the strength of mind to suffer as all the rest of them did. He was observed all the while to be drinking some cordials to keep him from fainting.' But Ludlow, who had now escaped from England and was on the continent, has a different story. When Cook was being quartered, he relates, one Colonel Turner called to the sheriff's men to bring Peters up and make him watch; and the executioner then came up to him, rubbing his bloody hands together, and asked him how he liked what he saw. Peters replied that he was not at all terrified and that the executioner might do his worst. And when he was on the ladder he said to the sheriff: 'Sir, you have butchered one of the servants of God before my eyes, and have forced me to see it in order to terrify and discourage me; but God has permitted it for my support and encouragement'.

Like the others Peters died at Charing Cross. It was he

who had taken the lead in the destruction of the old monument, declaring that 'it was as old as popery itself, and that it had caused more superstition and done more mischief than any pulpit in England had done good'.

During the next three days all the remaining regicides were condemned to death, and those who had been previously sentenced were brought to execution. On Wednesday 'Thomas Scott, railing, and Gregory Clements, howling', in the words of an eye-witness, died at Charing Cross. They were followed by Scroop and Jones, who showed more courage and dignity. Evelyn 'met their quarters mangled & cutt & reaking, as they were brought from the Gallows in baskets on the hurdle'.

The neighbourhood of Charing Cross was in fact becoming somewhat unsavoury. The place had been chosen as a public example, in sight of the spot where Charles I had suffered. But after the eighth hanging the inhabitants of the neighbouring streets complained of the smell of burnt bowels a petitioned the King that no more executions should be held there. So Hacker and Axtell, the former without remorse and the latter with tears and prayers, were hanged at the more conventional Tyburn. Hacker, who had had only a small part in the proceedings against the King, was spared from quartering.

This was the end. Ten men had now died, and the King and Hyde both felt that enough blood had been shed. The rest of the sentences were suspended until the King, by the advice of Parliament, should decide whether they were to be carried out.

The *Parliamentary Intelligencer* had a footnote:

'Twill be expected that we tell you how the dead bodies of the several persons executed are disposed. The friends of Mr *Carew* and Mr *Hacker* begg'd their respective bodies; *Axtell's* Quarters are not yet boil'd; *Harrison's* Quarters are not yet disposed of; *Cook's* head and *Harrison's* (a Councellor and Attorney) are set upon Poles on *Westminster Hall*; the heads of the rest upon *London-bridge*, and their Quarters at several Gates.

Part II: Autumn

Pepys saw some of the limbs hung up at Aldersgate: 'a sad sight to see.' 'A bloody week this and the last have been,' he commented.

Sunday, October 21, to Saturday, October 27. Ecclesiastical affairs had taken a back seat during the enthralling business of dissecting the regicides. But discussion on the religious settlement had been going on behind the scenes, and on Monday a full-dress conference was held at Worcester House to discuss the draft royal declaration which had been brought forward in its first form on September 4. The King himself was present, with the Lord Chancellor, the Duke of Albemarle, the Marquess of Ormonde, the Earl of Manchester and a number of bishops; the leading members of the Presbyterian party were Baxter, Reynolds and Calamy.

A little progress was made. The Presbyterians were willing to agree to episcopal government provided the bishops would admit the advice of presbyters; the Book of Common Prayer could be accepted as the common rule of worship if liberty to dispense with certain ceremonies were granted. None of this was repugnant to the King's ideas; but he wanted to go further in the matter of toleration. After discussion had gone on for some time, Hyde produced, on behalf of his master, a further proposal. The King, he said, had been petitioned by the Independents and Anabaptists, and he now proposed that 'others also be permitted to meet for religious worship, so be it they do it not to the disturbance of the peace; and that no justice of peace or officer disturb them'. At this suggestion there was an ominous silence. Everybody knew what was in the King's mind; he wanted to extend the toleration to all, including Catholics. And neither Anglicans nor Presbyterians were prepared to grant this. At last Baxter spoke up. His party did not desire rigorous severity, he said, but they distinguished between tolerable and intolerable opinions; and papists and Socinians were intolerable. To this the King replied that there were laws enough against the papists already. Baxter's answer was that the question was whether or not they should be enforced.

Upon this the conference broke up. The King was bitterly disappointed. He had failed to win the support of either party on the one point about which he really cared.

Three days later a watered-down version of the declaration was published. Certain concessions were made to the Presbyterians. A stricter observance of the Lord's Day was to be enforced and the preaching of bishops encouraged; suffragan bishops were to be appointed in the larger dioceses; no bishop was to ordain or to exercise church censure without the advice or assistance of the presbyters; rural deans were to assist in confirmation, admission to the Lord's Supper and catechising; deans and chapters were to be appointed from among the most learned and pious presbyters of dioceses; no bishop was to exercise any power but according to the laws of the land; learned men were to be appointed to review and amend the liturgy; and individuals were to be left at liberty in the matter of kneeling at the sacrament, the cross in baptism, bowing at the name of Jesus, the oath of canonical obedience and the use of the surplice. The pledge given in the Declaration of Breda was repeated: that no man 'shall be disquieted or called in question for Differences in Opinion on Matters of Religion, which do not disturb the Peace of the Kingdom'. Beyond this nothing specific was said of toleration for other than Anglicans and Presbyterians.

While the Worcester House conference was in progress, word was received that the Chancellor's daughter was in labour in the same building. The Duke of York was still in a panic of indecision whether to regard himself as married or not; but the King decided that the time had come for him to act. He ordered the Chancellor to admit to his daughter's bedside a committee consisting of the Marquess and Marchioness of Ormonde, the Earl of Manchester, Sir Edward Nicholas, the Countesses of Sunderland and Cork and the Bishop of Winchester. In the presence of the rest the Bishop interrogated Anne. He asked who was the father of her child; she said the Duke of York. He asked if she had ever known any other man; she answered 'with many imprecations' that she had not. Finally he asked if she and the Duke were married; she replied that they were, and that there were witnesses who, in due time, would avow it.

The lords and ladies present were completely convinced that she was speaking the truth, and so reported to the King. Lady Ormonde went to the Duke and told him what had passed, and the wretched James came to his senses. Berkeley at the same time confessed that the story he had told was untrue, and the Duke, anxious to atone for his behaviour, was only too glad to recognise the fact of his marriage. As Anne gave birth to a son, the King, who had never wavered in his support, declared her to be the Duchess of York. And he emphasised that he bore no ill-will towards his Chancellor by informing him privately of his intention to raise him to the peerage.

But the most redoubtable enemy of the match had still to be encountered. Queen Henrietta Maria, accompanied by her youngest daughter, was on her way to England, breathing fire and slaughter at every step. The original and ostensible object of her journey was to promote the marriage of her daughter with Monsieur; the primary purpose was now to break the marriage of her son with Anne Hyde. The Duke of York and the Princess Royal, the former doubtless in a high state of nervousness, set out for Dover on Wednesday to await her arrival. On Saturday the King followed.

Traffic and parking problems were exercising the attentions of His Majesty's ministers. The streets were cluttered up with hackney coaches, and a proclamation was issued enjoining 'that no Person of what estate, degree or quality soever, keeping or using any Hackney Coaches, or Coach-Horses, do from and after the 6th of November next, suffer the said Coaches and Horses or any of them to remain in the Streets or Passages of the Cities of London or Westminster to be there hired, but that they keep them within their respective Coach-houses, Stables or Yards'.

Sunday, October 28, to Saturday, November 3. The Duke of York met his mother and sister at sea with the whole fleet and conducted them into Dover Harbour; he was most attentive and, finding that it was a day of abstinence, arranged for a supply of sturgeon for them and their fellow-Catholics. Among the Queen's attendants was the Capuchin Father Cyprien de Gamache, who was enchanted with the warmth of the reception they received.

Prince Rupert had joined the King and the Princess Royal, and the three of them met the Queen at Dover on October 30. King Charles was delighted to see his beloved 'Minette', whom he had not met for many months. A magnificent banquet followed. The King's chaplain said grace, but as soon as he had done so Father Cyprien rose and, making the sign of the cross, said in a loud and grave tone: 'Benedic Domine nos, et haec tua dona quae de tua largitate sumus sumpturi, per Christum Dominum nostrum.' The King, the Queen and others stood while he said this second grace. 'The Puritans, the Independents, the Quakers, of whom the town of Dover is full,' recorded Father Cyprien with some satisfaction, 'and who are sworn foes to the ceremonies of the Church, and particularly to the sign of the cross, were highly astonished at the liberty which I took to make it thus publicly at the table of the Protestant King.'

Next morning he astonished them still more. He said Mass openly in a large apartment with all the doors open. Some who watched, he commented, 'were sensibly touched with the reverence with which we treated those high and sacred mysteries, which they compared with the meanness and nakedness of their Lord's Supper'. But others were inflamed with rage.

The royal cavalcade reached Whitehall on Friday. The Queen had not seen her old home for nineteen years, and the memory of old times and the warmth of her welcome perhaps softened her anger, for she seems to have let her son James down comparatively lightly. But she was coldness itself to Hyde, whom she had always regarded as her enemy; and she refused to receive her daughter-in-law or recognise her as the Duchess of York. King Charles's answer was to create the Chancellor Baron Hyde of Hindon.

Another faithful servant now honoured was Dr John Barwick. He had been among the most ardent and the most selfless of those working in London for a restoration. The King had wanted to make him Bishop of Carlisle, but Barwick had refused lest it be thought he had advocated episcopacy for reasons of personal ambition. So he became Dean of Durham and took up office on All Saints' Day.

On October 28 five bishops were consecrated in Westminster Abbey. They were Gilbert Sheldon of London, Humphrey Henchman of Salisbury, George Morley of Worcester, Robert Sanderson of Lincoln and George Griffith of St Asaph.

On the following day Sir Richard Brown was installed as Lord Mayor. The Merchant Taylors provided the Lord Mayor's Show, which was on an imposing scale; among the pageants was one portraying the Royal Oak and King Charles's escape at Boscobel.

The Venetian Senate ordered the immediate building of two special gondolas for the King of England. The East India Company offered free passage to any persons 'desirous to settle upon the healthful island of St Helena'.

WINTER

Sunday, November 4, to Monday, November 12. The first business in the House of Lords when Parliament reassembled on November 6 was the introduction of Lord Hyde of Hindon. He had, of course, already taken his seat on the Woolsack as Lord Chancellor, but hitherto he had had no place as a peer. The induction took place with due ceremony. Hyde left the Woolsack with the Great Seal in his arms and, walking between Lord Roberts and Lord Hatton and with Garter King of Arms going before, was led to the seat of the junior baron. That done, he took his place once more on the Woolsack.

The Commons' first act was to vote a gift of £10,000 to

Princess Henrietta. Later in the week letters of thanks were read from her and also from her mother and sister, who had previously received gifts. The young Princess, who had been brought up in France from infancy, 'excused herself that she could not do it so well in the English tongue, which she desired to supply with an English heart'.

Sir Heneage Finch brought in a Bill to attaint Oliver Cromwell and other dead regicides. It was read a first time, but the ardent William Prynne was in a hurry. Saying that the traitors of 1648 had read their Bill for the trial of the King twice together, he moved an immediate second reading of the new measure. He got his way. Next a Bill was introduced for giving effect to the Worcester House Declaration on religion.

On Saturday a debate took place on a Bill to prevent married women leaving their husbands; it was proposed that they should not be allowed alimony, nor have their debts paid, if they went away without consent. The Bill was read a first time, but some members expressed misgivings. Sir John Northcot said it was not improper for him as an old man to speak up for the ladies; he raised the possibility of a young man marrying a rich old woman and then leaving her, by which she might be ruined. Mr Bamfield said it was fit that women should have a livelihood, though not power to ruin their husbands by their own debts. The final speech in favour of the Bill was made by Prynne, who said that if it were laid aside 'those that had ill wives would call for it again within a day or two'.

The negotiations for the French marriage were hanging fire. King Charles was not enthusiastic; he was far from anxious to bestow his favourite sister on the odious little pervert that Philip of Anjou was known to be. She, on the other hand, did not seem to mind the prospect, and her mother was an ardent advocate. Another French envoy, the Comte de Soissons, had arrived to speed the matter up, but had little success.

Pepys, the rising young *parvenu*, revealed the most despicable side of his nature in his dealings with his own family.

His father suggested that he and his wife should take his young sister, Paulina or 'Pall', to live with them. Pepys agreed, on condition that she should come 'not as a sister in any respect, but as a servant'. The wretched Pall humbly accepted the offer.

Tuesday, November 13, *to Saturday, November* 17. The Bill to prevent wives leaving their husbands came up again in the House of Commons, and another light-hearted debate took place. Prynne, who seems to have found the Bill great fun, spoke once more in its favour, 'though he never had a good or bad wife in his life'. Mr Walpole said the measure was so severe that if a bridge were made from Dover to Calais all the women in England would leave. England, he added, was according to the proverb a women's heaven; it would now be their hell. But the champions of women's rights were in a minority; the Bill was read a second time.

In the Lords a committee reported in favour of restoring the Dukedom of Norfolk to the Earl of Arundel. It also revealed that this nobleman, now to become England's premier duke, was a hopeless lunatic, living in Italy with a physician constantly in attendance. However, he had the best house in Padua, with twelve servants and all things fitting for his quality.

The disbandment of the Army was proceeding apace; by the end of the week only eight regiments remained to be paid off. England, which had never taken kindly to militarism, had been becoming increasingly restive under the burden. On Wednesday the Commons considered a petition from the inn-keepers and victuallers of Windsor, who complained that three hundred soldiers had recently been quartered on them. They had been compelled to lend them sixpence a day each, besides providing lodging, fire and candles and cooking their meals. The House agreed to forward the petition to the King.

King Charles had reluctantly withdrawn his objections to the marriage of his sister and the Duke of Anjou, and Soissons hurried back to Paris to put the proposed terms before the French King. The match-making Henrietta had now turned her attentions to marrying her eldest son off; the favourite candidate was Hortense Mancini, one of the lovely and dashing nieces of Cardinal Mazarin. Charles had known Hortense in her days of exile, but he was not so sure that he wanted her as a bride. In any case he was in no hurry.

Lord Hyde had been elected to the Chancellorship of Oxford, recently laid down by Richard Cromwell. The Vice-Chancellor, Proctors and heads of houses waited on him at Worcester House to confer the honour. Hyde received them with the stately grace that was his. He was sorry, he told them, that they had lost a chance of making a new friend. He himself was so much their friend already that no honour or addition could make him more so.

Sunday, November 18, *to Saturday, November* 24. It had always been understood that when the Convention Parliament had completed the essential work of the Restoration it should give place to another. The King, therefore, now announced that the dissolution would take place on December 20. This would give the members a Christmas holiday, and the King and his advisers would have leisure to prepare for the Coronation, which was tentatively fixed for January. Elections for the new Parliament would take place early in the New Year.

There was in truth not very much left for the Parliament to clear up. The Commons had prepared a declaration to put in force all the laws against Catholics of the time of Queen Elizabeth, but the King let it be known that the suggestion was repugnant to him and the Lords let the matter rest. As for the remaining regicides, no attempt was made to press the suspended sentences. On Monday Pepys met Lord Southampton, who gave him a lift in his coach to Whitehall. The Treasurer, whom he found a very good-natured man, told him the King was a man of such compassion that he believed that, if the law would allow, the regicides would be wholly pardoned.

With the advance of winter London was returning to its pre-civil-war gaiety, and the theatres were thronged. On

Part II: Winter

Monday the King, his mother and Princess Henrietta were the guests of the Duke of Albemarle at the Cockpit in Whitehall; after supper there was a performance of Ben Jonson's *The Silent Woman*. The revels went on all night, but the King caused some offence by preferring French music to English.

Next day Pepys paid his first visit to the King's House near Lincoln's Inn Fields, London's newest and biggest theatre, just opened under the management of Thomas Killigrew. The play he saw was *Beggars Bush* by Beaumont and Fletcher, and the star was Michael Mohun, who had come to England at the Restoration with a great reputation earned abroad.

In one case a play led to tragedy. Some lively spirits had been watching Davenant's *Unfortunate Lovers*, in which a duel takes place on the stage. Proceeding to the Fleece Tavern, some of them drew their swords and re-enacted the duel to demonstrate where the actors had gone wrong. This was a dangerous game after generous potations, and Sir Robert Gaskoll was wounded in the hand; he fell over backwards and the man who had wounded him, a Scotsman, at the same time tripped forwards. Sir Robert was run through the body, and died half an hour later.

Wild weather was reported from Guernsey. On Friday there was such a thunderstorm as nobody could remember. Mr Merchant, a gentleman of Port Town, ran for shelter to a windmill, where he found three horses tied, the middle one struck dead and the others unharmed. On the stairs sat a woman, her breast grievously burned. Inside the mill were three men, lying one upon another; two were dead and the third had a scorched leg.

At home the Thames overflowed its banks, and boats were rowed in the streets of Westminster.

Sunday, November 25, to Saturday, December 1. The Bill to give legal effect to the Worcester House Declaration produced a long debate in the House of Commons. The House was uneasy at the provisions, but there was a general reluctance to reject a plan which had the personal authority of the King;

Prynne voiced a widespread sentiment when he commented on the wonder that would be felt should the Commons throw out the Bill after giving thanks to His Majesty for the Declaration. In these circumstances Sir Allen Broderick suggested postponing the awkward decision; he moved that the Bill should be laid aside till the calling of the new Parliament. He was supported by Sir Thomas Meeres, who said that to pass the Bill would be to make all papists and other dissenters rejoice, since it would remove all conformity in the Church. This was the prevailing temper of the House; wrapped up in a blanket of rhetoric, it amounted to a deep distaste for any degree of toleration. When the House divided the votes were 157 for, and 183 against, a second reading, and the measure was laid aside.

'So there is an end of that Bill,' wrote Andrew Marvell prophetically, 'and for those excellent things therein. We must henceforth rely onely upon his Majesty's goodnesse, who, I must needs say, hath hitherto been more ready to give than we to receive.'

Queen Henrietta had planned to return to France this week; but she was persuaded to stay till after Christmas. Charles could not let his mother go without escorting her to the coast, and he was busy in London just now with preparations for the dissolution. This was the official reason, but doubtless he hoped, if he could get her to stay a little longer, to reconcile her with the Duchess of York, whom she still refused to receive.

Henrietta was still pressing for the Mazarin marriage. Meanwhile new obstacles were reported to have arisen in the matter of young Henrietta and Prince Philip. This, wrote Giavarina, was much to the distress of the intended bridegroom, who was 'apparently consumed with desire for the consummation of the nuptials'. From what is known of the temperament of Monsieur this hardly seems very likely.

The title of a new book advertised in *Mercurius Publicus* struck a note that was to echo increasingly through the literature of the new era:

Part II: Winter

The Horn Exalted: Or, Room for Cuckolds, Being a Treatise concerning the Reason and Original of the word Cuckold, and why such are said to wear Horns. Also an Appendix concerning Women and Jealousie. Sold at several Booksellers.

Tench, the carpenter who had built the scaffold on which Charles I had died, was arrested and committed to the Gatehouse; he was said to have installed rings and pulleys by which the King could be held down if he resisted. On the same day Johnston of Wariston was proclaimed a traitor in Edinburgh.

Sunday, December 2, to Tuesday, December 11. On December 2 seven more bishops were consecrated in the Abbey. They were John Cosin of Durham, William Lucy of St David's, Benjamin Laney of Peterborough, Hugh Lloyd of Llandaff, Richard Sterne of Carlisle, Brian Walton of Chester and John Gauden of Exeter. The consecrator was the Archbishop of York, by commission of the Archbishop of Canterbury.

This week a start was made on tackling the thorny problem of land that had changed hands during the interregnum. A royal commission was appointed to examine the whole question, and its exalted composition shows the paramount importance attached to its work. Albemarle, Ormonde, Hyde and Nicholas were all members.

Nothing had yet been decided concerning the fate of the regicides still in prison; the Commons again deferred the matter, but appointed a committee to consider it. But at least they could deal with the dead. On Friday they passed a resolution 'that the carcasses of Oliver Cromwell, Henry Ireton, John Bradshaw and Thomas Pride, whether buried in Westminster Abbey or elsewhere, be with all expedition taken up, and drawn upon a hurdle to Tyburn, and there hanged up in their coffins for some time, and after that buried under the said gallows'. On the following Monday the Lords concurred in the proposal.

The Scots acted in an opposite direction. The remains of the gallant James Graham, Marquess of Montrose, who had been hanged as a traitor in Edinburgh in 1650 for fighting for his King, were taken from their place of ignominy and given honourable burial.

The Duke of York was getting down to the serious task of reorganising the administration of the Navy. On Tuesday, December 4, he had a conference in Whitehall with Sir George Carteret and Pepys, at which the wasteful system of pay then in force was discussed. A new scheme was drawn up, to be shown to the King and then submitted to Parliament.

But the week ended with a naval tragedy. The rough weather had continued, and violent storms were reported from various parts of the country, particularly from the north of England. On Saturday the frigate *Assurance*, riding at anchor at Woolwich, took in so much water through her open portholes that she sank with the loss of twenty men. Pepys heard the news the following morning and rushed off to tell the Duke of York, who as soon as he could went down to Woolwich. On Tuesday Pepys himself followed, finding the ship under water with only the upper deck and the masts showing. In his capacity as a justice of the peace he examined one of the seamen suspected of negligence, but could find no reason to commit him.

In the midst of all this reports of a plot against the King had reached the Government; several arrests were made and the suspects examined. The Fifth Monarchy Men were believed to be at the bottom of the affair, the design being to murder the King and the Duke of Albemarle and set fire to Whitehall. Strong guards were set at the Palace and at all entrances to London.

On Sunday, December 9, the Duke of York's infant son, named James after his father, was christened at Worcester House. The King, Prince Rupert and the Duchess of Albemarle were the godparents.

Wednesday, December 12, to Friday, December 21. More than forty men were in prison in connection with the suspected plot against the King. The most important were Robert

Overton, a notorious Fifth Monarchy Man and a former Governor of Hull, and Desborough, who for the past few months had been at liberty. It was reported in some quarters that Lambert, from his cell in the Tower, was the guiding spirit. The King himself took part in examining the suspects, but little could be discovered. There was no concrete evidence, and the objects and details of the plot, if there was one, remained obscure. Disbanded officers were believed to be the principal offenders, and a proclamation was issued ordering all such to leave London and not to stay within twenty miles of the city without the permission of the Privy Council.

Parliament, which was due for dissolution on December 20, had as usual not concluded its business. A number of Bills were passed, the most important being concerned with the royal revenue. The Court of Wards was abolished and a regular income settled on the King, together with a month's assessment of £70,000 to meet the expenses of the Coronation, including the provision of new crown jewels.

Next the House of Commons discussed rewards for some of those who had helped King Charles after his escape from Worcester. Chief of these were Colonel Francis Wyndham, who had been his host in Dorset, and the brave and charming Jane Lane, who had ridden on a highly dangerous two-day journey to Bristol with the King disguised as her servant. There was some opposition to the granting of gifts to these two, on the grounds, first, that such a matter should be left to King Charles, and, second, that the House had no power to vote money other than to the King (though there were ample and recent precedents to the contrary). Wyndham, who was himself now a member of the House, stood up and said that his service to the King had been its own reward and that he desired no other. But the Commons' sense of gratitude won the day. Wyndham and Miss Lane were each voted £1,000, chargeable on the excise.

Another act of the Convention Parliament in its last days was to order the release of John Milton.

A curious move to discipline the House's own members

was recorded in the Commons on December 14. Serjeant Maynard moved that the Speaker should reprove all persons whom he observed talking, whispering or reading a paper. Very soon after, while a Bill was being read, the Speaker noticed some gentlemen talking near the Bar; whereupon it was ordered 'that every member of this House who shall stand in the passage by the door of this House shall forfeit 12d. to be paid to the Serjeant to the use of the poor of Westminster'.

A Bill for setting up a general letter office was read a third time. A proviso permitted carriers of the two universities to continue carrying their own letters, and the Commons settled down to a vehement argument as to whether Oxford or Cambridge should be named first. Mr Swinson maintained that if the usual formula were adopted it would be thought that there were more Oxford than Cambridge men in the House. Sir George Reeves protested against two sister universities being made to quarrel like women about place. Sir Thomas Meeres said that if the proviso passed as it stood it would show that Oxford men could fast better than Cambridge men, as most of the latter had gone to dinner. At length the formula 'both universities' was adopted.

Princess Henrietta was at Tunbridge Wells, and King Charles passed a scribbled note across the Council table to Hyde. 'I would willingly make a visit to my sister at tunbridge for a night or two at farthest,' he wrote; 'when do you think I can best spare that time?'

Hyde minuted back: 'I know no reason why you may not for such a tyme, (2 nights) go the next weeke, about Wensday, or Thursday, and returne tyme enough for the adiournement; which yett ought to be the weeke followinge. I suppose you will goe with a light Trayne.'

Back came the royal answer: 'I intend to take nothing but my night bag.'

This was too much for Hyde's sense of decorum, and he wrote: 'Yes, you will not go without 40 or 50 horse!'

'I counte that parte of my night bag,' replied His Majesty.

The King does not appear to have carried out his plan,

and by December 19 the Princess was back at Whitehall. On that day the Princess Royal was taken ill, and it was soon known that she had the same complaint that had killed her brother Henry. The younger sister was quickly moved to St James's Palace to be out of the way of infection. Two days later the Princess Royal was reported to be dangerously ill.

The Duchess of York was now accepted by all except the Queen. The Duke appeared publicly with her at the theatre, and she held court at Worcester House, where Evelyn was among those who went to pay their respects.

Saturday, December 22, to Tuesday, December 25. The Houses of Parliament were still not ready, and the dissolution had to be postponed till after Christmas. On Saturday the King sent them a message saying that he would come on Monday to pass such Bills as were ready; Parliament would then adjourn for Christmas, meet again on Thursday and Friday, and be dissolved on Saturday, December 29.

So on Christmas Eve King Charles went to the House of Lords and gave the royal assent to two Acts—for taking away the Court of Wards and Liveries and for impositions on beer, ale and other liquors. The King and his Parliament parted with mutual good will; but Christmas Eve was not to pass in so happy a mood. The Duke of Gloucester had died of smallpox on the day of the previous adjournment, and now, by a tragic coincidence, his eldest sister was to follow him to the grave, dying of the same disease on an exactly similar occasion. During the few days of her illness she had been growing rapidly weaker; on Friday, feeling that she was dying, she asked for a cordial to give her strength to receive the sacrament, of which she partook with great devotion. As she spoke of her coming death without fear or emotion, the King, who was spending every available moment at her bedside, burst into tears. Mary recommended the care of her son to him, and then made her will.

She rallied a little during the week-end, just as her brother had done at the same stage, and on Sunday appeared to be out of danger. But on Monday, while the King was at the House of Lords, he received a message that she was sinking. He hurried through the remaining ceremonies and hastened to the Palace in time to see his sister before her death. In her last hours the Princess's thoughts turned to the injustice she had done to her former maid of honour, and she expressed heartfelt contrition for the part she had played in the sufferings the Duchess of York had endured.

It was a sad Christmas for the King and the court. But throughout the country it was celebrated with joy and thanksgiving. The feast had been restored to the calendar by Order in Council; the rule of puritanism was over. Bishops preached in their cathedrals; Father Cyprien de Gamache said Mass in Whitehall Palace. Pepys had a turkey on Christmas Eve and chicken and a shoulder of mutton on Christmas Day.

Wednesday, December 26, *to Monday, December* 31. On Saturday the Princess Royal was given a stately funeral in Westminster Abbey, in contrast with the quiet burial of the Duke of Gloucester. The Duke of York walked behind the coffin, and others in the procession, which passed through the ranks of the Coldstream Guards (one of the only three regiments remaining), were the Marquess of Ormonde, the Earl of Manchester and Lord Hyde.

The King had withdrawn himself completely, and no foreign ambassador was able to approach him to offer condolences. The Duke of York was observed to be plunged in melancholy. As for Queen Henrietta, she felt that this was the culmination of all her misfortunes. She decided to leave for France as early as possible in the New Year, regardless of the weather which had rendered the country roads almost impassable. She declared roundly that if she stayed in England she would soon end her days. Her departure was fixed for January 2, and this time neither the King nor anybody else made any attempt to detain her.

Only for the dissolution of Parliament did the King emerge from his seclusion. In his speech from the throne he had high praise for the Convention, which he said should for ever be called 'the Healing and Blessed Parliament'. Its greatest achievement, he added, was the passing of the Act of Indemnity and Oblivion, which engendered kindness and created confidence in the joint and common security of King and country. Anybody who ever attempted to persuade him to violate its provisions would be received like one who asked him to burn Magna Carta, cancel all the old laws, and erect a new government after his own invention and appetite.

So ended one of the most momentous years in English history. The summing-up can be left to the two most famous diarists of the time.

'At the end of the last and the beginning of this year,' wrote Samuel Pepys on January 1, 1661, 'I do live in one of the houses belonging to the Navy Office, as one of the principal officers, and have done now about half a year. After much trouble with workmen I am now almost settled; my family being, myself, Jane, Will Hervey, and Wayneman, my girle's brother. Myself in constant good health, and in a most handsome and thriving condition. Blessed be Almighty God for it. I am now taking of my sister to come and live with me. As to things of State.—The King settled, and loved of all. The Duke of York matched to my Lord Chancellor's daughter, which do not please many. The Queen upon her return to France with the Princess Henrietta. The Princess of Orange lately dead, and we into new mourning for her. We have been lately frighted with a great plot, and many taken up on it, and the fright not quite over. The Parliament, which had done all this great good to the King, beginning to grow factious, the King did dissolve it December 29th last, and another likely to be chosen speedily. I take myself now to be worth £300 clear in money, and all my goods and all manner of debts paid, which are none at all.'

John Evelyn wrote more succinctly: 'I gave God thankes for his many signal mercies to my selfe, Church & Nation this wonderfull Yeare.'

EPILOGUE

QUEEN Henrietta Maria returned to France early in January. Before she left, finding herself in a minority of one, she received the Duchess of York and embraced her as a daughter. She was also formally reconciled to Lord Hyde. She returned to her son's kingdom in 1662 with the intention of settling down permanently, but she was ill at ease in the unfamiliar atmosphere of Restoration England and three years later she went back to France, spending the remainder of her life at her château at Colombes. She died in 1669 in her sixtieth year.

Her sole surviving daughter, who accompanied her mother back to France, was duly married to Monsieur, now created Duke of Orleans, in March 1661. She was soon disillusioned with her degenerate husband, but contrived to enjoy herself at the French court, where she was honoured and fêted by all except Duke Philip. In 1670 she again visited her brother in England, spending a few weeks at Dover and negotiating there the famous secret treaty between the English and French kings. Within a month of her return to Paris she was dead, at the age of twenty-six, having been taken ill so suddenly that many people, including King Charles, suspected her husband of poisoning her. Modern historians, however, have tended to acquit Monsieur of such a crime.

The Duke of York's young son, created Duke of Cambridge in the New Year, lived less than seven months. Of the remaining seven children of the Duke and Duchess only two, Mary and Anne, grew up; both were destined to occupy the throne of England. In spite of this crop of deaths the marriage of James and Anne Hyde was happy. Anne's solid sense and even temperament exercised a profound influence on her husband; and he, though not faithful, maintained to the end his respect and affection for her. Shortly before her death in 1671 she was received into the Catholic Church, a move in which the Duke followed her at some date unknown.

The Duke of Albemarle remained one of King Charles's trusted counsellors, but he was never happy in politics and took no prominent part in public affairs. He performed one last great service to his country. When the plague broke out in London in 1665, he stayed at his post after nearly all the rest of the nobility had fled. With the Earl of Craven he maintained order in the city, and it was largely owing to him that complete chaos was avoided. In the following year he and Prince Rupert were made joint commanders of the Fleet in the second Dutch war; but the only action they fought was indecisive. Albemarle died in January 1670; his duchess survived him for less than a month.

His two faithful chaplains were both made Fellows of Eton; later each was instituted to a rich rectory in Sussex, Price at Petworth and Gumble at East Lavant. Gumble died in 1676; Price lived on till 1691.

Hyde, created Earl of Clarendon in 1661, remained Lord Chancellor till 1667. During that time he became more and more overbearing and relations between him and the King more and more strained. At length the humiliating failure of the Dutch war, for which he was little to blame, brought a united outcry from his enemies and gave King Charles a pretext for getting rid of him. The circumstances of his dismissal reflected little credit on the King, but his own conduct had made the breach inevitable. The Duke of York strenuously defended his father-in-law, but could not prevent an impeachment for high treason. By the advice of the King, sent to him privately through the Duke of York, Clarendon fled the country and spent the rest of his life in exile.

Ormonde, soon made a duke, never aspired to play more than a shadowy part in the government of England. His heart was in Ireland, and at the end of 1661 he was re-appointed to his old post of Lord Lieutenant of that country. He administered Ireland for most of the remainder of his long life, though with fluctuating fortunes owing to the machinations of political enemies. But he was always present behind the scenes as the confidential adviser of King Charles II, who had a greater respect for him than for any other man. His own loyalty to the monarch and the monarchy never wavered; he survived the King and died at the age of seventy-seven in the year of the Whig revolution.

Sir Edward Nicholas and Sir William Morrice remained joint Secretaries of State until 1662, when Nicholas retired in his seventieth year. Morrice stayed on for four more years, during which he found the hurly-burly of politics and intrigue increasingly distasteful; then he retired to his Devonshire estates and devoted the rest of his days to learning and literature.

Grenville was created Earl of Bath, a title Charles I had intended to confer on his father, Sir Bevil. Thereafter he held various appointments under Charles II, James II and William III and lived until 1701.

Mordaunt became Constable of Windsor Castle. He was impeached by Parliament in 1667, but was protected by the King; he then retired into private life and died in 1675.

As was expected, the regicides whose sentences of death were suspended were not hanged. When a Bill for their execution was introduced in the new Parliament, Clarendon passed a note to the King at the Council table proposing that the measure should be allowed to 'sleep in the Houses' and not be brought to him. Charles, who still felt that he could not in honour pardon the murderers of his father, agreed. 'I must confess I am weary of hanging except upon new offences,' he replied. So by tacit consent the executions were remitted, and the convicted men remained in prison. Three others, however, Okey, Barkstead and Corbet, who were captured later in Holland, were executed in 1662.

Another exception to the general rule of mercy was Vane. The new Parliament was more vindictive than its predecessor and insisted that he and Lambert should both be brought to trial. The King, who had agreed to the previous petition that their lives should be spared, was reluctant to reopen the

Epilogue

case; but he had also agreed that the decision should lie with Parliament, and he gave his consent. At the trial Vane boldly defended himself, justifying all that had been done against Charles I and asserting the sovereign power of Parliament. He was found guilty, and the King held that his attitude at his trial released him from the obligation to save his life. Vane was executed on Tower Hill.

Lambert had been removed to Guernsey, where he was allowed to live in semi-liberty with his wife and children. He was now brought back to face his trial, in which, in contrast with Vane, he was meek and submissive and admitted his offences. He was sentenced to death, then reprieved and sent back to Guernsey. In 1667, after a plot for his escape had been discovered, he was removed to the island of St Nicholas in Plymouth Sound. There, sixteen years later, he died.

Of the other Commonwealth leaders Haslerig died in the Tower early in 1661. Fleetwood was left at liberty, and lived in obscurity for another thirty years. Desborough was soon released after the plot scare in December 1660 and left the country. In 1666, being suspected of intrigues in Holland against the English Government, he was ordered to return on pain of being declared a traitor. He obeyed and was confined in the Tower; but the next year he was freed after examination and was allowed to spend the rest of his life in peace.

Ludlow, who lived until 1692, settled at Vevey in Switzerland, where he wrote his lengthy memoirs and resisted all attempts to draw him into republican plots. At the revolution he felt it was safe to return to England and appeared in London late in 1689. But he had mistaken the temper of the new régime; a proclamation was issued offering a reward for his arrest, and Ludlow, who was now over seventy, quickly escaped and made his way back to Vevey.

The last of all to die was Richard Cromwell. After the Restoration he left the country, living for a time in Paris and later at Geneva. About 1680 he returned unobtrusively

to England and settled down quietly at Cheshunt in Hert-
fordshire under the name of John Clarke. No attempt was
made to disturb him and he lived to the age of eighty-six,
dying at Cheshunt in 1712. His brother Henry had stayed
in England, likewise unmolested, and died at Spinney
Abbey, Cambridgeshire, in 1674.

Whether or not there was a plot against the King at the
end of 1660 was never established, but early in January 1661
a real Fifth Monarchy rising took place, led by the fanatical
preacher, Thomas Venner. There was some sharp fighting in
London, but the rebels were put down by the Guards and
the Trained Bands and Venner was hanged and quartered.

The gondolas from Venice had a difficult journey, being
damaged in their sea voyage round Italy and having to be
sent back for repairs. But they arrived in London with their
gondoliers in the summer of 1661. King Charles must by
then have come to the conclusion that the lake in St James's
Park was too small to accommodate them. They were sent
to Hampton Court, where they were used in river processions
on state occasions.

Charles II did not marry Hortense Mancini. Before the
end of 1660 a new candidate had been mentioned, the
Portuguese Princess Catherine of Braganza, and the King
married her in May 1662. During the twenty-three years of
their married life he treated her with respect and consideration, shielding her from the attacks of those who hated her as
a Catholic and resented her inability to produce an heir;
at the same time he amused himself with a host of mistresses
and made no attempt to hide his infidelities.

The bright dawn of the Restoration was soon overcast.
The Parliament elected in May 1661 was called the Cavalier
Parliament on account of its ardently royalist temper at the
outset. But it lived to see almost as many years as the Long
Parliament, and long before it was dissolved in 1679 it had
become a thorn in the side of the King. An opposition arose
determined to curb his power; it was led by the Earl of
Shaftesbury, formerly Sir Anthony Ashley Cooper, the most
treacherous and unscrupulous politician of the age.

Epilogue

The main points at issue were finance and religion. It was the policy of Shaftesbury, and of his minions in the House of Commons, to keep the King short of money unless he gave in to them in the matter of religion. The Worcester House Declaration was never put into effect. It was tacitly dropped, and the Church settlement took the shape of a return to an undiluted Anglicanism. Once in power the Anglicans consolidated their position; they opposed all efforts to accord toleration to nonconformists on the one hand and, still more, papists on the other. King Charles stood for toleration; lackadaisical on so many subjects, he cared deeply about this. Throughout the life of the Cavalier Parliament he made constant attempts to bring relief to tender consciences, attempts that were countered by more and more drastic measures on the part of the opposition, culminating in the brazen fiction of the Popish Plot.

From his long duel with Shaftesbury King Charles at last emerged the victor. But he did not live long enough to set the seal on his victory. After his death his brother James, more ardent in his ideals but lacking Charles's political subtlety, charged bull-headed at all obstacles. In the Declaration of Indulgence of 1687 he proclaimed complete freedom of worship for all Christians. The result was disastrous. The Bishops refused to co-operate, the opposition politicians, coming to be known as Whigs, entered into treasonable correspondence with the King's nephew William of Orange, son of his sister Mary, and King James was driven from his throne. With him was defeated the spirit of tolerance, so far in advance of the time, that was the peculiar contribution to history of the Stewart dynasty. Thenceforward the Crown was increasingly at the mercy of the politicians.

Yet all that was regained in 1660 was not lost in 1688. Monarchy in the old sense received its death blow with the fall of James II, but the outward forms remained, symbols of the reverence for tradition and the sense of order and dignity that are the safeguards of civilisation. The men and women who welcomed Charles II to London on May 29,

1660, had seen with their own eyes what happens when those symbols are trampled in the mud. Never since that day have their descendants allowed themselves to fall into the dark and gloomy abyss of republicanism.

BIBLIOGRAPHY

Abbreviation	*Author and Title*
Acts of the Interregnum	Firth, C. H., and Rait, R. S.: Acts and Ordinances of the Interregnum (1911). Vol. II.
Baker	Baker, Sir Richard: A Chronicle of the Kings of England, with continuations (the continuation for the Restoration is probably by Sir Thomas Clarges) (1733 edition).
Barlow	Barlow's Journal of his Life at Sea. Transcribed from the Original Manuscript by Basil Lubbock (1934).
Barwick	Barwick, Peter: Life of Dr John Barwick, Dean of St Paul's (ed. Barwick, G. F., 1903).
Baxter	Reliquiae Baxterianae, or Mr Richard Baxter's Narrative of the Most Memorable Passages of his Life and Times. Faithfully Publish'd from his own Original Manuscript by Matthew Sylvester (1696).
Blundell	Cavalier: Letters of William Blundell to his Friends, 1620–1698. Edited by Margaret Blundell (1933).

Bibliography

Abbreviation	Author and Title
Bulstrode	Bulstrode, Sir Richard: Memoirs and Reflections upon the Reign and Government of King Charles the Ist and King Charles the IId. (1721).
Burnet	Burnet's History of His Own Time (1838 edition).
Cartwright	Cartwright, Julia: Madame, a Life of Henrietta, Daughter of Charles I and Duchess of Orleans (containing letters) (1894).
Clarendon's Life	The Life of Edward Earl of Clarendon, in which is included a Continuation of his History of the Grand Rebellion. Written by Himself (1827 edition). Vol. I.
Clarendon S.P.	State Papers collected by Edward Earl of Clarendon. Vols. III and IV (1786).
Clarendon's Rebellion	The History of the Rebellion and Civil Wars in England, by Edward Earl of Clarendon (1826 edition). Vol. VII.
Clarke	The Life of James the Second, King of England. Collected out of Memoirs Writ of his own Hand. Published from the original Stuart Manuscripts in Carlton House, by the Rev. J. S. Clarke (1816). Vol. I.
Clarke Papers	The Clarke Papers (ed. Firth, C. H., 1901). Vol. IV.

Bibliography

Abbreviation	Author and Title
Commons Journals	Journals of the House of Commons (reprinted, 1813). Vols. VII and VIII.
Council Notes	Notes which passed at Meetings of the Privy Council between Charles II and the Earl of Clarendon, 1660–1667 (ed. Macrae, W. D., 1896).
Court & Times	The Court and Times of Charles the First, including Memoirs of the Mission in England of the Capuchin Friars in the Service of Queen Henrietta Maria, by Father Cyprien de Gamache (1848). Vol. II.
Cowley	Abraham Cowley: Poems (ed. Waller, A. R., 1905).
Dryden	The Poems of John Dryden (ed. Kinsley, J., 1958).
Eglesfield	Eglesfield, Francis: Monarchy Revived: being the Personal History of Charles the Second. Reprinted from the Edition of 1661 (1822).
Eng. Hist. Doc.	English Historical Documents, 1660–1714 (ed. Browning, A., 1953).
Evelyn	The Diary of John Evelyn (ed. de Beer, E. S., 1955). Vol. III.
Fanshawe	Memoirs of Lady Fanshawe, wife of Sir Richard Fanshawe, Bt. (ed. Marshall, Beatrice, 1905).

Bibliography

Abbreviation	*Author and Title*
Fox	The Journal of George Fox: a revised edition by John L. Nickalls (1952).
Grammont	Memoirs of the Court of Charles II, by Count Grammont: edited by Sir Walter Scott (1891 edition).
Guizot	Guizot, M.: History of Richard Cromwell and the Restoration of Charles II: translated by Andrew R. Scoble (1856). Vol. II (containing Bordeaux's dispatches).
Gumble	Gumble, Thomas: Life of General Monk, Duke of Albemarle (1671).
Hartmann	Hartmann, C. H.: Charles II and Madame (containing letters of Princess Henrietta) (1934).
Heath	Heath, James: A Chronicle of the Late Intestine War; to which is added a Continuation to the present year 1675 (1676).
	Historical Manuscripts Commission:
H.M.C. Bath	Marquess of Bath (1907).
H.M.C. Dartmouth	Earl of Dartmouth (1887).
H.M.C. Edmonstone	Sir Archibald Edmonstone (1909).
H.M.C. Le Fleming	S. H. Le Fleming (1890).
H.M.C. Leybourne-Popham	F. W. Leybourne-Popham (1899).
H.M.C. Morrison	Alfred Morrison (1884).
H.M.C. Ormonde	Marquess of Ormonde (1902).

Bibliography

Abbreviation	Author and Title
H.M.C. Portland	Duke of Portland (1899).
H.M.C. Sutherland	Duke of Sutherland (1876).
H.M.C. Verney	Sir Harry Verney (1879).
Hutchinson	Memoirs of the Life of Colonel Hutchinson, by his Widow Lucy: Edited from the original manuscript by the Rev. Julius Hutchinson. Revised by C. H. Firth (1885).
Kennet	A Register and Chronicle, Ecclesiastical and Civil: from the Restoration of King Charles II (Kennet's Register) (1728).
Kingdomes Int.	The Kingdomes Intelligencer (newspaper, 1661).
Letters	Bryant, Arthur: Letters, Speeches and Declarations of King Charles II (1935).
Lister	Lister, T. H.: Life and Administration of Edward, Earl of Clarendon. Vol. III (Letters and Papers) (1837).
London's Diurnal	London's Diurnal (newspaper, 1660).
Lords Journals	Journals of the House of Lords. Vol. XI. (1660).
Lower	Lower, Sir William: A Relation in Form of Journal, of the Voiage and Residence which the most Excellent and most Mighty Prince Charles II Hath made in Holland (1660).

Bibliography

Abbreviation	*Author and Title*
Ludlow	Memoirs of Edmund Ludlow (ed. Firth, C. H., 1894). Vol. II.
Marvell	The Complete Works in Verse and Prose of Andrew Marvell, M.P. (ed. Grosart, A. B., 1875). Vol. II.
Merc. Civ.	Mercurius Civicus, or the Cities Intelligencer (newspaper, 1660).
Merc. Pol.	Mercurius Politicus (newspaper, 1660).
Merc. Pub.	Mercurius Publicus (newspaper, 1660).
Mordaunt	Letter-Book of John Viscount Mordaunt, 1658–1660 (ed. Coate, Mary, 1945).
Newcome	The Autobiography of Henry Newcome (ed. Parkinson, R., 1891). Vol. I.
Newton	Newton, Lady: The House of Lyme from its Formation to the End of the Eighteenth Century (1917).
Nicholas Papers	The Nicholas Papers: Correspondence of Sir Edward Nicholas, Secretary of State (ed. Warner, Sir George, 1920). Vol. IV.
Nicholl	Nicholl, John: A Diary of Public Transactions, 1650–1667 (1836 edition).
Occurrences	Occurrences from Foreign Parts, with an Exact Accompt of the Daily Proceedings in Parliament (newspaper, 1660).

Bibliography

Abbreviation	Author and Title
Old Parl. Hist.	The Parliamentary or Constitutional History of England (Old Parliamentary History) (1763). Vols. XXII and XXIII.
Ormonde Papers	Original Letters and Papers, found among the Duke of Ormonde's Papers (1739). Vol. II.
Parl. Hist.	The Parliamentary History of England (1808). Vols. III and IV.
Parl. Int.	The Parliamentary Intelligencer (newspaper, 1660).
Pepys	Diary of Samuel Pepys (ed. Wheatley, H. B., 1946 edition). Vol. I.
Perfect Occurrences	Perfect Occurrences of the most Remarkable Passages in Parliament, with other Moderate Intelligence (newspaper, 1660).
Pub. Int.	The Publick Intelligencer (newspaper, 1660).
Reresby	The Memoirs of Sir John Reresby: Edited from the Original Manuscript by James J. Cartwright (1875).
Rugge	Mercurius Politicus Redivivus: A Collection of the most materiall Occurences and Transactions in Publick Affaires. By Thomas Rugge ('Rugge's Diurnal', MS. in British Museum). Vol. I.
Sandwich	The Journal of Edward Montagu, First Earl of Sandwich (ed. Anderson, R. C., 1929).

Bibliography

Abbreviation	*Author and Title*
Secret Hist.	The Secret History of the Court and Reign of Charles the Second, by a Member of the Privy Council (1792). Vol. I.
Select Tracts	Masères, F.: Select Tracts Relating to the Civil Wars in England (containing 'The Mystery and Method of His Majesty's Happy Restauration' by John Price, originally printed 1680) (1815).
Skinner	Skinner, Thomas: Life of General Monk, Duke of Albemarle(1724).
Somers Tracts	A Collection of Scarce and Valuable Tracts, particularly from the Library of Lord Somers (1812). Vol. VII.
S.P. Charles II	Calendar of State Papers, Domestic Series, of the Reign of Charles II, 1660–1661 (ed. Green, Mary Everett, 1860).
S.P. Commonwealth	Calendar of State Papers, Domestic Series (Commonwealth, Vol. XIII, 1886).
State Trials	Cobbett's Complete Collection of State Trials. Vol. V. (1810).
Thurloe, S.P.	A Collection of the State Papers of John Thurloe, by Thomas Birch (1742). Vol. VII.
Townshend	Diary of Henry Townshend, of Elmley Lovett, 1640–1663 (ed. Willis Bund, J. W., 1915).

Bibliography

Abbreviation	Author and Title
Venetian S.P.	Calendar of State Papers from the Archives and Collections of Venice. Vol. XXXII (ed. Hinds, A., 1931).
Verney Memoirs	Verney, Margaret M.: Memoirs of the Verney Family during the Commonwealth (1894). Vols. III and IV.
Wariston	Diary of Sir Archibald Johnston of Wariston (ed. Ogilvie, J. D., 1940). Vol. III.
Whitelock	Whitelock, Bulstrode: Memorials of the English Affairs (1732).
Wood	The Life and Times of Anthony Wood, 1632–1695, collected from his Diaries and other Papers by Andrew Clark (1891). Vol. I.

REFERENCES

PART I

January 1.
Baker, 593. Select Tracts, 749.
Skinner, 179–180. Gumble, 192.
Burnet, 55–56. Ludlow, 206. Barwick, 118–120. Nicholl, 269–270.
Pepys, 1–4. Merc. Pol., 1011.

January 2.
Clarke Papers, 238. Ludlow, 206.
Baker, 593–594. Commons Journals, VII, 801–803. Select Tracts, 749–750. Whitelock, 692. Skinner, 180–181. Gumble, 192–197. Pepys, 7.

January 3.
Gumble, 197–199. Select Tracts, 750. Skinner, 181. Parl. Hist. III, 1572. Somers Tracts, 98. Whitelock, 692. Pub. Int., 1005–1006. Guizot, 329.

January 4.
Pepys, 7–9. Whitelock, 692. Baker, 593. Select Tracts, 750–751. Skinner, 182. Gumble, 199–203. Letters, 79. Mordaunt, 155–160. Barwick, 125–128. Kennet, 5–7.

January 5.
Baker, 593. Skinner, 182–185. Gumble, 203–204. Pepys, 9–10. Commons Journals, VII, 803. Whitelock, 692. Venetian S.P., 108–109.

January 6.
Commons Journals, VII, 804. Whitelock, 693. Somers Tracts, 99. Wariston, 166–167. Venetian S.P., 108–109. Clarke Papers, 240. S.P. Commonwealth, 303.

January 7.
Mordaunt, 160–161.

January 8.
Gumble, 204, 207–209.

January 9.
Parl. Hist., 1572. Commons Journals, VII, 805. Whitelock, 693–694. Pepys, 12–14. Ludlow, 201. Wariston, 168–169. Venetian S.P., 110. Old Parl. Hist., XXII, 43. Pub. Int., 997.

January 10.
Merc. Pol., 1079.

January 11.
Baker, 593. Select Tracts, 751. Whitelock, 693. Skinner, 187–188. Gumble, 207–209.

January 12.
Parl. Hist., III, 1572. Commons Journals, VII, 808–810. Whitelock, 693. Gumble, 209–215. Baker, 594. Evelyn, 239. Kennet, 19.

January 13.
Commons Journals, VII, 811–812. Whitelock, 693. Gumble, 215–216. Baker, 594. Select Tracts, 751–752. Skinner, 188.

January 14.
Select Tracts, 752–753. Skinner, 188. Wariston, 169.

References

January 16.
Mordaunt, 152–153, 167, 170. Ormonde Papers, 300–302. Parl. Hist., III, 1572–1573. Commons Journals, VII, 813. Somers Tracts, 99. Whitelock, 693. Baker, 594. Select Tracts, 753. Nicholl, 269. Skinner, 189–190. Gumble, 216–217.

January 17.
Pepys, 19–22. Mordaunt, 163–166. Ludlow, 201. Venetian S.P., 111–113. Rugge, 47.

January 18.
Ludlow, 206–207. Skinner, 190–192. Gumble, 217–221. Mordaunt, 165–166. Wariston, 170. Venetian S.P., 111–113.

January 19.
Mordaunt, 166–169. Ludlow, 202, 207–208, 211. Commons Journals, VII, 815–816. Whitelock, 693. Baker, 594. Select Tracts, 753. Ormonde Papers, 305–306. Skinner, 192–193. Gumble, 221–222.

January 20.
Pepys, 23–25. Baker, 594.

January 21.
Clarke Papers, 247–254. Baker, 594. Select Tracts, 753. Whitelock, 693. Pepys, 26. Parl. Hist., III, 1573. Commons Journals, VII, 818. Somers Tracts, 99. S.P. Commonwealth, 319.

January 22.
Clarke Papers, 254–258. Evelyn, 240. Baker, 594–595. Select Tracts, 754. Skinner, 193–195.

January 23.
Baker, 595. Select Tracts, 754–755. Whitelock, 693–694. Skinner, 195. Gumble, 222–224. Clarke Papers, 258–260. Ludlow, 208–209. Pepys, 27–28. Parl. Hist., III, 1573. Wariston, 172.

January 24.
Skinner, 196–197. Gumble, 224–227.

January 25.
Pepys, 30.

January 26.
Acts of the Interregnum, 1355–1403. Whitelock, 694. Commons Journals, VII, 823. Pepys, 31–32.

January 27.
Baker, 596. Skinner, 197. Select Tracts, 755–756. Pub. Int., 1048.

January 28.
Baker, 596. Select Tracts, 755–756. Skinner, 197–199. Gumble, 224–227. Letters, 79–80. Wariston, 173. Cartwright, 53.

January 30.
Ludlow, 211, 213. Baker, 596. Commons Journals, VII, 826. Whitelock, 694.

January 31.
Whitelock, 694. H.M.C. Sutherland, 153. Rugge, 55.

February 1.
Pepys, 37. Pub. Int., 1058. Old Parl. Hist., XXII, 80. Select Tracts, 756–757.

February 2.
Pub. Int., 1067. Pepys, 38–39. H.M.C. Leybourne-Popham, 144. Guizot, 342. Baker, 596. Select Tracts, 757. Skinner, 200–201. Lister, 83–84.

February 3.
Venetian S.P., 114–115, 117. Pub. Int., 1066–1068. London's Diurnal, 4–5. Merc. Pol., 1069–1070, 1084, 1107. H.M.C. Leybourne-Popham, 143–144. Guizot, 342–343. Baker, 596. Ludlow, 215–216. Select Tracts, 758. Skinner, 204–205. Gumble, 227–228. Eglesfield, 221.

References

February 4.
Pub. Int., 1066–1068. Merc. Pol., 1084. Venetian S.P., 117. Skinner, 205. Gumble, 228–229.

February 5.
H.M.C. Leybourne-Popham, 145. Select Tracts, 758–759. Clarendon S.P., III, 669–670.

February 6.
Merc. Pol., 1082–1083. London's Diurnal, 5. Venetian S.P., 115–116. H.M.C. Leybourne-Popham, 145. Guizot, 340–344. Baker, 596–597. Ludlow, 217. Gumble, 229–234.

February 7.
Pepys, 44.

February 8.
Venetian S.P., 116–117. Guizot, 345. Baker, 597. Ludlow, 218. Old Parl. Hist., XXII, 91. Gumble, 234–235. Eglesfield, 221.

February 9.
Pub. Int., 1093–1094. Pepys, 46–47. Venetian S.P., 116–117. Guizot, 345–347. Clarendon's Rebellion, 405–409. Baker, 597–598. Ludlow, 218–220. Commons Journals, VII, 838. Gumble, 236–244. Evelyn, 241.

February 10.
Pub. Int., 1094. Pepys, 48. Venetian S.P., 117. H.M.C. Leybourne-Popham, 146–148. Guizot, 347–348. Baker, 598. Gumble, 244–245. Kennet, 53–54.

February 11.
Pub. Int., 1094. Merc. Pol., 1110. Pepys, 48–52. Venetian S.P., 118–119. H.M.C. Verney, 483. Evelyn, 242. Whitelock, 695. Gumble, 245–255. Guizot, 348–351. Burnet, 156. Clarendon's Rebellion, 409–411. Baker, 598–599. Select Tracts, 767–768. Bulstrode, 209–210. Eglesfield, 222.

February 12.
Pepys, 52. Clarendon's Rebellion, 429–423. Kennet, 58.

February 13.
Venetian S.P., 119. Old Parl. Hist., XXII, 128. Wood, 304.

February 14.
Old Parl. Hist., XXII, 130.

February 16.
Merc. Pol., 1109–1110. Pub. Int., 1019. Pepys, 56. Venetian S.P., 120. Clarendon S.P., III, 682.

February 17.
Pub. Int., 1019. H.M.C. Verney, 483. Newcome, 118.

February 18.
Pub. Int., 1019–1020. H.M.C. Leybourne-Popham, 154–155. Guizot, 356. Baker, 600–601. Old Parl. Hist., XXII, 131–132.

February 20.
Pepys, 59. Ludlow, 233–235. Skinner, 240–241. Venetian S.P., 121.

February 21.
Merc. Pol., 1119–1122. Pepys, 59–61. Venetian S.P., 121–122. H.M.C. Bath, 141. Guizot, 358–363. Newton, 208. Baker, 601. Ludlow, 235–236. Commons Journal, VII, 846–847. Select Tracts, 772–775. Gumble, 263. Bulstrode, 210. Eglesfield, 223–224. Kennet, 63–65.

February 22.
Venetian S.P., 129. Thurloe, S.P., 823. Commons Journals, VII, 848.

February 23.
Pepys, 62–63. Guizot, 365. Old Parl. Hist., XXII, 137. Whitelock, 696.

References

February 25.
Pepys, 63–65. H.M.C. Leybourne-Popham, 159, 161–162. Thurloe, S.P., 824.

February 27.
Pepys, 68–69. Commons Journals, VII, 855.

February 28.
Merc. Pol., 1142. Ludlow, 244.

February 29.
Verney Memoirs, 469–470.

March 1.
Merc. Pol., 1142. Pepys, 71. Venetian S.P., 127. Old Parl. Hist., XXII, 147. Commons Journals, VII, 857.

March 2.
Pub. Int., 1141. Pepys, 72. H.M.C. Ormonde, 334. Old Parl. Hist., XXII, 148. Commons Journals, VII, 858.

March 4.
Nicholas Papers, 198.

March 5.
Pub. Int., 1149. Occurrences, 754. Pepys, 75. Venetian S.P., 130. H.M.C. Ormonde, 335. Guizot, 373–376. Nicholas Papers, 198–199. Ludlow, 241. Parl. Hist., III, 1582.

March 6.
Merc. Pol., 1157. Pepys, 75–76. Nicholas Papers, 199–200.

March 7.
Pepys, 79. Venetian S.P., 128, 130. H.M.C. Ormonde, 335. Guizot, 376–377. Nicholas Papers, 200–201. Commons Journals, VII, 866.

March 8.
Venetian S.P., 128–129. Guizot, 376–377. Verney Memoirs, III, 472. Nicholas Papers, 201, 205. Old Parl. Hist., XXII, 154.

March 9.
Merc. Pol., 1183. Pepys, 80–81. Venetian S.P., 130–131. Nicholas Papers, 203. Fox, 369.

March 12.
Merc. Pol., 1174. Acts of the Interregnum, 1425.

March 13.
Baker, 602.

March 14.
Guizot, 381. Verney Memoirs, III, 472. Whitelock, 698.

March 15.
Pub. Int., 1174. Pepys, 84–85. Venetian S.P., 132. Guizot, 382. Ludlow, 249–250. Old Parl. Hist., XXII, 157. Whitelock, 698.

March 16.
Pub. Int., 1174. Pepys, 86. Venetian S.P., 133–134. Guizot, 385–386. Clarendon's Rebellion, 442–443. Verney Memoirs, III, 473. Ludlow, 250. Parl. Hist., III, 1584. Lister, 90–91. Eglesfield, 224.

March 17.
Thurloe, S.P., 858. Baker, 604–605. Clarendon's Rebellion, 442–444. Select Tracts, 785–786. Kennet, 85–86.

March 19.
Venetian S.P., 134. Clarendon's Rebellion, 444–445. Select Tracts, 786. Baker, 606. Skinner, 274–276. Pepys, 88. Guizot, 386–387. Kennet, 87–88.

March 20.
Skinner, 276. Pepys, 89–90. Thurloe, S.P., 861–862.

March 21.
Wariston, 177.

March 22.
Venetian S.P., 133.

References

March 23.
Pepys, 92. Baker, 606. Wariston, 179. Sandwich, 73.

March 24.
Pub. Int., 1189. Letters, 80–81. Wariston, 179–180.

March 26.
Parl. Int., 212.

March 27.
Clarendon S.P., III, 706. Merc. Pol., 1206. Letters, 83. Wariston, 180.

March 28.
Merc. Pol., 1194, 1206.

March 29.
Merc. Pol., 1199.

March 30.
Clarendon's Rebellion, 445–451. Baker, 606.

April 1.
Pub. Int., 1203. Pepys, 96.

April 2.
Parl. Int., 209.

April 3.
Clarendon's Rebellion, 451. Kennet, 104–105.

April 4.
Clarendon's Rebellion, 451–470. Letters, 84–86. Baker, 606. Barwick, 145. Lower, 5–6. Select Tracts, 791. Kennet, 105–110.

April 5.
Merc. Pol., 1219. Venetian S.P., 137.

April 6.
Parl. Int., 239.

April 8.
Pepys, 100.

April 9.
Parl. Int., 225.

April 10.
Merc. Pol., 1216.

April 11.
Merc. Pol., 1253–1254. Pepys, 102–103. Guizot, 407. Clarke Papers, 267. Rugge, 121.

April 12.
Parl. Int., 256. Whitelock, 699.

April 16.
Parl. Int., 256. Merc. Pub., 256.

April 18.
Baker, 607. H.M.C. Sutherland, 146.

April 19.
Letters, 89.

April 20.
Venetian S.P., 140. Baker, 607.

April 21.
Parl. Int., 272. Merc. Pub., 271. Pepys, 107–108. Baker, 607. Gumble, 283.

April 22.
Merc. Pub., 269–270. Baker, 607–608. Gumble, 283–286. Heath, 441–442.

April 23.
Parl. Int., 273. Pepys, 108–109.

April 24.
Merc. Pub., 272. Venetian S.P., 141. H.M.C. Leybourne-Popham, 179. Guizot, 415–416. Baker, 608. Clarendon S.P., III, 734–735. H.M.C. Edmonstone, 171–172. Ormonde Papers, 328. Eglesfield, 226.

April 25.
Guizot, 412–414. Venetian S.P.,

140-141. H.M.C. Edmonstone, 171. Clarendon's Rebellion, 477–478. Baker, 609. Lords Journals, 3. Parl. Hist., IV, 13–14. Gumble, 288–289. Commons Journals, VIII, 1. Pepys, 110.

April 26.
Merc. Pub., 265. Guizot, 414–415.

April 27.
Baker, 609. Ormonde Papers, 329–330. Clarendon S.P., III, 734. Gumble, 289–290.

April 28.
H.M.C. Sutherland, 167. Baker, 609. Clarendon S.P., III, 736.

April 29.
Ormonde Papers, 326–327.

April 30.
Parl. Int., 280. Venetian S.P., 142. Baxter, 217. Clarke Papers, 268.

May 1.
Merc. Pub., 281–282. Pepys, 113–115. Venetian S.P., 142–143. Guizot, 419–420. Baxter, 218. Baker, 612. Lords Journals, 8–9. Parl. Hist., IV, 23. Merc. Civ., 31.

May 2.
Baker, 613.

May 3.
Parl. Int., 304. Merc. Pub., 315. Pepys, 116–117. Lords Journals, 11. Commons Journals, VIII, 10–11. Barlow, 42. Lower, 7–8. Sandwich, 75.

May 4.
Parl. Int., 304. Pepys, 118–119. Whitelock, 701. Lower, 7. Lister, 104–106.

May 5.
Parl. Int., 304. Pepys, 121. Baker, 614. Old Parl. Hist., XXII, 271.

May 7.
Parl. Int., 301. Merc. Civ., 32. Merc. Pub., 304. Pepys, 121–122. Lords Journals, 15–16. Old Parl. Hist., XXII, 273. Clarendon S.P., III, 739–740.

May 8.
Merc. Pub., 300–302. Parl. Int., 310, 320. Venetian S.P., 146. H.M.C. Leybourne-Popham, 182. Wood, 315. Baker, 614. Clarendon S.P., III, 742–743. Lower, 12–13. Eglesfield, 228. Kennet, 139–142.

May 10.
Merc. Pub., 305–306. Letters, 90–91. Thurloe, S.P., 912–913. Lords Journals, 22–23. Commons Journals, VIII, 21–22. Ormonde Papers, 336. Sandwich, 75. Guizot, 428.

May 11.
Perfect Occurrences, 32. Pepys, 125–126. H.M.C. Leybourne-Popham, 182. Sandwich, 75.

May 12.
Parl. Int., 320. H.M.C. Sutherland, 150. Hutchinson, 246–249. Commons Journals, VIII, 24–25. Townshend, 39.

May 13.
Merc. Pub., 317.

May 14.
Merc. Pub., 317–318, 322, 324–330, 336. Parl. Int., 337–340. Pepys, 128–130, 134. Venetian S.P., 149. Clarendon's Rebellion, 496–497. Ludlow, 269–270. Old Parl. Hist., XXII, 287. Townshend, 40–41. Nicoll, 283–284. Barlow, 42. Lower, 24–30, 43. Sandwich, 76.

May 15.
Clarendon's Rebellion, 497. Merc. Pub., 336. Pub. Int., 161–162. H.M.C. Sutherland, 206. Lords Journals, 29. Old Parl. Hist., XXII,

References

289. Lower, 30–35. Sandwich, 76.
Venetian S.P., 148–149.

May 16.
Merc. Pub., 336. Pub. Int., 162.
Clarendon's Rebellion, 498–503.
Baker, 614–615. Lower, 50–53.

May 17.
Merc. Pub., 336. Pub. Int., 162–
163. Letters, 91–92. Baker, 615.
Sandwich, 76.

May 19.
Pepys, 139. Lower, 68.

May 20.
Parl. Int., 351. Merc. Pub., 341.
Pepys, 139. Lower, 73–82.

May 21.
Merc. Pub., 336. H.M.C. Suther-
land, 150. Baker, 615. Ludlow, 271.
Commons Journals, VIII, 39.

May 22.
Parl. Int., 352. Baker, 615. Barlow,
43. Lower, 85–102. Pepys, 141–
144. Lords Journals, 36. Gumble,
381–383. Sandwich, 76. Guizot,
431–432.

May 23.
Parl. Int., 352. Pepys, 144–147.
Venetian S.P., 153. H.M.C. Le
Fleming, 24–25. Eng. Hist. Doc.,
59. Baker, 615. Old Parl. Hist.,
XXII, 308. Barlow, 43–44. Lower,
44, 102–108. Sandwich, 76–77.
Fanshawe, 120–121. Heath, 450.

May 24.
Evelyn, 245.

May 25.
Parl. Int., 352. Blundell, 93. Pepys,
149–151. Venetian S.P., 154–155.
H.M.C. Le Fleming, 24–25. Eng.
Hist. Doc., 59–60. Guizot, 435–436.
Clarendon's Rebellion, 504. Claren-
don's Life, 321–326. Baker, 615.
Barlow, 44–45. Gumble, 383–385.
Dryden, 23. Sandwich, 77–78.
Fanshawe, 121.

May 26.
Parl. Int., 352. Merc. Pub., 342,
349. Letters, 92. H.M.C. Sutherland, 145. Clarendon's Life, 326.
Baker, 615. S.P. Commonwealth,
446.

May 27.
Pepys, 152–153. Clarendon's Rebel-
lion, 504. Sandwich, 78. Merc.
Pub., 342.

May 28.
Parl. Int., 348. Merc. Pub., 349–
350. Eng. Hist. Doc., 60. Clarendon's Life, 326. Baker, 615.
Gumble, 386.

May 29.
Merc. Pub., 350–352. Parl. Int.,
359. Letters, 92. Venetian S.P.,
155. H.M.C. Le Fleming, 25–26.
H.M.C. Sutherland, 167–168. Evelyn, 246. Eng. Hist. Doc., 60.
Guizot, 437–438. Clarendon's Rebellion, 504–505. Clarendon's Life,
326–328. Baxter, 218. Baker, 615–
616. Ludlow, 274. Commons Journals, VIII, 49. Select Tracts, 800.
Cowley, 430–431. Gumble, 387–
393. Fanshawe, 122. Eglesfield,
229–230. Heath, 451–453. Rugge,
147–150.

PART II

May 30–*June* 2.
Guizot, 438–439. Somers Tracts,
423–425. Ludlow, 275. Lords
Journals, 47–51. Old Parl. Hist.,
XXII, 330. Cartwright, 57. Parl.
Int., 366. Venetian S.P., 155–159.
Baker, 618. H.M.C. Sutherland,
205.

References

June 3-9.
Evelyn, 247. Old Parl. Hist., XXII, 343-345. Commons Journals, VIII, 56-57, 60. Hartmann, 15. S.P. Charles II, 39. Pub. Int., 233. Venetian S.P., 158. Somers Tracts, 436-437. Townshend, 47. H.M.C. Sutherland, 153, 168. Pepys, 162.

June 10-16.
H.M.C. Sutherland, 153-154, 168. Old Parl. Hist., XXII, 347-350, 354. Townshend, 50. Merc. Pub., 381. Parl. Int., 400. Commons Journals, VIII, 65-66. Kennet, 179-181.

June 17-23.
Pepys, 165, 168-169. H.M.C. Dartmouth, 3. Commons Journals, VIII, 66-68. Merc. Pub., 414-416, 429-430. H.M.C. Sutherland, 154, 168. Venetian S.P., 164.

June 24-30.
Pepys, 170-175. Merc. Pub., 412-413. Parl. Int., 431. Venetian S.P., 168. Commons Journals, VIII, 77. Kennet, 187-189.

July 1-7.
Merc. Pub., 428, 430-431, 462. Old Parl. Hist., XXII, 365. Pepys, 179. Venetian S.P., 170. H.M.C. Sutherland, 154, 206. Evelyn, 250-251. Ludlow, 284.

July 8-16.
Pepys, 180-182, 185. Old Parl. Hist., XXII, 373-376. Townshend, 54-55. Parl. Int., 461-462, 464-465, 673-674. Venetian S.P., 173. H.M.C. Portland, 229. Lords Journals, 90. Commons Journals, VIII, 95.

July 17-21.
Pepys, 188-189. Lords Journals, 99.

July 22-31.
Lords Journals, 101-102. Nicoll,
296. Parl. Int., 495-496. Letters, 100-101. Baker, 619. Ludlow, 287-288. Newton, 213. Merc. Pub., 552.

August 1-12.
Reresby, 46. Ludlow, 290-291. Lords Journals, 114. Pepys, 202-205. H.M.C. Sutherland, 174. Old Parl. Hist., XXII, 405, 419.

August 13-18.
Parl. Int., 521, 539-540, 553. Merc. Pub., 532-534. Pepys, 206-208. Cartwright, 63. H.M.C. Sutherland, 168.

August 19-25.
Merc. Pub , 566, 587. Venetian S.P., 189. Lords Journals, 136, 143-144. Parl. Int., 560. Commons Journals, VIII, 135. Kennet, 236.

August 26-31.
Parl. Int., 553. Reresby, 47. Old Parl. Hist., XXII, 455, 463-466. Commons Journals, VIII, 140-141. Merc. Pub., 568. Letters, 102-103. Lords Journals, 147-150. Venetian S.P., 193-194. Kennet, 239-241.

September 1-8.
Pepys, 217-220. H.M.C. Sutherland, 156, 174. Merc. Pub., 574-576. Venetian S.P., 156, 196. Grammont, 162. H.M.C. Morrison, 445. Clarendon's Life, 371-372. Clarke, 387. Baxter, 259-264. Old Parl. Hist., XXII, 468-472. Sandwich, 80-81. Lords Journals, 156, 163. Parl. Int., 592. Kennet, 247.

September 9-15.
Merc. Pub., 592, 608. Pepys, 221-223. Venetian S.P., 197-198. H.M.C. Sutherland, 156, 174. Reresby, 47-48. Lords Journals, 164, 170-176. Sandwich, 81. Old Parl. Hist., XXII, 476-478. Parl. Int., 607-608. Evelyn, 257. Burnet,

References

299–300. Clarke, 386. Baker, 621. Secret Hist., 145–146. S.P. Charles II, 266.

September 16–22.
Grammont, 162–163. Clarendon's Life, 371–383. Clarke, 387–388. Kennet, 264. Pepys, 224–228. Merc. Pub., 608. Barlow, 46. Venetian S.P., 201. Sandwich, 81. Parl. Int., 623. Burnet, 312–313. H.M.C. Le Fleming, 26–27.

September 23–29.
Parl. Int., 624. Pepys, 229–233. Venetian S.P., 203–204. H.M.C. Sutherland, 156, 169, 174. Clarendon's Life, 383. Barlow, 46. Sandwich, 82. Merc. Pub., 623. H.M.C. Portland, 238. Townshend, 63.

September 30–*October* 6.
Grammont, 163–165. Clarendon's Life, 382–384. Kennet, 270–272. Parl. Int., 647, 659. Pepys, 236. Council Notes, 11. Venetian S.P., 208.

October 7–13.
Kennet, 272–279. Parl. Int., 647, 651–656, 665–672. Somers Tracts, 440–452. Pepys, 239–242. Ludlow, 303–308. H.M.C. Sutherland, 157. Venetian S.P., 208. Burnet, 282. Heath, 462–466. State Trials, 988–1145.

October 14–20.
Merc. Pub., 668–672. Parl. Int., 676, 678–684, 688. Pepys, 242–245. Burnet, 281–282. Ludlow, 312–314. H.M.C. Sutherland, 174–175. Evelyn, 259. Kennet, 281–286. Townshend, 63. Heath, 466–467. State Trials, 1145–1230.

October 21–27.
Grammont, 165–166. Clarke, 387–388. Kennet, 279–281, 287–293. Merc. Pub., 683–684. Parl. Int., 689–690, 704. Pepys, 246–249.

H.M.C. Sutherland, 157, 175, H.M.C. Morrison, 445. Clarendon's Life, 386–393. Venetian S.P., 212–214. Eng. Hist. Doc., 365–366. Burnet, 315–316. Baker, 620–621. Ludlow, 301.

October 28–*November* 3.
Venetian S.P., 214–216, 228–229. H.M.C. Sutherland, 157. Evelyn, 259. Court & Times, 415–417. Merc. Pub., 708. Clarendon's Life, 387–388. Barwick, 163–164. Pepys, 254. H.M.C. Sutherland, 200. Baxter, 283. Baker, 621.

November 4–12.
H.M.C. Sutherland, 157. Lords Journals, 176. Parl. Hist., IV, 141. Merc. Pub., 701, 720–721, 739. Old Parl. Hist., XXIII, 6–9. Pepys, 259–261. Venetian S.P., 217–218. Kennet, 306–309.

November 13–17.
Lords Journals, 184. Venetian S.P., 218–219. H.M.C. Sutherland, 200. Old Parl. Hist., XXIII, 13. Parl. Int., 757. Commons Journals, VIII, 184. Marvell, 17–18.

November 18–24.
H.M.C. Sutherland, 196, 200. Pepys, 266–268. Lords Journals, 189. Merc. Pub., 823. Venetian S.P., 221.

November 25–*December* 1.
Merc. Pub., 772, 776. Pepys, 272–273. H.M.C. Sutherland, 169. Old Parl. Hist., XXIII, 27–30. Marvell, 26–27. Venetian S.P., 223.

December 2–11.
Kennet, 323–326. Pepys, 277–285. Marvell, 29. Parl. Int., 783–786, 808, 822. Merc. Pub., 791, 807. Venetian S.P., 226–229. Lords Journals, 202, 205. Townshend, 65. H.M.C. Sutherland, 158, 196.

References

December 12–21.

Council Notes, 21. S.P. Charles II, 412. Venetian S.P., 228, 230–231. Parl. Hist. IV, 162. Parl. Int., 823–824. Pepys, 286–287. Lords Journals, 214, 219. Old Parl. Hist., XXIII, 54–56, 58–61. Marvell, 36. H.M.C. Sutherland, 201. Merc. Pub., 823–824. Evelyn, 264.

December 22–25.

Evelyn, 264. Lords Journals, 224.

Pepys, 288. Merc. Pub., 834, 839. Venetian S.P., 235. Burnet, 300. Clarendon's Life, 392. Clarke, 386. Townshend, 65. Secret Hist., 153–154. Cartwright, 78. Court & Times, 417. Kennet, 331–332.

December 26–31.

Venetian S.P., 235, 237. Kingdome's Int., 9. Baker, 622. Commons Journals, VIII, 237. Pepys, 291–292. Evelyn, 265. Heath, 470.

INDEX

Index

Index